Directing for the Stage

Lloyd Anton Frerer

Fort Hays State University

NTC Publishing Group
Lincolnwood, Illinois USA

Executive Editor: John T. Nolan
Sponsoring Editor: Marisa L. L'Heureux
Interior design: Ophelia M. Chambliss
Cover design: Paul Uhl
Interior art: Paula Weber
Director art: Kieran Ratzlaff
Production Manager: Rosemary Dolinski

Excerpts from *The Rainmaker* and *Blue Denim* are used by permission of the copyright holders.

CONTENTS

PREFACE

This book is written for students of directing for the theatre. Because such students have widely varying levels of training and experience, the book cannot assume that the readers will have a thorough background in theatre. For example, Chapter 1, which surveys the responsibilities of the director, may appear to be rather elementary to some readers. The more sophisticated reader should view this chapter as a review of information that he or she has long known. Many young directors have had little acting experience, while others may have spent numberless hours on the stage. Chapter 11, which deals with acting and actors, will prove a greater revelation to the former group than to the latter.

Directing for the Stage begins with a section that guides students immediately into the specific process of analyzing and staging a scene from a play. Because students usually deal with scenes rather than full plays in classroom situations, and because students often must begin their first projects before they have had time to read much of the material in the textbook, this section of the book offers the basic information to get them started. Instructors of directing who approach the subject differently may find reading the chapters of the text in an alternative order to be more appropriate. For example, if the students do not begin their projects in scene direction early in the term, the instructor might have students skip over Chapters 2 and 3, reading them at a more appropriate time in terms of the organization of that particular course.

Throughout the text, I use examples from my own directing experience, particularly in the staging of scenes from *The Rainmaker* and *Blue Denim* and in the sample script analyses of *Night of the Iguana, Uncle Vanya,* and *Play It Again, Sam.* This last play is used as a running example in the text, from its choice for production through its analysis, casting, rehearsal, and performance. *Sam* was chosen because it is a well-written, contemporary theatre piece that does not present extraordinary difficulties for the beginning director. *Iguana* and *Vanya* were chosen for the opposite reason: Because they are dense and difficult works. An example drawn from my experience should be recognized for what it is—neither the perfect way to do things nor the only approach but rather as one way in which a theatrical problem was resolved in actual practice. No doubt instructors will provide students with many examples from their own careers in directing, as well.

Directors ultimately must discover their own method of directing, a way of attacking a production that succeeds for them. This book recommends one such method that involves a form of creative staging with the actors (as opposed to preblocking the action outside of rehearsals). If the approach of the directing instructor differs in some ways from that suggested by this book, so much the better for the student, who will be exposed to more than one method of staging.

For the most part, the text and its examples refer to the small theatrical organization in the amateur theatre—for example, in universities and community theatres. Nevertheless, the basic principles and strategies of stage directing presented in the text relate equally well to larger theatrical organizations, both amateur and professional.

This book is about *directing* plays. Although much material about acting is included, it is not a substitute for a good acting textbook. While all areas of theatrical training are of use to a director, this book does not deal in detail with stagecraft, scene design, or the history of the theatre. My goal is to introduce the student to both the artistic and practical nature of the director's job; surely, that is task enough for one book.

A Final Note

I wish to apologize for shortcomings in this text concerning the staging of dramatic works for the theatre. Again and again, I have returned to various sections of the book to add some minimal information about subjects that I felt had been neglected in earlier drafts. For example, whereas information concerning designers and their relations with directors has been expanded, little has been said about the budgeting process—which is essential knowledge for those involved in play production. Similarly, information about the individual coaching of actors and the use of improvisation as a directorial tool seems less than adequate.

More important, I hope that readers will take seriously my admonition to take any and all suggestions made in this text with a grain of salt. There are legitimate exceptions to every rule and amazingly creative new approaches to be discovered for solving old problems. Knowledge of the traditional tools and methods has always been considered essential for the training of any artist. Once that knowledge has been absorbed, artists should feel free to break new ground, to use their own unique intuition in the process of conceptualizing and creating new works of art for the theatre.

Acknowledgments

In creating a textbook dealing with a subject that I have studied and practiced over many years, I am obliged to all those who both taught and directed me, all those who authored texts that influenced my thinking, and those friends and colleagues who gave their encouragement. First, thanks go to John Dietrich, author of the textbook that was the basis of training for most of my generation. In at least two instances, I use his ideas in this text, but my unconscious debt surely is greater. I am grateful to my mentors in graduate schools: Malcolm Sillars and O. G. Brockett. I acknowledge those who taught me directing in formal classroom situations: Bob Davis, Robert L. Rivera, Waldon Boyle, James Brock, and Lael Woodbury. An equal debt is owed to those who actually directed me as an actor, a list of names too numerous to recount here. Finally, I owe thanks to colleagues and friends, particularly to Stephen Klein at Mississippi State, and Sandra Rupp, Kathy Meier, Bill Watt, and Stephen Shapiro at Fort Hays State University in Kansas.

Lloyd Anton Frerer

PART 1

The Process of Directing

In the first section of this book, the overall job of the director will be described, followed by the analysis and staging of an example scene from a play. While the survey of the tasks of an artistic director outlined in Chapter 1 is common to most textbooks concerned with directing, the detailed study of a particular scene is not. Careful attention is given in Chapter 2 to the reasons for and rules of movement for actors on the stage, followed by a step-by-step analysis of the acting scene. In Chapter 3, an actual staging of that scene is recorded, allowing the reader to see all of these principles brought together in action. Rather than trying to imagine a theoretical staging of the scene, the author chose to describe the way things happened in reality, the actual interaction between a director and actors. Thus, the reader will be armed with an understanding of directing as a practical and action-packed dynamic process when he or she encounters a more detailed explanation of each of the director's tasks, chapter by chapter, in the later sections of the book. Welcome to the world of the director in the theatre.

CHAPTER 1

RESPONSIBILITIES OF THE DIRECTOR

Directors imagine and initiate a theatrical production. They embue it with a sense of mission, inspiring their coworkers with a sense of ensemble. They focus the disparate production elements into an integrated and meaningful dramatic experience. . . . They create dramatic events.

(Cohen and Harrop 1984, 10–11)

In this chapter, we will survey the responsibilities of the director of a play. Later in the book, most of these responsibilities will be discussed in greater detail. Assuming that you are in the process of attending a class in play directing, early projects in directing may be assigned soon. With that in mind, the first section of the book will cover enough basic information for you to begin directing immediately.

Because the director of a stage production is responsible for the entire resulting project, his or her job often may seen without limits. Although specific tasks are often delegated to someone else, the director is responsible because he or she is the chief officer and must worry about every task in the theatre. In contrast, when acting in a production, a performer need only worry about his or her own work. If another actor has problems, that is too bad, but that is not his or her responsibility. However, when the actors or technicians make mistakes, those mistakes are the director's responsibility. While the breadth of the director's responsibility is large, the actual tasks encompassed vary with the directing situation.

In professional circumstances such as a motion picture or a Broadway play, the person responsible for the overall production is called the **producer.** The director's job is more narrow; he or she is responsible only for the artistic aspects of the production. Someone else takes care of the money, pays the bills, and does the organizational tasks.

Many high school and college directors, on the other hand, are their own scene designers, lighting technicians, publicists, and so on. In most community theatres, for example, the only responsible person—often the only person on salary—is the director; everyone else is a volunteer, often with limited experience and available time.

What then, is the director's position in the theatre? The director is the person who provides inspiration and artistic unity for the play, the person responsible for making sure that the whole production happens in a timely and successful fashion. Aside from being caught up in peripheral production tasks, what are the central artistic jobs of the director? Specifically, the director chooses the play, analyzes the script, sets up the auditions and casts the roles, guides the play through a series of rehearsals, and, finally, views and evaluates the results. Now let us look at each of these tasks, one by one.

Play Selection

Selecting a script is the first and one of the most important tasks of the director. That decision is often limited to or controlled by a number of outside factors in both the amateur and professional theatre. For example, if the show is part of a season, the director's options may be limited. If a theatre season contains three contemporary comedies, a director may choose a serious play for the fourth entry. Or, if three contemporary plays are scheduled, a director might choose a classic for the fourth slot.

Play Selection Committees

The director might not be the only voice in the script selection. In a number of community theatres, the board of directors or some other committee reads plays and submits a list to the director. Fortunately, because few directors enjoy being entirely trapped by others' choices, some leeway is provided. For example, a group of plays may be suggested from which the director can choose one he or she prefers to stage.

Professional Assignment

In the professional theatre, the director may be offered a job that involves no choice, but because the director needs the job, he or she would be willing to direct anything. At times, the professional director is responsible for suggesting a project, but just as often the project is a producer's idea or a studio's idea, and the director is just hired on. *Gone with the Wind* has always been considered to be a David O. Selznick project. Although Selznick was the producer, not the director, he had complete artistic control of the film's production.

Commercial Considerations

The choice of plays may well be colored by commercial considerations. A college director may have more freedom of choice than a community theatre director would have, simply because the community theatre must break even or profit at the box office. Therefore, the director might choose more popular plays that will draw larger audiences. The college director, on the other hand, does not have to make money with the play because the theatre is subsidized by the university as a service for the students and other members of the audience. The director can take a chance on a Greek classic or a Shakespearean piece, something that might not be a popular smash-hit. Clearly, directors' situations often limit their freedom of choice.

Practical Considerations

The choice of play may also be limited by practical and logistical considerations. How many actors and actresses are needed? How difficult are the roles? If directors do not have a very talented actor available, they will not choose to produce *Hamlet*. For that matter, if twenty male performers are not available, it will be difficult to produce many of Shakespeare's plays. In other words, directors must look closely at any play they are considering and decide if it can be done by their group. Does the play require numerous or more complicated sets than can be built? Is it a costume extravaganza? One advantage of doing a contemporary play is that the actors can wear their own clothes. A classic piece requires costumes, and even if the talent is available to sew costumes, they are extremely expensive. Clearly, such considerations concern budget and personnel—money to pay for the materials and talented personnel to do the work. Both must be available before deciding on a particular play.

Personal Considerations

Directors choose a play for many different reasons. More than likely, the main reason is that they like the play. They had some experience with it, either reading it or seeing a production, and were taken by it. As artists, we react to things and assume that other people will react to them in a similar fashion. We find such-and-such a play to be funny or touching or inspiring, and we choose to produce it for our audience because we are sure they will feel the same way that we did. Directors, then, are making a choice based upon their own personal judgment and are also attempting to assess the type of play their audience might enjoy.

Script Analysis

Having chosen the piece, the director must now determine the effect of the play and how to put the play together in order to achieve that effect. This is a complex process, one that will be discussed in detail later in the book. Ultimately, the director will arrive at a plan for his or her production, often called the director's vision or concept of the play. Throughout this book, a particular production of Woody Allen's *Play It Again, Sam* will be used as an extended example of the directing process. Details of this artistic analysis for *Play It Again, Sam* will be found in Chapter 5.

After choosing a play, the director must reread the play in more detail for technical reasons, looking at props, sound effects—anything that might become a problem. For example, at the opening of *Sam,* the main character is watching a Humphrey Bogart film, *The Maltese Falcon,* on television. The director might try to find a videotape copy of this movie because it is required by the script. Details of this practical analysis for *Sam* will be found in Chapter 7. In this way, the director reads through the script, making lists of problems to be solved. Then, he or she would read the script again, looking for good audition scenes. Directors want to discover strong scenes between particular characters, making note of their location in the script. Then, when actors read for those roles at an audition, the director knows exactly where to locate moments that allow the actors to deal with the characters at some length. At this stage in the directing process, the director will read the script a number of times, each for a different purpose, as part of the analysis of the play.

Auditions and Casting

Numerous methods are used to audition actors for a play. Traditionally, the actors are assigned scenes from the play to read aloud. The director hears how they sound, sees how they look, takes notes, and tries to fit people into the roles. If the director has been around a certain theatre for some time and has come to know some of the performers, it is difficult not to picture certain people in certain roles, to sense that such-and-such an actor might play a particular role well. In general, it is a mistake to precast a role in mind before auditions, unless that role has unusually difficult requirements, such as great acting skill (necessary for a role such as Hamlet) or specific musical talent for a major musical comedy role, so that such preplanning is not only wise, but necessary. The point is: At an audition that is open to all, the director should keep an open mind.

A cold reading is not the only type of audition. One may ask actors to audition with memorized work. Many actors have scenes prepared from different plays they have done and can give three or five minutes of **memorized audition pieces**. This kind of tryout typically is done as a general audition for summer theatre work. Casting directors from a number of theatres are present, and they expect the actors to demonstrate their skills with a memorized audition. At all musical auditions, the performer is expected to arrive with a prepared song number, even when the dialogue portion of the audition is to be read cold.

One advantage of the **open audition** is that the director can see all the people who might be cast standing together onstage. They can be auditioned together in different combinations. In the film industry, the director seldom has this advantage. After looking at the actor's picture and reading his or her credits in the screen actor's book, the director calls the actor in for an interview. The actor may read a few lines with the director or with another person whom the director has recruited for that purpose, but the director seldom sees the performer with anybody else he or she is planning to cast. Such a combination of personal interview and audition is common on the professional theatre level, as well.

Whatever the form of audition, the director is trying to get the best cast members for the roles in the play. Analysis of a role has uncovered certain specific characteristics, and the director is looking for a performer who seems to demonstrate a closely matching set of characteristics. When reading the play, the director should avoid picturing unnecessary details of the characters' appearance.

Unless directors have a great pool of talent, the more specifically they picture a role, the less likely they are to find someone who will fit that role. Because roles allow for great variation of characteristics, they can be played by a variety of people. For example, a role might require the character to seem mature and dynamic, but other characteristics such as height or hair color would not matter. The director is looking for a performer who has those few key characteristics that truly are important to the role.

The director must be wary of visuals in the audition, as there is a tendency for looks to dominate. It is better to listen carefully and choose performers who are able to act the character, even if they do not look like the character. One can change the way people look on stage—make a short woman tall by putting her in heels and a high hairdo or make a plain person look quite striking. At one audition, the skinniest actor in the talent pool was cast as Falstaff—Shakespeare's big, fat comic character—but he was the funniest and most skilled actor. That director knew what he was doing; padding an actor to make him or her look heavy onstage is easy. The worst mistake a director can make is to cast a performer based solely on appearance and find that he or she cannot act the role believably.

Rehearsals

Once the director has cast the play, the rehearsals begin. The rehearsal period consumes the most time in directing and is divided into a series of different kinds of rehearsals.

Reading Rehearsals

The first rehearsals are **reading rehearsals,** in which everyone sits down and reads through the play aloud, each actor reading his or her own role. The director, having previously analyzed the play, now listens to the cast read the play, discussing each important moment, trying to bring about an agreement concerning who the characters are and what the play is all about.

One common approach for the director at this time is to have the actors write autobiographies of their characters and, perhaps, something about their characters' aspirations. What would their characters wish to be happening in their lives a year from now, five years from now? The script tells about a day or a week in the life of the character. Based upon the clues given in the script, the actor writes the life story of his character, imagining reasonable events to fill in the gaps not specifically explained in the script. The purpose of this exercise is to create a three-dimensional human being. Everyone has a past. If actors are to believe in their characters as real persons, they should invent a past life for their characters. At the next rehearsal, performers read their autobiography aloud and the cast members discuss whether the conclusions seem sensible and appropriate to the play. For example, if the character of the butler decides for no logical reason that his mother was a mass murderer, the cast will soon throw cold water on that idea.

Thus, the first section of the rehearsal period is dedicated to the reading and analysis of the play. How many rehearsals are devoted to that purpose? That depends upon the difficulty of the play itself. For the Woody Allen play, two or three rehearsals will suffice because the actors will get into the play and come to understand the characters rapidly. On the other hand, if one of Shakespeare's plays was chosen, the reading rehearsals might last a week or more. Because the poetic language of such a play is extremely difficult, even for experienced performers, a substantial portion of the rehearsal time would be devoted to reaching a clear understanding of the meaning of each and every phrase. However long it takes, the director and the actors must have a basic understanding of the meaning of every event and of the motivation behind every event in the play before they move into the next phase of rehearsals.

Blocking Rehearsals

Next, we come to what are called **blocking rehearsals.** It is during these rehearsals that the director and the actors create the major movement of the play. Onstage, going through the lines of the script, the director moves the actors around, or they move themselves under the director's guidance, and once particular movements are determined, the actors write their characters' movements in the margins of their scripts. A number of days are spent on this process, going through the play scene by scene. A few more days will be spent running through the play act by act, practicing, polishing, and correcting any problems that might be noticed in the blocking. Blocking rehearsals constitute a major portion of the art of directing and will be discussed in greater detail later in the text.

Line Rehearsals

Once the action of the play is arranged on the stage, a segment of rehearsals (called **line rehearsals**) usually is devoted to the memorization of lines. How much of the rehearsal period is devoted to each segment? For our example, *Play It Again, Sam* will have a five-week rehearsal, opening in the middle of the fifth week. Two or three days will be spent in reading and analysis, followed by ten days of blocking. Therefore, reading and blocking will take the first two weeks. Then, we will spend a week learning lines, weaning the actors from dependence on their scripts until they know both the dialogue and the movement by heart. Ideally, everyone will have the show memorized by the end of this week.

Alternate organizational patterns exist for accomplishing the same ends. For example, some directors like to block one act, learn it, and polish it before going on the next act. Actors should not learn the lines until they have learned a great deal about the script. The more they know about their characters and the way things are going to happen in the play, the more likely they are to deliver their lines in an appropriate manner. If memorization is held off until all the movement has been blocked, the actors will know exactly what they are doing, as well as what they are saying, at any moment. This knowledge will affect the way they say their lines. Once they memorize a line in a particular way, young, inexperienced actors are seldom able to say it in any other way; they are locked into a certain pattern of delivery. By waiting until he or she discovers what the line means from the experience of numerous rehearsals, the actor has a better chance of memorizing that line with an appropriate pattern of delivery.

Final Rehearsals

Now that the overall action is set and the lines are memorized, the **final rehearsals** begin. The fourth week is devoted to **polishing rehearsals.** Polishing involves development of the crucial details, such as levels of intensity, emotion, and timing. The fifth and final week will begin with a **technical rehearsal,** followed by a series of **dress rehearsals,** leading to the opening night of the play. Up to this point, the cast has been working without costumes, using makeshift props, and relying on card-table chairs for the proper furniture. At the technical rehearsal, all the details are added. Suddenly, the actors have to adjust to scenery, costumes, makeup, and lighting after rehearsing for weeks just imagining all these things. In the following rehearsals, the play will be done exactly as it is to be done in the actual performance so that both the actors and the stage technicians can practice their jobs; these final, polished run-throughs of the play are the dress rehearsals. Thus, for *Play It Again, Sam,* the final week will consist of a technical rehearsal on Sunday, followed by three dress rehearsals before the play opens to its first-night audience on Thursday.

Performances

Nothing has been said about performances up to this point, because the director's job is officially over when the play opens and the performances begin. In New York, for instance, the professional director's contract ends on opening night. Certain conditions require a continued commitment to the show—for example, replacement of cast members in a long-run hit—but otherwise the director's job is over. During the performance, the show is controlled by the stage manager. The director may be sitting in the audience, waiting for the opening night reviews; regardless, he or she is looking for a new directing assignment the moment the last show opens.

In nonprofessional theatre, the major portion of the director's work is finished on opening night; however, certain responsibilities remain during the run of the show. Usually, the director will spend some time in the dressing room before the opening performance, reassuring the actors, giving them confidence, keeping the atmosphere cool and friendly to avoid nervous reactions they may have about facing an audience for the first time. The actors have depended on the director for many weeks, and they will continue to depend on the director during the performances. The director has been the eyes of the audience for them all the way through rehearsals. They depended on the director to make sure they were doing a good job out there and to tell them so. They will want to know how well the show went on a particular night and whether it was as good as the performance of the previous night. The actors expect the director to be there because of the emotional relationship which has been created between them throughout the rehearsals.

Evaluation

Finally, after the production has closed, the director should attempt to objectively evaluate his or her work. During the production, everyone's ego is heavily involved—who needs criticism at this point? Better to wait a week or two for this self-evaluation. Such **evaluation,** however, is important for directors. What can they learn from this experience that will make them better directors next time? How can they avoid making the same mistakes? Perhaps the director had a bad relationship with an actor throughout the rehearsal. What was wrong? If the director ever works with somebody like that again, how can he or she improve the relationship? Perhaps one actor did not succeed in their performance; audience members said the actor was terrible. What could the director have done to make that performer more successful? Is there anything that could have been done that was missed? We are talking about the evaluation of our directing work for our own personal growth. A little honest objectivity may lead to a great deal of improvement in the director's next show.

It should be pointed out that directors may differ in their rehearsal time. Five weeks is the minimum—many directors rehearse at greater length. Some directors, such as Marshall Mason of the Circle Repertory, spend considerable time with "table work" (reading and discussion), while Joanne Akalaitis of the Public Theatre likes to get the actors on their feet early. Each aspect of the director's tasks will be discussed at greater length later on in this text.

Summary

In this chapter, we have surveyed the overall job of the director. Typically, the director chooses and analyzes the play, arranges the auditions and casts the play, and leads the cast through a series of rehearsals. The director is the person who provides inspiration and artistic unity for the play, the person responsible for making sure that the whole production takes place in a timely and successful fashion.

First, the director makes a "profound analysis" in order to develop a "unique perception" of the "particular world" of the play; next, the director joins with the actors and the other members of the production team to discover ways to "embody" that world; finally, the production is brought before the audience as a unified and accessible experience which invites them to discover the world of the play for themselves.

(Benedetti 1985, 11)

CHAPTER 2

STAGING A SCENE
The Analysis

In the second and third sections of this book, beginning with Chapter 4, each of the different aspects of the director's tasks will be dealt with in order, from choosing a script to the final production. However, now that we have surveyed the overall job of the director, let us concentrate on the type of task a beginning director is most likely to have: the staging of a single scene from a play. The scene used as an example will be one from *The Rainmaker* by N. Richard Nash. We will look at a way of analyzing the scene as well as the reasons for and rules of stage movement. We shall then apply these concepts to the scene itself, first with a reading and analysis of the script and, finally, with the description of the actual **blocking** of the action. A second example of this process of scene analysis and blocking will be provided in Chapter 15.

When working with a full-length play, from moment to moment, the director is working with one small segment of that play. Therefore, directing a scene is much the same as directing the whole play; one follows a similar process. The production duties are greater when doing a full play because the director requires props, appropriate costumes and furniture, proper lighting, and the like. However, for training purposes, these technicalities can be minimized.

The director can analyze a scene in much the same way he or she might approach a larger piece. One can ask of the scene: Who is the **protagonist,** or main character? About who or what is the **antagonist** in conflict with the main character? What is the scene about—does it have a **climax,** or high point of emotion and intensity? In a small way, scenes usually have a structure similar to that of whole plays, and they also build up to some high point or climax.

Analysis of Beats

The particular term we will use in our analysis of the scene comes from **method acting.** Konstantin Stanislavsky, a Russian director whose major work was done close to the turn of the twentieth century, developed a system of actor training which, in America, is commonly called **method acting.** One hears about performers such as Marlon Brando being described as method actors; this means that they were trained in this system. Most acting schools, both professional and university-level, use some variation of Stanislavsky's method here in America.

Stanislavsky called the smallest analytical unit in a play a **beat.** A beat is a segment of the scene, no matter how long, in which the characters maintain both a continuous purpose or goal and the same method of achieving that goal. A beat might be two or three lines long, or it might be a whole page long; there is no specified length. The length depends upon the characters' goals and what they are doing to achieve those goals at that moment. For example, a wife is trying to get her husband to take her to Hawaii instead of to a ball game in Kansas City. At first, she tries to seduce him with sweet talk. When that tactic fails, she gets angry and demands to have her way. Although her purpose and his response remain constant, each new tactic used to get him to change his mind would constitute a new beat. In this imaginary scene, we assume that she is the protagonist, that he is the antagonist, and that the climax of the scene would come when she finally wins him over or when she becomes so frustrated that she takes out a pistol and shoots him. This example is rather melodramatic but nonetheless demonstrates a series of beats rising to a climax.

At times, the beat does not change simultaneously for both characters. Sometimes, one character will go on consistently for a number of lines after the other has changed beats before realizing what has happened. One cannot always draw a line across the page and say, "That is where the new beat starts, no question about it." Just as often, the choice is a matter of sensitive judgment.

Discovering the beats is a way of analyzing a scene which Stanislavsky developed for actors. The actor wants to know each time his purpose changes and each time the other character's purpose changes so that he or she can understand his character and react to those changes. Marking out all the beats in the script and writing each new change of purpose or tactic in the margin is a very useful way for actors to analyze the scene, and it can be helpful for the director as well. In practice, many actors make these discoveries instinctively; they don't write out the separate beats. Nevertheless, they are aware of these moments of change. The more aware the actor can be of the moments when the beat changes, the more the actor will play the moment properly and effectively, because these are the moments when new things happen in terms of line delivery, emotional attitude, and movement. Thus, we will study our scene from *The Rainmaker* in terms of beats, allowing those beats to lead us into actual movement on the stage.

The Basis of Movement

What is the basis for actor movement on the stage? Many directors and textbooks have illustrated the following idea, but it was brought home most clearly to this author by George Kernodle, head of the theatre department at the University of Arkansas. At the time, Dr. Kernodle was the visiting director for a production of Shakespeare's *Twelfth Night* at the University of Iowa. Most Shakespearean scenes consist of two or three characters and an empty stage; there is not even a bench on which to sit. My experience had involved plays with objects on the stage which I would use as an excuse for movement: go to the bench, cross behind the couch, sit at the table, and so on. Kernodle said that movement has nothing to do with the furniture; acting movement onstage is based on characters moving toward or away from one another. Because the furniture is incidental to movement, the director should find it just as easy to block a scene between two characters on an empty stage as to direct them on a stage with furniture. Of course, furniture lends variety to a scene, but the basis of blocking is the movement of characters toward and away from one another. The purpose of this movement is to demonstrate the relationship between the characters from moment to moment. For example, you are angry with me, and, as a result, you turn your back on me or walk away. If you are sympathizing with me or want something from me, you will probably move toward me. The physical movement illustrates the emotional relationship, the event that is happening between the characters. Obviously, in real life, it is possible to tell someone that you love them without moving toward that person. But, in drama, the actor should take every opportunity to make the movement that is appropriate to the emotional situation.

Thus, the director wants the actors to **physicalize** as well as to vocalize the emotional relationships; that is the underlying basis of blocking the action. The director and actors read the scene and analyze the beats, attempting to discern what is happening in the characters' relationship, the changing relationship between those characters during the scene. This knowledge will then be used to create the movement of the characters toward and away from one another, movement which illustrates their fluctuating emotional relationship from moment to moment.

The Amount of Movement

People probably move more onstage than they do in real life. For the most part, the director will use every excuse for movement, because watching people just standing around and talking can and does get boring. A phrase used in reference to television soap operas is "talking heads," meaning that all the characters do in soaps is stand around the room and talk; they seldom move or do anything physical. A stage play can be just like that—nothing but talking heads. Take, for example, a conversation between two people sitting at a table. In reality, it would be perfectly reasonable if they sat at that table for the entire conversation. However, such a scene could become a deadly bore on stage. Therefore, the director looks for sensible reasons to move those actors, using every opportunity offered by the script to make the play more visually interesting.

One rule of tempo states that the greater the amount of movement in a play, the faster the play seems to go by. Of course, tempo in this sense is an illusion. We've all attended 50-minute lectures that just seemed to whiz by, as well as 50-minute lectures that felt like they were 150 minutes long. One technique that makes a stage play seem to take place in a shorter period of time is the addition of more physical movement to the blocking. Think of action-packed movie scenes such as car chases; these scenes always seem more lively and fast-paced than scenes with people just sitting around and talking.

Common wisdom tells us that comedy needs more movement than tragedy. Certainly, comedy requires a sense of pace to keep it quick, light, hectic, funny, while a serious piece can afford to be slower and more dramatic. Nevertheless, if the director wants the pace of either type of play to seem quick instead of slow and boring, one way to achieve that quality is to create more movement in the blocking.

Stage Locations

Because we are discussing stage movement, let us look at common descriptive terminology for the stage. Onstage, the directions left and right are opposite of those for the audience. Commonly called **stage right** and **stage left,** these directions are from the actor's point of view while facing the audience. An actor directed to "cross left" will move to his or her left, which is to the right of the director facing the stage. The direction toward the audience is called **downstage;** the direction away from the audience is called **upstage.** This terminology comes from the period between 1650 and the beginning of the twentieth century, when stage floors were actually raked or tilted upward, away from the audience. Thus, when actors came downstage, moving toward the audience, they were literally walking downhill. "Center," as in the center of the stage, refers to a particular location, so directions for movement can be given to the actor thusly: move center, move down center (or simply cross down), or cross up left or down right. In these examples, only "center" means a particular place on the stage. All other commands simply require the actor to move in a certain direction from the place in which he or she is standing at that moment.

Figure 2.1 shows the stage divided into a grid of squares, each square with a label. The three squares on stage left are called "up left," "left center," and "down left." If your set designer wants to put a table left center, you will find it useful to understand what that means in terms of stage location. But for actual stage movement, such a grid is minimally useful. A comment from the director indicating that an actor should cross left to a chair would result in a movement by that actor from wherever he or she is onstage to the chair, as well as a notation in the margin of the actor's script: "XL to chair." And "XDL" means cross in a down left direction from the current position onstage. It has no relation to the down left square on the grid.

Rules for Movement

In the majority of staging situations, the director is dealing with a **proscenium stage,** an arrangement in which the audience views the action from out front, all looking in the same direction. The general principles for movement on the stage relate to this particular form of staging, allowing the audience to see the actor more clearly and focusing the audience attention on a particular actor at any one moment. These principles are the "common wisdom," and, as such, should be

Figure 2.1

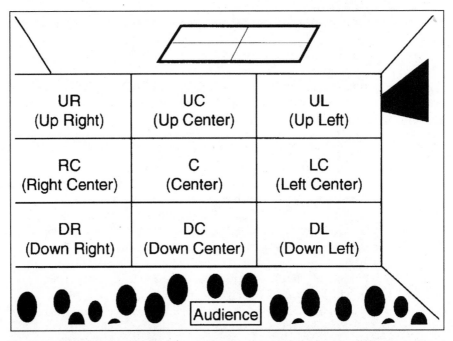

A stage divided into descriptive areas. All directions are from the actor's perspective when facing the audience. In marking a script for movement, the annotation "X" stands for *cross,* so "XC" denotes a movement *cross center,* "X DR to table" means to *cross down right to the table,* "X to her" means *cross to her,* and so on. This type of shorthand will be used to describe the blocking of a scene in Chapter 3.

taken with a grain of salt. In most cases, the director might as well follow the common wisdom, simply because it makes good sense; it works. When a particular situation seems to provide good reason for doing so, it is acceptable to break the rules. Otherwise, one would do well to follow the tradition, which provides sensible rules of thumb and a clear path to follow.

Improving Visibility

The audience wants to see the actors' faces and hear their voices clearly; therefore, a number of rules exist regarding opening the actor's face and body to view. Unless it is necessary to do so, actors should never turn their backs on the audience. Of course, turning one's back might create an unusual special effect; however, if nothing is to be gained by this, why turn a back to the audience? Thus, actors spend most of their time either facing the audience or turned one-quarter to the left or to the right, facing down left or down right. In real life, two people in conversation naturally face one another. When actors face each other they are in profile—a half turn away from the audience. Two actors in conversation onstage usually open their bodies one-quarter turn toward the audience, avoiding such a profile position for most situations. While experienced actors will operate this way instinctively, the director may have to teach new performers to **open up,** as they may feel more natural standing in profile. Experienced actors have an uncanny way of playing face-on to the audience, even when they are in conversation with other actors. They find ways to be wide open to the audience while making it look quite natural.

When actors turn around onstage, they should turn downstage so that their faces are always toward the audience. A large gesture, such as pointing at something across the stage, should be done with the upstage hand so that the body remains open to the audience. An actor should kneel on the downstage knee, again so that the body remains open to the audience. Each of these simple rules accomplishes the same goal: providing the audience with a clear view of the actor.

The **arrangement** of actors onstage has symbolic as well as practical values. A character may seem to be isolated by other characters onstage or entrapped by them, simply because of the way those actors are placed on the stage. Even the actor's degree of turn toward or away from the audience has subtle implications. The quarter-turn position provides a high degree of intimacy; profile positions are more remote; and a three-quarter turn away from the audience seems almost antisocial.

Focusing Attention

Another series of traditions for stage movement deals with control of the attention of the audience. The director wants to focus the attention on the actor who has the most important lines or business at a particular moment. Thus, as a general rule, the actor may move during his or her own lines, but remains still when another actor speaks his lines. Generally, the director wants the audience attention focused on the actor who is talking. If that actor moves about at the same time, he or she will draw even more attention. But if everyone else is moving around onstage, the audience will be distracted. They won't know where to look. On the other hand, if the director wished to focus attention on the reaction of one actor to another, the listener might sensibly make a sudden move while the speaker remained still. Movement controls attention, while simultaneous movement often can be confusing. By following this rule, the director is able to shift the audience's attention from one actor to another at will, avoiding confusion.

When an actor reciting lines passes another actor onstage, he or she should cross downstage of that person. If the moving actor passes behind the listener, attention might pass to the listener, who is more prominent and visible for that brief moment. Of course, circling around another actor while trying to talk him or her into something or arguing is an appropriate movement. In this case, the actor would circle upstage to avoid turning a back on the audience. This is not a case of simply crossing past another actor on stage.

For inexperienced actors, turning their back on a person to whom they are talking seems difficult and unnatural. When moving away from another actor onstage, they will have a natural tendency to turn immediately and face the other person, even though that turn may put their back toward the audience. Yet, an actor crossing away from another, moving down left or down right while talking, looks very natural on the stage. Not only that, a negative movement, such as a cross away from another actor, is often a necessary tool for the director.

The director may have to work with actors until they become comfortable delivering lines with their backs to the listener and their faces to the audience, saving the movement of turning toward the listener for a particularly appropriate moment, if at all. Movement units, such as standing up, sitting, crossing, and turning around, are best used one at a time. One could cross and turn around on a single line of dialogue, but a better sense of movement is created when one crosses on one line and saves the turn for a succeeding line. Of course, characters who are upset or angry will often run a series of such movement units together, jumping up from a chair, then crossing and turning around on the same line, for example.

The preceding discussion of stage movement is a summary of basic but key rules. Once the director understands the desired goals to be achieved, inventing movements which fulfill these goals is not difficult. For the most part, following these traditions of stage movement, while choosing movements that illustrate the emotional relationship of the characters at each moment by having them move toward or away from one another, should provide the director with the tools necessary for the development of blocking.

Background of the Scene

The scene that we will stage as an example of the process of directing is the first of two scenes that take place in a tack room, at the close of the second act of *The Rainmaker* by N. Richard Nash. The director will explain the background of the play to the actors, because, in order to understand the scene and its ramifications, the actors must know how the scene fits into the rest of the play. The actors will then read the scene aloud, and we shall discuss the action in terms of its beats.

The story takes place in Nebraska—a country story about farmers and ranchers—during a terrible drought. It concerns a family named Curry: a father, two sons, and a daughter. The father is easygoing, whereas Noah, the older brother who runs the ranch, is conservative, domineering, and dictatorial. Noah is constantly giving his teenage brother, Jimmy, a hard time. Jimmy is a charming, comic screw-up, and Noah tries to discipline the boy "for his own good." The daughter, Lizzie, is the central character. Lizzie is in her twenties, really quite young, but she lives in a culture that assumes that if a girl is not married by the time she graduates from high school, she is on the way to becoming an old maid. And Lizzie is not married, a fact which has the whole family worried, including Lizzie. She reads a lot; she is very bright, straight-laced, and not a real beauty. In general, the atmosphere that surrounds Lizzie scares the boys away; thus, her father and brothers are always trying to get her together with someone, to fix her up with a date, but their efforts never seem to work out.

Into this situation comes a hustler. His name is Bill Starbuck, and he is selling himself as a rainmaker. The police are on his trail, which will lead to a clash with the local sheriff and deputy toward the close of the play. The father and Jimmy, being romantics, take to this colorful intruder immediately; but Noah and Lizzie, being practical and sensible, become angry. Making rain—what a stupid idea! Nevertheless, the father hires Starbuck. The relationship between Lizzie and Starbuck is extremely negative from the start, in part because he is forward and a little flirtatious with her, which clearly makes her nervous.

Just before our scene, the family has had a major argument in the house. Thinking he is doing it for her own good, Noah tells Lizzie, "Nobody's gonna come ridin' up here on a white horse. Nobody's gonna snatch you up in his arms and marry you. You're gonna be an old maid! And the sooner you face it, the sooner you'll stop breakin' your heart." Lizzie is devastated. She runs out of the house in tears, carrying blankets that have been promised to Starbuck so that he can sleep in the tack room. Having just had a traumatic emotional experience, she arrives at the tack room to find a stranger whom she does not like.

Scene Analysis ⚞

Once this background information has been given, the actors begin their reading of the script.

STARBUCK: Who's that? (He rises tautly.) Who's there?

LIZZIE: (LIZZIE stands at rear of tack room, trying not to look into the room. She is carrying the bed linens. Trying to sound calm) It's me—Lizzie.

(STARBUCK starts to put on his shirt. An awkward moment. Then
        LIZZIE without entering the room, hands him the bedding
        across the threshold.)

LIZZIE: Here.

STARBUCK: What's that?

LIZZIE: Bed stuff—take them.

STARBUCK: Is that what you came out for?

LIZZIE: (After a painful moment) No—I came out because—(She finds it
        too difficult to continue.)

STARBUCK: (Gently) Go on, Lizzie.

LIZZIE: I came out to thank you for what you said to Noah.

STARBUCK: I meant every word of it.

LIZZIE: What you said about Jim—I'm sure you meant that.

STARBUCK: What I said about you?

LIZZIE: I don't believe you.

STARBUCK: Then what are you thankin' me for? What's the matter,
        Lizzie? You afraid that if you stop bein' sore at me you'll like
        me a little?

LIZZIE: No . . . (And she starts to go.)

STARBUCK: (stopping her) Then stay and talk to me! (As she hesitates)
        It's lonely out here and I don't think I'll sleep much—not in a
        strange place.

LIZZIE: Then I guess you never sleep. Running from one strange place to
        another.

STARBUCK: (With a smile) Not runnin'—travelin'.

Let us stop and discuss what is happening here. Starbuck and Lizzie talk
about bed linens, a mundane exchange until he asks if that was her reason for
coming. He implies that the linens were just an excuse, that she wants something
else. She admits to another reason, and we have a new beat. Something new is
happening between them. She thanks him for defending Jimmy from Noah, but
when he pushes the point to what he said about her, she has a quick, negative
reaction which begins another new beat. Starbuck begins talking about his life as
a rainmaker, and Lizzie goes along with the idea. The actors continue reading.

LIZZIE: Well, if that's the kind of life you like. . . .

STARBUCK: Oh, it's not what a man likes—it's what he's got to do. Now what would a fella in my business be doin' stayin' in the same place? Rain's nice—but it ain't nice all the time.

LIZZIE: (Relaxing a bit) No, I guess not.

STARBUCK: People got no use for me—except maybe once in a lifetime. And when my work's done, they're glad to see me go.

LIZZIE: (Caught by the loneliness in his voice) I never thought of it that way.

STARBUCK: Why would you? You never thought of me as a real rainmaker—not until just now.

LIZZIE: I still don't think it! (Now she starts to go more determinedly than before.)

STARBUCK: Lizzie—wait! Why don't you let yourself think of me the way you **want** to?

LIZZIE: (Unnerved) What do you mean?

STARBUCK: Think like Lizzie, not like Noah.

LIZZIE: I don't know what you're talking about.

Lizzie doesn't believe that Starbuck is a rainmaker; her attitude changes as she backs off, and we have a new beat. See how easily that new beat leads to movement. She says, "I still don't think it!" and turns or moves away from him. Starbuck begins a new tactic, trying to win her over.

STARBUCK: Lizzie! What are you scared of?

LIZZIE: You! I don't trust you!

STARBUCK: Why? What don't you trust about me?

LIZZIE: Everything! The way you talk, the way you brag—why, even your name!

STARBUCK: What's wrong with my name?

LIZZIE: It sounds fake! It sounds like you made it up!

STARBUCK: You're darn right! I did make it up!

LIZZIE: There! Of course!

STARBUCK: Why not? You know what name I was born with? Smith! Smith, for the love of Mike, **Smith**! Now what kind of handle is that for a fella like me! I needed a name that had the whole sky in it! And the power of a man! Star—buck! Now there's a name—and it's mine!

LIZZIE: No it's not! You were born Smith—and that's your name!

STARBUCK: You're wrong, Lizzie! The name you choose for yourself is more your own than the name you were born with! And if I was you I'd choose another name than Lizzie!

LIZZIE: Thank you—I'm very pleased with it!

Starbuck defends himself by standing up for his name after Lizzie puts him down. Now he will get even by attacking her name, thus beginning a new beat. She attacked his name, putting him on the defensive; now he attacks her name and she is on the defensive. With each new beat, there is a change in mood which becomes the motivation for movement. What kind of movement? Starbuck is a very colorful character. He is the kind of person who might jump up onto chairs or tables. Because he is an itinerant preacher and a showman, he can do much more outlandish things than the conservative Lizzie can do. For example, this author has seen productions in which, during Starbuck's line about needing a name with the whole sky in it—and the power of a man, actors jump up onto a chair, or a table, or a bale of hay. The first time the author saw this scene, the actor picked up a chair, holding it high in the air, aimed at the ceiling. The possibilities are numerous because a colorful character allows for large, unusual types of movement.

Three or four times, Lizzie starts to leave the tack room, an obviously repetitive situation. The director would have to find a variety of ways to stage this. Perhaps Starbuck calls her back one time. Maybe he gets between her and the door another time. How far would he go? That depends on who these characters are. Would they actually touch one another? The director and actors study the possibilities, looking for different ways to handle the situation.

STARBUCK: Oh no you ain't! You ain't pleased with anything about yourself! And I'm sure you ain't pleased with "Lizzie"!

LIZZIE: I don't ask **you** to be pleased with it, Starbuck. I **am**!

STARBUCK: Lizzie! Why, it don't **stand** for anything!

LIZZIE: It stands for me! **ME**! I'm not the Queen of Sheba—I'm not Lady Godiva—I'm not Cinderella at the Ball!

STARBUCK: Would you like to be?

LIZZIE: Starbuck, you're ridiculous!

STARBUCK: What's ridiculous about it? Dream you're somebody—be
            somebody! But Lizzie?—that's nobody! So many millions of
            wonderful women with wonderful names! (In an orgy of
            delight) Leonora, Desdemona, Caroline, Annabella, Florinda,
            Christina, Diane! (Then with a pathetic little lift of his
            shoulders) Lizzie.

LIZZIE: Goodnight, Starbuck!

Again she starts to leave, and he will begin a new tactic, trying to keep
her from going. This section also presents the actor with a problem. How does
one deal with a great long list of women's names? Can they be varied so the actor
won't sound like he's reading a telephone book? The director might help the actor
by finding a new gesture or movement to go with each of the names toward
the end of the list, a way to make each name new and different from the one that
went before.

STARBUCK: (With a sudden inspiration) Just a minute, Lizzie—just one
            little half of a minute! I got the greatest name for you—the
            greatest name—just listen! (Then, like a love lyric) Melisande.

LIZZIE: (Flatly) I don't like it.

STARBUCK: That's because you don't know anything about her! But when
            I tell you who she was—lady, when I tell you who she was!

LIZZIE: Who?

STARBUCK: She was the most beautiful— She was the beautiful wife of
            King Hamlet!—Ever hear of him?

LIZZIE: (Giving him rope) Go on!—go on!

The stage direction, "giving him rope," indicates a new beat for Lizzie, while
he goes right on, unaware of her plan. By means of movement and delivery,
Lizzie lets the audience know that she is aware that Starbuck is about to weave
a big lie. She intends to let him continue until he has made a complete fool
of himself.

STARBUCK: He was the fella who sailed across the ocean and brought
            back the Golden Fleece! And you know why he did that?
            Because Queen Melisande begged him for it! I tell you, that
            Melisande—she was so beautiful and her hair was so long and

curly—every time he looked at her he just fell right down and died! And this King Hamlet, he'd do anything for her—anything she wanted! So when she said: "Hamlet, I got a terrible hankerin' for a soft Golden Fleece," he just naturally sailed right off to find it! And when he came back—all bleedin' and torn—he went and laid that Fleece of Gold right down at her pretty white feet! And she took that fur piece and she wrapped it around her pink naked shoulders and she said: "I got the Golden Fleece—and I'll never be cold no more!"—Melisande! What a woman! What a **name**!

LIZZIE: (Forlornly) Starbuck, you silly jackass. You take a lot of stories—that I've read in a hundred different places—and you roll them up into one big fat ridiculous lie!

Let us stop at this point, not only for the new beat but also for an obvious acting problem. Starbuck delivers a lengthy solo; how does the director help the actor to keep such a monologue interesting? First, the director might want to find a neutral location for Lizzie; since she has nothing to do for quite some time, she might sit down while she listens to Starbuck. Then, Starbuck could act out his story in great detail—climbing on couches, chairs, bales of hay, whatever is available, when he "sails off to find the golden fleece." And he might end up crawling around, writhing on the floor when he returns "all bleeding and torn." After all, his character allows for such outlandish behavior.

Clearly, Lizzie causes a new beat with her reaction to his story. After leading him on, pretending to believe him, she cuts him down to size. His feelings are hurt, and he turns the attack on her. Her honest and touching response, revealing her most desperate longing, constitutes the next beat.

STARBUCK: (Angry, hurt) I wasn't lyin'—I was dreamin'!

LIZZIE: It's the same thing!

STARBUCK: If you think it's the same thing then I take it back about your name! Lizzie—it's just right for you! I'll tell you another name that would suit you—Noah! Because you and your brother—you've got no dream!

LIZZIE: (With an outcry) You think all dreams have to be your kind! Golden fleece and thunder on the mountain! But there are other dreams, Starbuck! Little quiet ones that come to a woman when she's shining the silverware and putting moth flakes in the closet!

STARBUCK: Like what?

LIZZIE: Like a man's voice saying: "Lizzie, is my blue suit pressed?" And the same man saying: "Scratch between my shoulder blades." And kids laughing and teasing and setting up a racket! And how it feels to say the word "Husband"!—There are all kinds of dreams, Mr. Starbuck! Mine are small ones—like my name—Lizzie! But they're **real** like my name—real! So you can have yours—and I'll have mine! (Unable to control her tears).

STARBUCK: (This time he grabs her fully, holding her close.) Lizzie—

LIZZIE: Please—

STARBUCK: I'm sorry, Lizzie! I'm sorry!

LIZZIE: It's all right—let me go!

STARBUCK: I hope your dreams come true, Lizzie—I hope they do!

LIZZIE: They won't—they never will!

The beat changes for Starbuck immediately. What can he say? How can he help her? His choice leads to a revelation for both of the characters and the climax of the scene.

STARBUCK: Believe in yourself and they will!

LIZZIE: I've got nothing to believe in!

STARBUCK: You're a woman! Believe in that!

LIZZIE: How can I when nobody else will?

STARBUCK: **You** gotta believe it first! (Quickly) Let me ask you, Lizzie—are you pretty?

LIZZIE: I'm a woman! A plain one!

STARBUCK: There's no such thing as a plain woman! Every real woman is pretty! They're all pretty in a different way—but they're all pretty!

LIZZIE: Not me! When I look in the looking glass—

STARBUCK: Don't let Noah be your lookin' glass! It's gotta be inside you! And then one day the lookin' glass will be the man who loves you! It'll be his eyes maybe! And you'll look in that mirror and you'll be more than pretty!—you'll be beautiful!

LIZZIE: (Crying out) It'll never happen!

STARBUCK: Make it happen! Lizzie, why don't you think "pretty"? and take down your hair! (He reaches for her hair.)

LIZZIE: (In panic) No!

STARBUCK: Please, Lizzie! (He is taking the pins out of her hair. Taking her in his arms) Now close your eyes, Lizzie—close them! (As she obeys) Now—say: I'm pretty!

LIZZIE: (Trying) I'm—I'm—I can't!

STARBUCK: Say it! Say it, Lizzie!

LIZZIE: I'm—pretty.

STARBUCK: Say it again!

LIZZIE: (With a little cry) Pretty!

STARBUCK: Say it—mean it!

LIZZIE: (Exalted) I'm pretty! I'm pretty! I'm pretty! (He kisses her. A long kiss and she clings to him, passionately, the bonds of her spinsterhood breaking away. The kiss over, she collapses on the sacks, sobbing.) (Through the sobs) Why did you do that?!

STARBUCK: (Going beside her on the sacks) Because when you said you were pretty, it was true! (Her sobs are louder, more heartrending because, for the first time, she is happy.) Lizzie—look at me!

LIZZIE: I can't!

STARBUCK: (Turning her to him) Stop cryin' and look at me! Look at my eyes! What do you see?

LIZZIE: (Gazing through her tears) I can't **believe** what I see!

STARBUCK: Tell me what you see!

LIZZIE: (With a sob of happiness) Oh, is it me?! Is it really me?!

Whereas Lizzie's attitude remains constant in resisting his arguments, Starbuck goes through a series of beats, trying new tactics to convince her. As far as we can tell from this scene, the kiss might be just another in Starbuck's series of tactics. But we discover in the final act of the play that he has fallen in love with her. Does he intend to kiss her? Probably not. It just happens. Nevertheless, the kiss is a major turning point in both of their lives.

This first read-through of the scene and analysis of the beats will make the events of the scene clear to the actors. A second read-through will provide them with a greater understanding of their characters' purpose in the scene from one moment to the next. Thus, the actors will recite the dialogue in a much more appropriate manner. They will know how to say the lines because they will understand the meaning behind each line—the **subtext** underlying the surface text of the actual script.

Some overall analysis of the scene is necessary. What happens in our scene? What is it all about? We begin the scene with two people who are very antagonistic toward one another, but by the close of the scene, they are kissing. Therefore, the scene is about the change from opponents to lovers in the relationship between the two characters. That is the action of the scene, and the kiss is the climax. Lizzie changes her opinion of herself, the low self-image she has lived with all her life. At first, Starbuck tries to con Lizzie, but he ends up trying to help her and, inadvertently, falling in love with her. At the end of the play, Starbuck asks Lizzie to go away with him. Because he is in danger of losing her, the local deputy sheriff finally gets up the courage to propose to her as well. Lizzie really is pretty now. She has two men who want to marry her. Therefore, this change in Lizzie is the major action of the whole play, *The Rainmaker*.

Summary

In this chapter, we have surveyed the reasons for stage movement, and we have applied a particular method of analysis to a single scene from the play, *The Rainmaker*. In the next chapter, we will show how this information was used to create an actual staging of that scene. The concepts presented in this chapter concerning movement on the stage are of crucial importance to directors. The basic reasons that motivate movement, as well as ideas dealing with the amount of movement needed, should be reviewed again and again. In Chapter 3, we shall see these concepts in action.

CHAPTER 3

STAGING A SCENE
The Blocking

In order to demonstrate the process involved in blocking the scene from *The Rainmaker,* the actual staging of the scene by this author was recorded during a university class in play directing. The director's comments to his actors and audience involved not only *The Rainmaker* but also principles of staging in general, because both actors and audience were learning to direct plays.

Planning the Set

Having read and analyzed the scene in detail with the actors, exactly as was done in the previous chapter, the next task was to plan a setting. A more detailed discussion of the subject of set design will be included in Chapter 7. For our purposes here, the director explained that the entire play would involve three settings, which would be on the stage simultaneously. The Curry house—which is the major locale—would take up a large portion of the center stage. Two other locations would be used: the sheriff's office and the tack room. Generally, these are smaller sets, one down left and the other down right. Therefore, we decided upon an extremely simple, small set for the tack room. At stage right we used a sturdy table and a few chairs with their backs against the table to simulate bales of hay. In effect, we had created two levels of bales: a lower one developed by the seats and a higher one by the table top. At stage center was a simple sawhorse. At stage left was the doorway, indicated by two folding chairs; we also used a few folding chairs to define the location of the back wall of the tack room. The bales of hay were at an angle to the audience, not facing front or in full profile, but rather at a quarter turn away from the audience. It is important to determine the exact location of the characters when the lights come up at the opening of any scene. Starbuck, we decided, would be sitting on the hay bales.

Blocking the Action

At this point, the blocking began. However, the director immediately noticed that his actress was following the stage directions printed in the script. Many scripts, such as those from Samuel French or Dramatists' Play Service, will have blocking printed in them, quite a bit of which was not in the original play. In publishing these scripts for amateur use, they have added some of the blocking from the prompt book of the Broadway production. Actors will follow these directions as law unless the director cautions against the practice. Assuming that our new production has different actors and a different set, such blocking written in the script should be ignored, for the most part.

STARBUCK: Who's that? Who's there?

LIZZIE: It's me—Lizzie.

The actress walked into the room on her line. The director asked whether this character would to that. He reminded the actors of the relationship which would control their movement toward or away from one another; Lizzie doesn't like Starbuck, and she is afraid of him. Therefore, she would stay away from him, remaining in the doorway (see Figure 3.1). The actors begin again.

STARBUCK: Who's that? Who's there?

LIZZIE: (She is carrying the bed linens. Trying to sound calm.) It's me—Lizzie.

Because the actor playing Starbuck did not move, the director stopped the scene to point out that Starbuck would have to cross over to Lizzie in order to get the blankets from her. The actors began again, only to be stopped so that the director could caution the actor to cross on his own line of dialogue, as much as possible.

STARBUCK: Who's that? Who's there? (Rise)

LIZZIE: (She is carrying the bed linens. Trying to sound calm.) It's me—Lizzie. Here.

Figure 3.1

STARBUCK: What's that? (<u>X TO HER</u>)

LIZZIE: Bed stuff—take them.

STARBUCK: Is that what you came out for?

LIZZIE: (After a painful moment) No—I came out because—(She finds it too difficult to continue.)

STARBUCK: (Gently) Go on, Lizzie.

LIZZIE: I came out to thank you for what you said to Noah.

STARBUCK: I meant every word of it.

The director asked whether Starbuck wanted Lizzie to stay. Would he remain that close to her? The actor decided that he would walk back into the room as soon as he had the blankets in hand. The director agreed that Starbuck would give Lizzie some space in order not to scare her away. Starbuck crossed back to the sawhorse while saying "Is that what you came for?"

STARBUCK: Is that what you came out for? (<u>X TO SAWHORSE</u>)

LIZZIE: (After a painful moment) No—I came out because—(She finds it too difficult to continue.)

STARBUCK: (Gently) Go on, Lizzie. (<u>TURN TO HER</u>)

LIZZIE: I came out to thank you for what you said to Noah.

STARBUCK: I meant every word of it.

LIZZIE: What you said about Jim—I'm sure you meant that.

STARBUCK: What I said about you?

LIZZIE: I don't believe you.

STARBUCK: Then what are you thankin' me for?

The director asked if Starbuck was not beginning to feel uncomfortable, staying in the same place for such a long time. The actor agreed. What could Starbuck be doing? It was decided that he should continue his cross all the way to the bales and make up his bed during this early conversation with Lizzie. We began again, and, having given Lizzie this much space, she automatically entered the room on her "thank you" line, crossing to the edge of the sawhorse (see Figure 3.2).

STARBUCK: Who's that? Who's there?

Figure 3.2

LIZZIE: (She is carrying the bed linens. Trying to sound calm) It's me—
           Lizzie. Here.

STARBUCK: What's that? (<u>X TO HER</u>)

LIZZIE: Bed stuff—take them.

STARBUCK: Is that what you came out for? (<u>X TO BALES</u>)

LIZZIE: (After a painful moment) No—I came out because—(She finds it
           too difficult to continue.)

STARBUCK: (Gently) Go on, Lizzie. (<u>TURN TO HER</u>)

LIZZIE: I came out to thank you for what you said to Noah. (<u>X TO
           SAWHORSE</u>)

STARBUCK: I meant every word of it.

LIZZIE: What you said about Jim—I'm sure you meant that.

STARBUCK: What I said about you?

LIZZIE: I don't believe you.

Clearly, the last line called for a negative movement. It was decided that
Lizzie should move down left, away from Starbuck, keeping her back to him. The
director asked the actors to pick up the scene from the line, "I came out to thank
you for. . . ."

LIZZIE: I came out to thank you for what you said to Noah.

STARBUCK: I meant every word of it.

LIZZIE: What you said about Jim—I'm sure you meant that.

STARBUCK: What I said about you? (<u>TURN TOWARD HER</u>)

LIZZIE: I don't believe you. (<u>XDL</u>)

STARBUCK: Then what are you thankin' me for? What's the matter,
Lizzie? You afraid that if you stop bein' sore at me you'll like
me a little? (<u>X TOWARD HER</u>)

LIZZIE: No . . . (And she starts to go) (<u>X TO DOOR</u>)

STARBUCK: (stopping her) Then stay and talk to me! (As she hesitates)
It's lonely out here and I don't think I'll sleep too much—not
in a strange place.

Starbuck had moved toward Lizzie, and everyone approved of that choice.
The director suggested that the actor make that move a more definite and direct
one, rather than just drifting toward her. Lizzie's movement, however, is manda-
tory, required by the script. Starbuck's line, "Stay and talk to me," clearly implies
that Lizzie is attempting to leave.

The majority of movement onstage is a matter of choice; however, a few
movements are required by the script—that is, without those movements, the
script makes no sense. The director told about a production of *California Suite*
in which a number of required movements were ignored. For example, in one
scene the actor said to the actress, "Sit up! Sit up!" but the woman actually was
standing up at that moment. Obviously, the line required her to be lounging or
lying down.

Notice how this method of blocking develops. The director and actors invent
the movement together. They read the script until they come to a point where
something new is needed. The actors and/or director suggest a new movement.
They go back to the point in the script where the blocking was satisfactory, and
work their way forward again until some new problem appears. Such overlap-
ping and repetition of the reading of dialogue may seem tedious on the written
page, but that is how the actual process of blocking occurs. The director encour-

ages the actors to try a movement when they feel the urge. The director can agree with that movement, suggest that it go in a different direction, or suggest that no movement is appropriate at that moment. The director also may initiate a movement when none is forthcoming from the actor. Both director and actors should be sensitive to the fact that the actors have been standing in the same place for too long and back up to find some reason to move.

Returning to the scene. When Lizzie began to exit from the tack room, she backed up toward the door. The director made the point that backing up onstage shows fear or awe on the part of the character. If those extreme emotions are inappropriate, then backing up looks unnatural and should be avoided. We began again from Lizzie's "I don't believe you."

STARBUCK: Then what are you thankin' me for? What's the matter, Lizzie? You afraid that if you stop bein' sore at me you'll like me a little? (<u>X TOWARD HER</u>)

LIZZIE: No . . . (And she starts to go) (<u>X TO DOOR</u>)

STARBUCK: Then stay and talk to me! (As she hesitates) It's lonely out here and I don't think I'll sleep much—not in a strange place. (<u>X UP OF SAWHORSE</u>)

LIZZIE: Then I guess you never sleep. Running from one strange place to another. (<u>TURN TO FACE HIM</u>)

STARBUCK: (With a smile) Not runnin'—travelin'.

LIZZIE: Well, if that's the kind of life you like . . .

STARBUCK: Oh, it's not what a man likes—It's what he's got to do. Now what would a fella in my business be doin' stayin' in the same place? Rain's nice—but it ain't nice all the time.

LIZZIE: (Relaxing a bit) No, I guess not.

STARBUCK: People got no use for me—except maybe once in a lifetime. And when my work's done, they're glad to see me go.

LIZZIE: (Caught by the loneliness of his voice) I never thought of it that way.

STARBUCK: Why would you? You never thought of me as a real rainmaker—not until just now.

LIZZIE: I still don't think it! (Now she starts to go more determinedly than before.)

The action stopped twice during this beat. Once he reached the sawhorse, Starbuck wanted to move but did not know where to go. Lizzie also felt stuck in the doorway. After discussing the possibilities, the artists decided that Starbuck could straddle the sawhorse, avoiding a negative move away from or toward Lizzie which might seem threatening. Now she could move toward him during the beat. This movement led to him standing up face to face with her, when he said, "You never thought of me as a real rainmaker." In order to make this work, Starbuck had to pull his leg over the sawhorse at some point so that he was sitting forward and could easily stand up to face her (see Figure 3.3). Finally, it was decided to have Starbuck prevent Lizzie's exit this time, putting himself between her and the door.

LIZZIE: Then I guess you never sleep. Running from one strange place to another. (<u>TURN TO FACE HIM</u>)

STARBUCK: (with a smile) Not runnin'—travelin'.

LIZZIE: Well, if that's the kind of life you like . . .

STARBUCK: Oh, it's not what a man likes—it's what he's got to do. Now what would a fella in my business be doin' stayin' in the same place? Rain's nice—but it ain't nice all the time. (<u>HE STRADDLES THE SAWHORSE</u>)

LIZZIE: (Relaxing a bit) No, I guess not. (<u>X IN A BIT</u>)

STARBUCK: People got no use for me—except maybe once in a lifetime. And when my work's done, they're glad to see me go. (<u>PULL LEG OVER SAWHORSE</u>)

LIZZIE: (Caught by the loneliness in his voice) I never thought of it that way. (<u>X TO SAWHORSE</u>)

STARBUCK: Why would you? You never thought of me as a real rainmaker—not until just now. (<u>RISE</u>)

LIZZIE: I still don't think it! (Now she starts to go more determinedly than before.) (<u>X TOWARD DOOR</u>)

STARBUCK: Lizzie—wait! Why don't you let yourself think of me the way you **want** to? (<u>X BETWEEN LIZZIE AND DOOR</u>)

LIZZIE: (Unnerved) What do you mean? (<u>TURNS AWAY FROM HIM</u>)

Having completed this beat, they began again, taking it from Lizzie's cross toward the door.

Figure 3.3

LIZZIE: I still don't think it! (<u>X TOWARD DOOR</u>)

STARBUCK: Lizzie—wait! Why don't you let yourself think of me the way you **want** to? (<u>X BETWEEN HER AND THE DOOR</u>)

LIZZIE: What do you mean? (<u>TURNS AWAY FROM HIM</u>)

STARBUCK: Think like Lizzie, not like Noah.

LIZZIE: I don't know what you're talking about. (<u>XDR</u>)

STARBUCK: Lizzie! What are you scared of?

LIZZIE: You! I don't trust you!

STARBUCK: Why? What don't you trust about me? (<u>X TO HER</u>)

LIZZIE: Everything! The way you talk, the way you brag—why, even your name!

STARBUCK: What's wrong with my name?

LIZZIE: It sounds fake! It sounds like you made it up!

STARBUCK: You're darn right! I did make it up!

Lizzie had crossed away from Starbuck, he had followed her, and now they were stuck in the down right corner with no place to go. In this common situation, the director must look for a line that will allow one of the actors to break out of the face-to-face confrontation. If Starbuck crossed toward center in frustration on "What's wrong with my name," then Lizzie could move toward him on her attack and away on her line of triumph.

LIZZIE: I don't know what you're talking about. (<u>XDR</u>)

STARBUCK: Lizzie! What are you scared of?

LIZZIE: You! I don't trust you! (<u>TURN TOWARD HIM</u>)

STARBUCK: Why? What don't you trust about me? (<u>X TO HER</u>)

LIZZIE: Everything! The way you talk, the way you brag—why, even your name!

STARBUCK: What's wrong with my name? (<u>XC</u>)

LIZZIE: It sounds fake! It sounds like you made it up! (<u>X TO HIM</u>)

STARBUCK: You're darn right! I did make it up! (<u>TURN TO FACE HER</u>)

LIZZIE: There! Of course! (<u>XDR</u>)

STARBUCK: Why not? You know what name I was born with? Smith! Smith, for the love of Mike, **Smith**! (<u>X TO HER</u>)

Up to this point, all was going well. The movement seemed appropriate and dynamic, action-packed rather than static and dull. What would Starbuck do during the upcoming speech about his name? It was decided to have him cross above the sawhorse and stand on it for the line about the sky and the power of man (see Figure 3.4).

STARBUCK: Lizzie! What are you scared of?

LIZZIE: You! I don't trust you! (<u>TURN TO FACE HIM</u>)

STARBUCK: Why? What don't you trust about me? (<u>X TO FACE HER</u>)

LIZZIE: Everything! The way you talk, the way you brag—why, even your name!

STARBUCK: What's wrong with my name? (<u>XC</u>)

Figure 3.4

LIZZIE: It sounds fake! It sounds like you made it up! (<u>X TO HIM</u>)

STARBUCK: You're darn right! I did make it up! (<u>TURN TO HER</u>)

LIZZIE: There! Of course! (<u>XDR</u>)

STARBUCK: Why not? You know what name I was born with? (<u>X TO HER</u>) Smith! Smith, for the love of Mike, **Smith**! (<u>XUC</u>) Now what kind of handle is that for a fella like me! (<u>CLIMB ON SAWHORSE</u>) I needed a name that had the whole sky in it! And the power of a man! Star—buck! Now there's a name—and it's mine!

LIZZIE: No it's not! You were born Smith—and that's your name! (<u>X TO EDGE OF SAWHORSE</u>)

STARBUCK: You're wrong, Lizzie! The name you choose for yourself is more your own than the name you were born with! And if I was you I'd choose another name than Lizzie!

LIZZIE: Thank you—I'm very pleased with it!

STARBUCK: Oh no you ain't! You ain't pleased with anything about yourself! And I'm sure you ain't pleased with "Lizzie"!

LIZZIE: I don't ask **you** to be pleased with it, Starbuck. I **am**!

STARBUCK: Lizzie! Why, it don't **stand** for anything!

LIZZIE: It stands for me! **ME**! I'm not the Queen of Sheba—I'm not Lady Godiva—I'm not Cinderella at the Ball!

STARBUCK: Would you like to be?

LIZZIE: Starbuck, you're ridiculous!

Starbuck can't stay up on the sawhorse forever. The logical time for a move is when he changes the beat by beginning his attack on Lizzie's name. At that moment, he jumped down from the sawhorse, right in front of her, or, to be more accurate, stage left of her. Her snippy response calls for a negative move, either left or right. The choice was for her to pass in front of him, crossing left, simply because the director did not want to be repetitive by sending her to the down right corner again.

STARBUCK: Now what kind of handle is that for a fella like me! I needed a name that had the whole sky in it! And the power of a man! Star—buck! Now there's a name—and it's mine! (<u>UP ON SAWHORSE</u>)

LIZZIE: No it's not! You were born Smith—and that's your name! (<u>X TO HIM</u>)

STARBUCK: You're wrong, Lizzie! The name you choose for yourself is more your own than the name you were born with! And if I was you I'd choose another name than Lizzie! (<u>JUMP DOWN</u>)

LIZZIE: Thank you—I'm very pleased with it! (<u>XL IN FRONT OF HIM</u>)

STARBUCK: Oh no you ain't! You ain't pleased with anything about yourself! And I'm sure you ain't pleased with "Lizzie"!

LIZZIE: I don't ask **you** to be pleased with it, Starbuck. I **am**! (<u>TURN TO FACE HIM</u>)

STARBUCK: Lizzie! Why, it don't **stand** for anything! <u>SIT ON SAW-HORSE</u>)

LIZZIE: It stands for me! **ME**! I'm not the Queen of Sheba—I'm not
Lady Godiva—I'm not Cinderella at the Ball! (<u>X TO HIM</u>)

STARBUCK: Would you like to be?

LIZZIE: Starbuck, you're ridiculous!

STARBUCK: What's ridiculous about it? Dream you're somebody—be
somebody! But Lizzie?—that's nobody! So many millions of
wonderful women with wonderful names! (In an orgy of
delight) Leonora, Desdemona, Caroline, Annabella, Florinda,
Christina, Diane! (Then with a pathetic little lift of his
shoulders) Lizzie.

LIZZIE: Goodnight, Starbuck!

The actors were inventing movements with ease by this point, but Starbuck
hit a snag when he arrived at the list of names. Because Lizzie has called him
"ridiculous," his first reaction is a negative one. It was suggested that he cross
down right and turn accusingly on "Lizzie—that's nobody!" Now he had a list
of names, exotic wonderful names, followed by a put-down, Lizzie . . . Yuck!—
just like the punch line of a joke. While Lizzie stood at the left edge of the
sawhorse, he tried a number of different movements, finally settling on a series
of movements, start and stop, which took him across the stage, down right
to down left, then up to Lizzie and around behind her, ending up on her
right, above the sawhorse, where he hit her with the punch line. She reacts
angrily, moving toward the door. In order to stop her, he tries a new tactic,
starting a new beat.

STARBUCK: What's ridiculous about it? Dream you're (<u>XDR</u>) somebody—be somebody! But Lizzie?—that's nobody! (<u>TURN
TOWARD HER</u>) So many millions of wonderful women
with wonderful names! (In an orgy of delight) (<u>XDL</u>)
Leonora, Desdemona, Caroline, Annabella, (<u>X TO HER</u>)
Florinda, Christina, Diane! (<u>X BEHIND HER</u>) (Then with a
pathetic little lift of his shoulders) Lizzie.

LIZZIE: Goodnight, Starbuck! (<u>XL</u>)

STARBUCK: (With a sudden inspiration) Just a minute, Lizzie—just one
little half of a minute! I got the (<u>X AROUND R END OF
SAWHORSE</u>) greatest name for you—the greatest name—
just listen! (Then, like a love lyric) Melisande.

LIZZIE: (Flatly) I don't like it.

STARBUCK: That's because you don't know anything about her! But when I tell you who she was—lady, when I tell you who she was! (<u>XDR</u>)

LIZZIE: Who? (<u>X TO SAWHORSE</u>)

STARBUCK: She was the most beautiful— She was the beautiful wife of King Hamlet!—Ever hear of him?

LIZZIE: (Giving him rope) Go on!—go on!

The latter series of movements was carefully arranged to allow Lizzie to sit down while Starbuck tells his long story about the golden fleece. The excuse for moving Starbuck away is that he is lying to her, making up names like King Hamlet as he goes along. Thus, he does not look her in the eye until she pretends to be taken in by the story. But his movement has the technical goal of clearing the space around the sawhorse so that she can be seated. For Starbuck's long solo, a series of movements were invented, toward and away from Lizzie, allowing him to act out the story as much as possible. He circled behind her, knelt at her feet, jumped up onto the bales of hay (see Figure 3.5), jumped back down, collapsed

Figure 3.5

Figure 3.6

on the floor "bleeding and torn," crawled to her, and finished sitting with his back against the sawhorse, to the right of Lizzie's feet (see Figure 3.6).

STARBUCK: (With a sudden inspiration) Just a minute, Lizzie—just one little half of a minute! I got the (<u>X AROUND END OF SAWHORSE</u>) greatest name for you—the greatest name—just listen! (Then, like a love lyric) Melisande.

LIZZIE: (Flatly) I don't like it.

STARBUCK: That's because you don't know anything about her! But when I tell you who she was—lady, when I tell you who she was! (<u>XDR</u>)

LIZZIE: Who? (<u>X TO SAWHORSE</u>)

STARBUCK: She was the most beautiful— She was the beautiful wife of King Hamlet!—Ever hear of him? (<u>TURN TO FACE HER</u>)

LIZZIE: (Giving him rope) Go on!—go on! (<u>SIT ON SAWHORSE</u>)

STARBUCK: He was the fella who sailed across the ocean and brought back the Golden Fleece! (<u>UP AND BEHIND HER</u>) And you know why he did that? Because Queen Melisande begged him for it! I tell you, that Melisande—she was so beautiful and her hair was so long and curly—every time he looked at her he just fell right down and died! (<u>KNEEL L OF HER FEET</u>) And this King Hamlet, he'd do anything for her—anything she wanted! So when she said: "Hamlet, I got a terrible (<u>RISE</u>) hankerin' for a soft Golden Fleece," he just naturally (<u>JUMP UP ON HAY</u>) sailed right off to find it! And when he came back—all bleedin' and torn—he went and laid that Fleece of Gold right down at her pretty white feet! (<u>FALL TO THE FLOOR</u>) And she took that fur piece and she wrapped it around her pink naked shoulders (<u>SIT AT HER FEET</u>) and she said: "I got the Golden Fleece—and I'll never be cold no more!"—Melisande! What a woman! What a **name**!

LIZZIE: (Forlornly) Starbuck, you silly jackass. You take a lot of stories—that I've read in a hundred different places—and you roll them up into one big fat ridiculous lie!

STARBUCK: (Angry, hurt) I wasn't lyin'—I was dreamin'!

LIZZIE: It's the same thing!

STARBUCK: If you think it's the same thing then I take it back about your name! Lizzie—it's just right for you! I'll tell you another name that would suit you—Noah! Because you and your brother—you've got no dream!

Clearly, this is a new beat. She makes fun of his silly story. He reacts negatively, accusing her of lacking dreams. She responds with her own story, a simple, honest, emotionally charged vision of her deepest desires. In contrast to Starbuck's acrobatics, Lizzie's story requires little in the way of movement. The decision was to have Starbuck rise and move away in anger, down right. At first, Lizzie would move toward him. Ultimately, she would go downstage center to tell her story (see Figure 3.7). Obviously, at the close, she heads for the door, and he must stop her, this time by physically taking hold of her.

LIZZIE: (Forlornly) Starbuck, you silly jackass. You take a lot of stories—that I've read in a hundred different places (<u>RISE</u>) and you roll them up into one big fat ridiculous lie!

Figure 3.7

STARBUCK: (Angry, hurt) I wasn't lyin'—I was dreamin'!

LIZZIE: It's the same thing!

STARBUCK: If you think it's the same thing then I (<u>KNEEL UP</u>) take it
back about your name! Lizzie—it's just right for you! I'll tell
you another name that would suit you (<u>RISE</u>)—Noah!
Because you and your brother—you've got no (<u>XDR</u>) dream!

LIZZIE: (With an outcry) You think all dreams have (<u>X TOWARD
HIM</u>) to be your kind! Golden Fleece and thunder on the
mountain! But there are other dreams, Starbuck! Little quiet
ones that come to a woman when she's shining the silverware
and putting moth flakes in the closet!

STARBUCK: Like what?

LIZZIE: Like a man's voice saying: "Lizzie, is my blue (<u>XDC FACING
AUDIENCE</u>) suit pressed?" And the same man saying: "Scratch

between my shoulder blades." And kids laughing and teasing and setting up a racket! And how it feels to say the word "Husband"!—There are all kinds of dreams (<u>TURN TO FACE HIM</u>) Mr. Starbuck! Mine are small ones—like my name—Lizzie! But they're **real** like my name—real! So you can (<u>GO TO EXIT</u>) have yours—and I'll have mine! (Unable to control her tears).

STARBUCK: (This time he grabs her fully, holding her close) Lizzie— (<u>FOLLOW AND GRAB HER</u>)

Starbuck is holding Lizzie in his arms near the door of the tack room as the finale of the scene begins.

LIZZIE: Please—

STARBUCK: I'm sorry, Lizzie! I'm sorry!

LIZZIE: It's all right—let me go!

STARBUCK: I hope your dreams come true, Lizzie—I hope they do!

LIZZIE: They won't—they never will!

STARBUCK: Believe in yourself and they will!

LIZZIE: I've got nothing to believe in!

STARBUCK: You're a woman! Believe in that!

LIZZIE: How can I when nobody else will?

STARBUCK: **You** gotta believe it first! (Quickly) Let me ask you, Lizzie— are you pretty?

LIZZIE: (with a wail) No—I'm plain!

STARBUCK: There! You see?—you don't even know you're a woman!

LIZZIE: I am a woman! A plain one!

STARBUCK: There's no such thing as a plain woman! Every real woman is pretty! They're all pretty in a different way—but they're all pretty!

LIZZIE: Not me! When I look in the looking glass—

STARBUCK: Don't let Noah be your lookin' glass! It's gotta be inside you! And then one day the lookin' glass will be the man who loves you! It'll be his eyes maybe! And you'll look in that mirror and you'll be more than pretty!—you'll be beautiful!

LIZZIE: (Crying out) It'll never happen!

STARBUCK: Make it happen! Lizzie, why don't you think "pretty"? and take down your hair! (He reaches for her hair.)

LIZZIE: (in panic) No!

STARBUCK: Please, Lizzie! (He is taking the pins out of her hair. Taking her in his arms.) Now close your eyes, Lizzie—close them! (as she obeys) Now—say: I'm pretty!

LIZZIE: I'm—I'm—I can't!

STARBUCK: Say it! Say it, Lizzie!

LIZZIE: I'm—pretty.

STARBUCK: Say it again!

LIZZIE: (With a little cry) Pretty!

STARBUCK: Say it—mean it!

LIZZIE: (Exalted) I'm pretty! I'm pretty! I'm pretty! (He kisses her. A long kiss and she clings to him, passionately, the bonds of her spinsterhood breaking away. The kiss over, she collapses on the sacks, sobbing.) (Through the sobs) Why did you do that?!

STARBUCK: (Going beside her on the sacks) Because when you said you were pretty, it was true! (Her sobs are louder, more heartrending because, for the first time, she is happy) Lizzie—look at me!

LIZZIE: I can't!

STARBUCK: (Turning her toward him) Stop cryin' and look at me! Look at my eyes! What do you see?

LIZZIE: (Gazing through the tears) I can't **believe** what I see!

STARBUCK: Tell me what you see!

LIZZIE: (With a sob of happiness) Oh, is it me?! Is it really me?! (Now she goes to him with all her giving)

End of act 2

Clearly, movement is indicated in the first portion of the segment, but once Starbuck lets Lizzie's hair down, the characters stay in the same location for the remainder of the scene. Therefore, since the earlier blocking must take the actors to the position where the kiss will take place, it might be prudent to choose that final position at this time. Given our set, the only logical locations were downstage center, on the floor, or up on the hay bales; we chose the hay bales at stage right. Bit by bit, the actors worked their way toward the hay during the early portion of the scene; Lizzie moving away on her negative lines and Starbuck following her with his entreaties. Finally, she was seated on the hay bales and he knelt in front of her. This was a better choice than having them sit side by side, simply because both of their faces could be seen more clearly (see Figure 3.8).

STARBUCK: (This time he grabs her fully, holding her close.) Lizzie—
(<u>GRABS HER</u>)

LIZZIE: Please—

STARBUCK: I'm sorry, Lizzie! I'm sorry!

LIZZIE: It's all right—let me go!

STARBUCK: I hope your dreams come true, Lizzie—I hope they do!
(<u>RELEASES HER</u>)

LIZZIE: They won't—they never will!

STARBUCK: Believe in yourself and they will!

LIZZIE: I've got nothing to believe in! (<u>TURN AWAY FROM HIM</u>)

STARBUCK: You're a woman! Believe in that!

LIZZIE: How can I when nobody else will? (<u>XR ABOVE THE
SAWHORSE</u>)

STARBUCK: **You** gotta believe it first! (Quickly) Let me ask you, Lizzie—
are you pretty? (<u>X TO HER</u>)

LIZZIE: (With a wail) No—I'm plain! (<u>KEEPING HER BACK TO
HIM</u>)

STARBUCK: There! You see?—you don't know you're a woman!

LIZZIE: I am a woman! A plain one! (<u>TURN TO FACE HIM</u>)

STARBUCK: There's no such thing as a plain woman! (<u>XL A FEW STEPS
AND TURN TO FACE HER</u>) Every real woman is pretty!
They're all pretty in a different way—but they're all pretty!

Figure 3.8

LIZZIE: Not me! When I look in the looking glass— (<u>X TO BALES</u>)

STARBUCK: Don't let Noah be your lookin' glass! It's gotta be inside you! And then one day the lookin' glass will be the man who loves you! It'll be his eyes maybe! (<u>X UP OF SAWHORSE</u>) And you'll look in that mirror and you'll be more than pretty!— you'll be beautiful!

LIZZIE: (Crying out) It'll never happen! (<u>SIT ON BALES</u>)

STARBUCK: Make it happen! Lizzie, why don't you think "pretty"? and take down your hair! (<u>X AND SIT UPSTAGE OF HER</u>) (He reaches for her hair.)

LIZZIE: (In panic) No!

STARBUCK: Please, Lizzie! (He is taking the pins out of her hair. Taking her in his arms) Now close your (<u>KNEEL IN FRONT OF</u>

HER) eyes, Lizzie—close them! (As she obeys) Now—say: I'm pretty!

LIZZIE: (Trying) I'm—I'm—I can't!

STARBUCK: Say it! Say it, Lizzie!

LIZZIE: I'm—pretty.

STARBUCK: Say it again!

LIZZIE: (With a little cry) Pretty!

STARBUCK: Say it—mean it!

LIZZIE: (Exalted) I'm pretty! I'm pretty! I'm pretty! (He kisses her. A long kiss and she clings to him, passionately.) (Through the sobs) Why did you do that?!

STARBUCK: Because (RISE) when you said you were pretty, it was true! (Her sobs are louder, more heartrending because, for the first time, she is happy) Lizzie—look at me!

LIZZIE: I can't!

STARBUCK: Stop cryin' and look (PULLING HER UP TO HIM) at me! Look at my eyes! What do you see?

LIZZIE: (Gazing through her tears) I can't **believe** what I see!

STARBUCK: Tell me what you see!

LIZZIE: (With a sob of happiness) Oh, is it me?! Is it really me?!

(THEY EMBRACE)

End of act 2

Running Through the Blocking

At the close of the rehearsal, the director must leave enough time to run through the scene or portion of the scene that has been blocked at that rehearsal. The run-through serves two purposes: First, it assures the director that the actors have written down, and will remember, all of their movements; second, it allows the director to see all these bits and pieces of movement run together at full speed in the flow of the scene. If some movements now seem awkward or inappropriate, the director has the opportunity to make corrections or changes before the actors begin to fix this blocking in their minds. In the run-through of this scene from *The Rainmaker*, Starbuck had difficulty climbing up onto the sawhorse, but the director assured him that it would happen more easily with further rehearsal. After Starbuck's list of exotic women's names, Lizzie said "Goodnight, Starbuck!" and left the stage completely. Because the actor had forgotten to write down that piece of blocking, he failed to stop her, which resulted in a big laugh from the audience. He wouldn't make that mistake again. Finally, the director pointed out to his class that this process of blocking creates a great deal of movement. The scene never remains static for very long.

Watching the Actors

Inexperienced directors often have a problem with the script. Because they do not feel confident, they sit with their noses in the script during the blocking, not watching the actors. Although the director is familiar with the script, he or she will not know what line is coming up next unless the script has been put to memory. This need to know what is coming up next tends to tie the director to the script. The solution is to let the actors tell the director—let them read a number of lines ahead. Listening to them read, the director recognizes the next sequence and its problems. Then, they back up, read the same sequence again, and work out the blocking. Beginning directors often feel insecure without that script in their hand. However, the director cannot watch the actors and the script at the same time, and blocking requires the director to watch the actors at every moment. By reading their lines, the actors will keep the director apprised of what is coming next; thus, the director can spend the time watching what the actors do; allowing his or her instincts and imagination full scope to see all the possible choices of movement, to seek out fresh and unexpected ways to present familiar and commonplace events, situations, and emotions.

As a final piece of advice, the director should realize that blocking rehearsals develop the large movement of a scene. This is not the proper time to work on minute details of gesture or line interpretation. The director will only confuse the actors by working on tiny, interpretive details at this point, when the actors are trying to bring the broadest aspects of the scene under control.

Summary

The possible approaches of directors to the blocking of a scene, as illustrated in this chapter, range from detailed **preblocking**—in which directors preplan every movement and gesture before they arrive at rehearsals—to complete improvisation—in which the actors work their way through the scene time after time, making new discoveries for themselves without interference or guidance from their directors. In theory, this textbook recommends an "ideal" balance of improvisational discovery by the actors with guidance and suggestions from the director when moments seem to go awry or an inspiration appears. When directing, as the example from *The Rainmaker* demonstrates, this author tends to intervene in the process of blocking more often than he would like. Further discussion of these issues, blocking in general and actor/director interaction, appear later in the text.

PART 2

Before Rehearsals Begin

In the previous section of the book, the overall job of the director was described, followed by the analysis and blocking of an example scene from a play. The following section of the book will take the reader from the point at which a script is chosen to the point of choosing a cast—that period of time which filmmakers call preproduction. Particular emphasis will be placed upon the analysis of the script.

The reader may not be aware that the role of director first appeared in the late nineteenth century along with the arrival of the movements called "realism" and "naturalism." Prior to this time, new plays were often given a first staging by their author. Thereafter, if a play remained in the repertoire, it continued to be presented in the traditional manner or was altered occasionally by the most powerful figure in the company, usually the star actor.

In general, staging prior to the late nineteenth century was unlike anything that we know today. In the French classical plays of the seventeenth and eighteenth centuries, for example, the actors simply formed a semicircle downstage center, seldom moving at all while delivering their lines. The story is told of Junius Brutus Booth—father of more famous sons, Edwin and John Wilkes—who, while touring America in the early nineteenth century as a visiting star performing with a cast of local actors, was approached by a young actor who had made his entrance from the wrong side of the stage. Booth brushed aside the young man's apology, saying something like, "Don't worry about it, my boy, you just come on, I'll find you." Stage blocking was seldom more specific than that in those years before the coming of realism. As long as the star could deliver his speeches while standing in the spotlight downstage center, everything was all right.

Realism had its beginning during the antiquarian movement of the late eighteenth century, at about the time of the American Revolution. Up to that time, the theatre took little note of history. Actors wore their own clothes onstage, no matter what the period of the play might be. No Roman togas for a production of *Julius Caesar,* for example; even Shakespeare's original production was done in Elizabethan, not Roman, clothing.

The antiquarian movement brought about the first interest in things antique or ancient. During the next century, more and more interest was paid to historically accurate costumes and scenery. Toward the end of the nineteenth century, many theatre people became interested in showing life on the stage as it was in everyday reality. The careful arrangement of the players onstage so that they looked lifelike and natural required the control of an outside observer; thus, the role of the director was born.

The Duke of Saxe-Meiningen in Germany and such figures as Augustin Daly and David Belasco in America are credited as being the first directors. In the early 1880s, a friend was surprised to meet Bronson Howard—America's most prominent playwright—on the street when he should have been at the staging of his latest play. Howard commented that he had turned the blocking over to a bright, young stage manager who had just come to Broadway from San Francisco, a fellow named David Belasco. Thus, the job of director was introduced to the American theatre.

CHAPTER

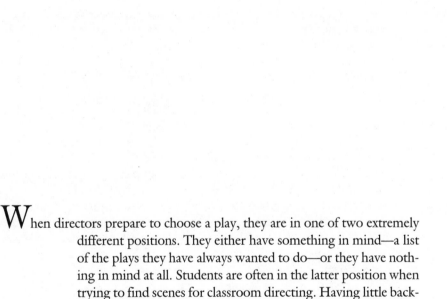

4

CHOOSING
THE PLAY

When directors prepare to choose a play, they are in one of two extremely different positions. They either have something in mind—a list of the plays they have always wanted to do—or they have nothing in mind at all. Students are often in the latter position when trying to find scenes for classroom directing. Having little background in theater, where does one find a scene? How many plays can a student be expected to read in order to find one scene for one of many assignments?

Finding a Scene

The best solution is to look in books that include collections of scenes for student actors. Many of these texts are available. Some have scenes from contemporary and twentieth-century plays; others mix contemporary and classic works. Some include scenes only from American plays, while others are devoted to scenes from motion pictures. Usually, a book of scenes introduces each piece with a description of the characters and the action in the play that has led up to the particular scene. Using such a book of scenes, the student director can survey a large number of choices in a relatively short period of time.

Putting the Scene in Context

Many theatre people object to the use of these scene books because students who choose a scene from such a book seldom take the time to read the entire play. This is a dangerous practice not only for students, but also for directors. One must know exactly how the scene fits into the play as a whole in order to truly understand the scene itself. For example, in the sample scene from *The Rainmaker,* we cannot know whether Starbuck is serious when he kisses Lizzie unless we know what happens in the remainder of the play. Such knowledge is essential to understanding a scene.

Once a script has been chosen from a scene book, the director must find and read a full copy of the play. A student-directed scene from Shakespeare's *King Lear,* the sixth scene of act 4, provides an example. In this scene, Gloucester is blind and distraught, wandering alone in the countryside. He asks poor Tom—who is, in reality, his own exiled son Edgar in disguise—to lead him to the Cliffs of Dover where he can commit suicide. Edgar leads Gloucester up onto a little mound of earth, telling him that he is at the Cliffs. Gloucester throws himself over the edge of the mound, but drops only two or three feet, then faints. When he revives, Edgar convinces him that his survival is a miracle, that God must want him to go on living. Thus Edgar (the son) saves his father's life with his strategy. However, nothing in the scene gives this strategy away; therefore, the student director, who had not read the whole play, did not know that poor Tom was someone else in disguise. In addition, it seemed that Gloucester actually fell from the Cliffs of Dover. By not reading the play, he had entirely missed the point of the scene.

Choosing a Script

Often, community theatre and high school directors will seek information about scripts. A standard suggestion is that they look at the catalogs of Samuel French or Dramatists' Play Service. These organizations act as **agents** for the majority of professional playwrights in dealing with amateur theatre organizations. Their catalogs are organized by size of the cast and give a very brief description of the play, comments from reviewers, number and types of sets required, and prices for royalties and scripts. **Royalties** for a typical play usually amount to fifty dollars for the first performance and thirty-five dollars for each succeeding performance. Musicals, however, command much greater royalties.

Another possible source of material is a series of books called *Best Plays*. An edition comes out each year in which the editors summarize in detail each of the ten best plays on Broadway that season. One director, having been away from New York City for five years and clearly feeling out of touch, read five editions of *Best Plays* a while back, discovering and producing a fine comedy by Larry Shue called *The Foreigner*.

Inspiration can come from looking at the seasons of other theatres in the state or region, or one can simply ask one's friends for advice. At a theatre conference, the author once asked his community theatre friends to suggest the latest, new, worthwhile play. Their unanimous recommendation was *Steel Magnolias,* a play which was not, at that time, released for amateur production. However, the directors were ready and waiting for the project.

The most exhilarating challenge for a director is to produce an original script. Most directors in the amateur theatre seldom have access to original works, but the opportunity to work with an author on the original creation of the artwork—to produce the world premiere—should be welcomed with enthusiasm when it comes along.

Many practical issues must be taken into consideration by the director when choosing a play. The number of actors and actresses available and their level of talent and experience will make a difference in choosing a play. The number of settings, costumes, lighting, and special effects, as well as the level of difficulty of each of these elements, must be considered. For example, *Steel Magnolias* takes place in a beauty salon. The set is not difficult, but it requires a group of professional beautician's chairs—items that may be troublesome to locate. *The Little Shop of Horrors* requires a giant talking plant that eats people. *Peter Pan* requires equipment that will allow the actors to fly on and offstage. Unless the production company can handle the practical problems contained in a particular script, the director should search for another play.

Challenging the Audience

A few years ago, the director of a small university theatre faced the task of choosing a musical. On the whole, this director did not like musicals and had little experience with them. With such a negative attitude, one might guess that he would have difficulty in picking a show. The show he finally chose was Steven Sondheim's *Company*. *Company* was selected for a number of reasons; unlike most musicals it did not have a very large cast, nor did it have a chorus or a dance troupe. It did not require a big orchestra, nor did it put major emphasis on dance numbers which require trained dancers and professional choreography as do such shows as *Chorus Line* and *Hello Dolly*.

Company was different from the musicals usually experienced by that audience—musicals in which nothing but sweetness and light abound. *Company* is the story of a young, swinging bachelor and his married friends. In his friends' marital relationships, he sees all that is wrong with the institution of marriage. Yet, in the end, he comes to recognize that surface relationships are worthless and that marriage, with all its flaws and stupidity, is preferable. *Company* has pot smoking, harsh language, sexy humor, and other elements that might not meet the expectations an audience would have for a musical. Not to mention the fact that the story dealt with something real and worthwhile. *Company* was chosen because the director wanted to provide his audience with a truly new experience.

So, at least one reason for choosing a play is to jolt the audience, to deliberately challenge them with a new and unexpected experience. The director should challenge his or her audience from time to time, taking the chance that some might be offended. Some years back, a director in a small town produced *Never Too Late,* a mild-mannered comedy without a single off-color word. Yet that director received a letter of complaint from one audience member who was offended by the use of the word "pregnant" onstage. Obviously, there is no way to please everyone.

Challenging the Actors

One community theatre director deliberately challenged his audience with his choice of a particular play in each season. Among a group of comedies, musicals, and mysteries—shows sure to please his audience—he would place one difficult play, such as *Virginia Woolf* or *A Man For All Seasons*. Not only was he attempting to broaden the taste of his audience to more sophisticated theatrical experiences, but he was also trying to provide more challenging roles for his actors.

As far as the performers are concerned, we have cautioned directors to make sure they have both the overall number of people needed for a particular play and the talent available for demanding roles. But actors must try new and different roles in order to develop their talent. The director should be willing to challenge them with more difficult roles rather than letting them repeat the roles they do easily. Also, directors should choose plays that provide the maximum opportunity for their players. High school directors choose shows with large casts because they have many students who would like to be in a play. The director should attempt to find scripts that encourage maximum participation.

Challenging the Director

The director chooses a show because he or she likes it, because he or she thinks that it is worthwhile and entertaining. The director chooses a play to give that particular experience to the audience. A script is chosen that will provide valuable opportunities for the actors. And directors should have as a goal, the idea of challenging themselves. Repeating the type of play that one does easily and successfully can become a trap for any director. A director who specializes in comedies should try some serious plays. A director who usually works with contemporary plays should be challenged by the production of a classic piece. The director who took on the musical *Company* was somewhat afraid of musicals. Being neither a musician nor a dancer, he felt that he had less control of the project. Not having done a musical for years, he found it more and more easy to avoid them. Finally, he just decided to jump in, to deliberately challenge himself with a difficult project.

Considering the Classics

Up to this point, we have discussed script choices in terms more practical than aesthetic in nature. But a theatrical production can do more than just entertain an audience; it can lift their spirits and expand their understanding of the world, of other human beings, of themselves. The theatre teaches us—not by preaching, but by experience. Just think how much of what we know about the world and the people in it is experienced not by being there in person, but by means of vicarious, dramatic encounters with an artistic reality, presented on a stage, a television, or a motion picture screen.

In choosing a script, directors have an opportunity to introduce their audiences to **classic** works of literature. Prior to the nineteenth century, most of the finest works of literature were plays. Across the centuries, there have been three eras of special literary excellence in the theatre: the classic plays of ancient Greece in the fifth century B.C.; the plays of the seventeenth century Renaissance represented by such playwrights as Lope De Vega in Spain, Molière in France, and

In the Director's Chair

David Garrick (1717–1779)

During the era prior to the development of the director as a separate and significant person in a theatrical production, there were actor-managers, who produced, directed, and played the lead role in a particular company. David Garrick is the most famous of these actor-managers. Garrick first became known as a great Shakespearean actor, particularly for his lead role in *Richard III* (1741). As manager of the Drury Lane Theatre from 1747 until 1776, Garrick made a number of significant theatrical innovations; for example, he was the first to conceal stage lighting from audience view, to end the seating of audience members on the edges of the stage, and to institute a more realistic style of acting. He took complete control of his productions, boldly rewriting most plays to suit his own ends. Garrick was also the author of some twenty plays, including *Lethe* (1740) and *The Enchanter* (1760).

Shakespeare in Britain; and the modern plays of the late nineteenth and early twentieth century playwrights such as Chekov, Ibsen, Hauptmann, Shaw, and O'Neill. Whether this modern era of great theatrical literature has ended or whether it continues up to the present is a matter of considerable debate which can only be resolved by future generations. Classic works of dramatic literature remain in the repertoire because they provide enduring insight into the human condition—experiences that have entertained and enlightened audiences across cultures, national boundaries, and the centuries.

Young directors are encouraged to study the classic plays and bring them to life for their own audiences, but first, perhaps some precautions are in order. In general, contemporary audiences tend to relate more easily to the comedies of the past, such as those of Molière and Aristophanes, rather than to the serious plays of, for example, Racine and Aeschylus. In classical and neoclassical tragedy, the dialogue often consists of long, set speeches rather than of conversation. This pattern of lengthy speeches presents a challenge to both actors and audience. By contrast, the plays of Shakespeare contain more conversation and more action. In general, classic plays have large casts; therefore, the director must have numerous available actors. And finally, the greatest pitfall for a young director in approaching scenes or plays by an author such as Shakespeare is excessive reverence and awe for the author. These classic plays are full of action, excitement, and fun. Solemn, overreverent, boring productions do the playwright a great disservice.

Summary

In this chapter, we have discussed sources for locating scripts, practical limitations that the director should observe when choosing a play, and possible goals the director might wish to consider. In choosing a play, directors want to provide new and valuable experiences for themselves, their performers, and their audiences. Once the play is chosen, the director's first step in preparing for the production is to study that playscript in order to understand the subtext of both the events and the characters. The complex process of script analysis will be discussed in detail in the following four chapters.

CHAPTER 5

SCRIPT ANALYSIS
Conflict
Structure

In this chapter, we shall discuss a particular form of script analysis and exemplify that analysis with a detailed study of *Play It Again, Sam.* Script analysis is an art, just as directing a play, painting, or writing a novel is an art. A sure sign of art is that there are no simple answers to all of the questions; thus, there is no absolutely correct way to analyze a script. The following method is just one of many ways to approach a script, recommended by its simplicity and practicality.

Conflict and Expectations

What is drama? What is a play? The author's favorite answer comes from Kenneth Burke, the brilliant twentieth-century philosopher, who describes the process of drama as the arousal and fulfillment of the audience's expectations. According to Burke, the performance arouses certain kinds of expectations in the audience and then fulfills those expectations—either in ways in which the audience thought they would be fulfilled or, perhaps, in ways that are a surprise to the audience. But in either case, the audience must feel satisfied and fulfilled, otherwise they will not like the play. In other words, the play raises certain questions and builds suspense. In order to be satisfactory to the audience, the play must answer those questions and relieve the suspense. If the main character has a problem, that problem must be solved in a manner that seems plausible and satisfying to the audience.

Usually, story lines are based in some kind of **conflict.** Story lines deal with a particular main character who has a problem that he or she must solve or a conflict with someone that must be resolved. This conflict is the basis of the story. Let us try to analyze and categorize these story conflicts. First, we have the main character—the hero, the good guy, the protagonist. Very often in drama, the main character may be a bad person such as a gangster or a murderer; therefore, we use a label that does not imply good or bad: protagonist. In the play's conflict, the opponent to the protagonist is the antagonist. Whereas protagonist is not a common word in our language, the term antagonist clearly implies someone who is antagonistic or opposed to something. Usually, the story has one main character, or protagonist. Think, for example, of the films of John Wayne or Clint Eastwood in which the star is clearly the protagonist. Nevertheless, some dramatists have used whole groups of people as protagonists, as in *The Weavers* by Gerhart Hauptmann, for example. In the famous play by Shakespeare, who is the protagonist—Romeo or Juliet? Perhaps both are protagonists because they are equally involved in the story's conflict. However, although there are other possibilities, the protagonist is usually a single character, male or female.

We can divide the concept of antagonist into one of three types or categories: person versus person, person versus self, or person versus outside forces. If the antagonist is another character or group of characters in the story, that conflict would be described as person versus person. When the story contains no obvious antagonistic character, internal conflict is most likely. In a person versus self conflict situation, the main character is both protagonist and antagonist. Let us create an example: In our story, the protagonist is a successful architect with a lovely wife and family. But he hires a new secretary and falls madly in love with her. Now he has a problem. Will he run off with this woman with whom he is having an affair—deserting the wife and children whom he loves? He is torn between his duty and this sudden new passion. Neither of these women is the antagonist; they both love him. The problem is within the man himself—a choice that he must make. The two women represent opposite goals rather than antagonists. The protagonist is his own antagonist; one part of him wants to remain with his family, while another part of him desperately wants this new love. Therefore, this conflict would be described as man versus himself.

If the antagonist is not personified in another character or in the protagonist, then the antagonist must be some kind of outside force, such as God, Mother Nature, or supernatural forces. Although the use of outside forces as antagonist is not common, some examples do come to mind. An airplane crashes in the mountains; will the passengers survive the freezing cold and lack of food? This is a survival story in which the weather is the antagonist. In the movie *Poltergeist,* the forces that attack the family are misty, ghostlike things. We never quite see them because they are somewhere on the other side of reality—unseen, outside forces. This type of conflict would be explained as person versus outside forces. Thus, we have described the three possibilities; the conflict must fall into one of these three categories, provided the story has a conflict to begin with.

Sequence of Events

The **sequence of events** in the story will complicate and build on the conflict until, finally, the conflict is resolved. The protagonist either wins or loses. For example, in the most simple of melodramas, we find a character such as James Bond versus Dr. No or some other evildoer. Bond is sent on a mission—an event that begins the conflict. In our structure, this event would be called the **initial incident,** or the "inciting incident." When a drama begins, the conflict usually does not yet exist; then, something happens to kick off the conflict—a clear initial incident. However, there are exceptions to every typical pattern. In some stories, the conflict is already in existence when the drama starts. And, in many dramas, the initial incident is difficult to pin down. The conflict seems to just drift in, getting more and more serious until the audience becomes aware that the protagonist has a real problem. However, in most stories, one can point to some obvious moment when the conflict appears—when the audience first becomes aware of it.

After the initial incident, the tension created by the conflict becomes stronger and stronger in the sequence of following events until the story reaches a climax in which the problem is solved. In the old westerns, the good guy finally faces off with the evil villain out in the street. They draw their guns and shoot, and one of them drops dead, usually the antagonist. The conflict is finished. The climax has been the turning point in the story; the protagonist has won, and the tension or suspense created by the conflict subsides. Whatever happens after that point is called the **conclusion**. Leaving behind the poor girl who loves him, the cowboy mounts his horse and rides off into the sunset.

Short stories often have no major complications between the initial incident and the climax, but most longer stories have numerous events and crises. Action-packed melodrama will contain a series of exciting and dangerous high points, just as its parallel, comic genre, farce or situation comedy, will contain a series of funny events or comic high points. Such events are often called **subclimaxes** or **crises,** in the sense that the protagonist faces some kind of crisis and survives, but the conflict continues. There is our hero, hanging from a cliff as the villain stomps on his fingertips. Will he survive? That is the mode of operation of the old time serials: stop at the peak of a crisis. Television shows also tend to stop for *advertisements* in the middle of crises. Although she is tied to the railroad tracks, our heroine manages to escape in the nick of time. However, because the villain also escapes, the conflict continues. Thus, this episode led to a crisis, but the climax is yet to come. Also, melodramas often have two climaxes, one which involves a spectacular event, such as a war, and another, smaller one which occurs later on and is actually the turning point that resolves the conflict—something akin to the famous one-two punch in boxing.

Complex Plots

The structure of a story—the playing out of its conflict—contains an initial incident, some crises, a climax (or two), and a conclusion. This simple story structure, called the **classical paradigm,** is often made more complex in two ways. Think of the novel *Huckleberry Finn:* Each new chapter is a new adventure. On the river, Huck and Jim float into a new town where they meet a bunch of crazy characters; this is the initial incident of a new story which leads to some climax. Then, they escape back to the river, traveling on to another initial incident with characters in the next town downriver, and another new story begins. Such a story, which is made up of a series of stories strung end-to-end with the same protagonist facing a new antagonist or new problem each time, is often called an **odyssey.** The word *odyssey* comes from the ancient Greek story by Homer, in which the protagonist, Odysseus, faces a whole series of antagonists on his journey home from the Trojan War, very much like Huck Finn's series of adventures on the Mississippi. For a contemporary example, let us look at *Raiders of the Lost Ark.* The story involves the protagonist's search for the lost ark. The film is structured as a series of five or six major adventures, each with its own major climax. In the first episode, the protagonist meets his old girlfriend in a bar while seeking a clue to the location of the ark high in the Himalaya Mountains. In the first climax, the whole building burns down while Nazis shoot at the hero and his girlfriend with machine guns; nevertheless, our hero wins. Then, on to the next episode, which takes place in the streets of a city in Egypt, where the climax is a battle with Arab swordsman and the kidnapping of the girlfriend. The protagonist steals the ark, but the villains always manage to steal it back, thus allowing the story to continue on to a new episode. One climax is a truck chase scene; the protagonist, on horseback, follows the truck containing the ark, climbs onto the truck, falls off and under the truck, only to climb back on again, single-handedly defeating dozens of villains. In the final climax, once the ark is opened, it destroys the bad guys, ending the conflict once and for all. Clearly, *Raiders of the Lost Ark* is an odyssey which takes the protagonist through a series of adventures, each one a new little story with its own initial incident and climax.

The second way to make a simple story structure more complex is to have more than one plot taking place simultaneously. This process involves more than one protagonist, each with their own conflict or problem. The typical soap opera contains this kind of structure; the reason it seems so complex is that there are four or five different stories going on at the same time. The show goes on indefinitely, because when one story reaches a climax, the other four stories continue to roll along. One character may disappear from the show, but a new character is added to create a new problem. However, if one breaks this seemingly complex story down into its parts, one finds a series of protagonists, each with a rather simple story of their own.

Stories with multiple plots—usually a major plot with **subplots**—have always been common in the British theatre. For example, the major story of Shakespeare's *King Lear* deals with Lear and the problems he has with his three daughters. A parallel subplot deals with Gloucester and the problems he has with his two sons. Each of these men is a protagonist in his own story, and the two stories are played out side by side, throughout the drama. Just as typical is a play with a serious main plot and a comic subplot. In the thirties and forties, Charlie Chan movies involved both a serious murder mystery and a silly subplot which featured Charlie's son and his friends—a bunch of comic characters, cracking jokes and doing pratfalls.

A play is a sequence of events in which a major conflict develops and is brought to its solution, in which the expectations of the audience are aroused and finally fulfilled. We are talking about the major problem, or conflict, that controls the action of the whole play. Every character has minor conflicts with other characters in a play, but these conflicts should not be confused with the major dramatic question.

Organic Unity

Organic unity is a concept developed by the romantics during the late eighteenth century. Romantics metaphorically envisioned a work of literature as a living, organic plant or animal. Each part of a living creature is necessary to the whole and is interdependent with the other parts. This organic unity is the desirable relationship between each part of a play; in other words, each scene should be necessary and vital to the whole play.

Unlike real life, drama cannot raise questions and leave them unresolved. In fact, every element of the play must be meaningful. In one original play, a number of peripheral characters were introduced in the first act who never reappeared in the story, because they simply were not important to the major action of the play. Although these scenes were true-to-life, they seemed strange in the drama. In a play, if a character is introduced, that character must be there for some reason, must be involved in the story for some specific purpose. The presence of a character raises audience expectation; the audience expects to understand the relevance of that character to the story. Superfluous characters have no place in a play.

Even more important, dramatic questions and conflicts cannot be raised and remain unresolved without leaving the audience dissatisfied. For example, in the motion picture *Norma Rae* (a film that brought Sally Field an Academy Award), two dramatic questions were raised. The story involves Norma Rae, a simple Southern girl married to a lovable but unsophisticated boy who lives in a small town with one factory. Everyone in the town works at that factory. It's the only job around, and the workers are exploited and treated badly. Into this situation comes a handsome, assertive, debonair unionizer from New York City. At first, everyone is against this outsider, but when he recruits Norma Rae she becomes more and more involved in his cause. Major conflicts arise because her husband, her family, and all of her friends work at the factory and see the union man from New York as their enemy. But the outsider is a revelation to Norma Rae. He introduces her to a life she had never known, teaches her about poetry and the arts, and she blossoms as a human being because of her association with him. Clearly, she is falling in love with him. The two dramatic questions raised in this story are: Will Norma Rae succeed in defeating the mean factory bosses by unionizing the workers; and, what will happen to the potential romance between a handsome stranger and a happily married woman?

At the end of the film, when Norma Rae convinces the workers to form a union, that question is resolved. However, the romantic question is never answered, leaving some members of the audience strangely unfulfilled. The tension created by the romantic relationship is vivid and powerful, leading to

In the Director's Chair

George II, Duke of Saxe-Meiningen (1826–1914)

George II is generally considered to be the first modern director, the first person to operate as the controlling force and guiding imagination behind a theatrical production, attempting to unify all of the elements of a dramatic production. The Duke formed a private resident group of actors at his court theatre (known as the Meiningen Company), where he directed the plays and designed the historically accurate costumes and scenery. Unlike his contemporaries, he held intensive rehearsals and arranged his actors in a disciplined and coordinated fashion. The Duke became famous for a number of innovations; for example, he placed the main actors within a scene among the crowd, rather than down center; he varied the stage by using platforms and different levels; he revolutionized the manner of staging crowd scenes; and he made early use of the box set and three-dimensional scenery. After 1874, his company toured throughout Europe, spreading its influence to such future innovators as Andre Antoine (see page 109) and Konstantin Stanislavsky (see page 123).

a scene that appears to be the climax of this conflict within Norma Rae. Norma Rae and the unionizer go swimming together in the nude. We expect him to make a pass at her, forcing her to respond, to make some choice between him and her husband. But our expectations are defeated because the scene abruptly ends without resolving the issue. The romance is never brought to a climax in the film; it is as if it had not existed in the first place. A noble person would not cheat on her husband, even briefly, and the filmmakers wanted the protagonist to seem heroic. But in doing so, they left a major dramatic question unresolved. Once a conflict has been set in motion, the audience will expect it to reach some climax. The French call such a climactic scene the *scène-à-faire,* or the scene that must be done.

Application of the Analysis

Now that we have looked at one particular method of script analysis, let us exemplify that method with a discussion of Woody Allen's *Play It Again, Sam*. In the first step, the director reads the play and makes a detailed summary. Memory tends to be vague. A full summary may well save the director from having to reread the play when trying to recall the exact order of events.

In the second step, the director summarizes the summary—making a very brief version of the major events of the play. Using this brief second summary, the director analyzes the sequence of events in order to determine the patterns of conflict, initial incident, climax, and conclusion. Finally, having gained an understanding of the action of the play, the director can draw some conclusions concerning the overall purpose and meaning of the script.

The following is this author's own summary of *Sam,* made when he directed the play. Some introduction seems appropriate so that the summary will be clear to the reader. The protagonist of the play is a character named Allan Felix, originally acted in both the stage and film version by Woody Allen himself. The script contains numerous dream sequences, daydreams, or memories, all of which seem to be happening in Allan's head. In particular, Allan dreams of being as successful and as confident as Humphrey Bogart was portrayed in the movies. In Allan's dreams, Bogart appears to give him advice.

During this reading, the director made a series of quick character notes for casting purposes. In this case, these notes will serve as an introduction to the characters in the play.

Characters

Nancy: His wife for 2 years—in her 20s—assertive and fun-loving—in some ways, a real bitch.

Dick: Young executive type—constantly leaves messages with his office—all his deals are failures.

Linda: A true romantic—does not like Dick's business view of life—Like Allan, a neurotic—works as a model—is a bit dingy.

Sharon: A nice, attractive girl—not a sex machine like Dream Sharon.

Gina: ?—quick goodnight at the door.

Vanessa: The liberated woman who has had many lovers.

Go-Go Girl: Just dances—says little.

Intellectual: A pretty blonde dressed like a hippie?

Barbara: A nice dream fulfilled—played by Dream Sharon.

Play It Again, Sam Summary

Act 1 Scene 1:   Allan's wife, Nancy, left him only 2 weeks ago—suddenly she appears as in a dream or flashback except that he actually talks to her. Bogart appears almost immediately to give him advice—then wife returns. His best friends, Dick and wife Linda, come by to commiserate with him. Dick immediately calls his office; she starts cleaning up the room. Dick sees life in terms of investments and business deals; Linda is a romantic, nervous wreck, forever in therapy, very much like Allan. She works at a modeling agency. She and Dick plan to fix Allan up for a dinner date that evening. Nancy reenters briefly as Allan objects to this whole idea. But they call a girl and he gives in. That evening, Allan worries as Bogy gives him macho advice.

Act 1 Scene 2:   Sharon appears in a dream as he would like her to be, with Allan acting like Bogy. Dick, Linda, and the real Sharon show up after Allan overprepares to create a macho/intellectual image. Constantly bragging while continually falling on his face, he makes a foolish impression rather than the brilliant one he intends.

Act 2:   Two weeks later, Allan reviews his disastrous adventures with women: seeing Gina to the door; getting turned down by Vanessa (the woman who has made it with everybody else in the world); being laughed at by the Go-Go Girl; turned off by the Intellectual girl at the art museum. Now a flashback with Linda at the park: he remembered her birthday with a dumb present. A flashback where he tells Dick he's neglecting Linda. Just then, Linda shows up, having anxiety because Dick is out of town. Enjoying their platonic relationship, they decide to cook dinner. After she goes out to the store a dream Linda comes to him. He feels guilty as Bogy and Nancy play good and evil angels on his shoulder. A dream Dick says he's dumping her and the dream Linda briefly appears to suddenly remind him she's his friend's wife! Linda returns with the groceries. Bogy encourages him to make a pass at her. A phone call from Dick interrupts. Allan continues, with Bogy coaching. Nancy comes in and shoots Bogy. Allan tries the kiss, fumbles it and she leaves—only to return and kiss him.

Act 3:   The next morning, Linda goes out to get stuff for breakfast and Allan daydreams Nancy in anguish over his success, becoming a nun; in dream scenes, Dick taking it with a stuff upper lip, like a man—suffering and in pain—dangerous like a Mafia Killer—and then the real Dick shows up at the door, worried that his wife is having an affair. Allan breaks up with a dream Linda who pulls a gun, like in a movie. Bogart shows him how to do it, breaking up with the dream Linda. When she returns, Linda and Allan break it off happily. Bogy and Nancy jump him as good and bad angels, she trying to destroy his confidence and Bogy trying to build it up. He decides to forget Nancy, doing her in. Bogy now leaves: "You don't need me anymore, kid." Doorbell rings and it is a new neighbor, Barbara, wanting to use the phone. Turns out she too is a film buff and one of Allan's fans. Curtain closes on this potential new romance.

In the play, the ex-wife and Bogart clearly are symbolic characters. The wife attacks Allan's confidence and destroys him. Bogart tries to build his confidence and convince him that he is a capable human being. The story is about a divorced man who had lost confidence in his ability to relate to women. Bogart and the wife represent two forces within him, one trying to buck him up and the other trying to make him give up in despair. After a series of comic failures with women, Allan realizes that Linda is the only girl he can talk to, the only one for whom he has any real feelings. He makes a successful pass at her. At the same time, they both feel guilty. She realizes that she loves her husband, and Allan realizes that he loves his friend too much to hurt him; and so, they break off their relationship.

Structural Analysis

Although we can discern the general aim, only by means of a second summary can we see the true structure of the play.

Play It Again, Sam

	1.1	Wife dumping on him—Bogart advising him.
Initial Incident:	1.2	Dick and Linda fix him up.
		Bogy and dream Sharon.
Climax:		He makes a fool of himself with the real Sharon.
	2	Dream disasters with a series of women.
Initial Incident:		He and Linda plan dinner with Dick out of town.
Climax:		Torn between the good and the bad, he finally kisses her.

	3	He daydreams Dick's reactions, benign to murderous.
Initial Incident:		Dick shows up, afraid he is losing Linda. Daydreams as Bogy shows Allan how to break it off.
Climax:		They break it off and remain friends.
Conclusion:		He dumps his dream wife and Bogy leaves him too. Potential new romance appears at door.

The opening event sets the situation: Poor Allan is clearly a failure. When his friends decide to fix him up, that is an initial incident. This leads to the climactic date with Sharon which turns out to be a total disaster. Allan is still a failure. At the opening of act 2, he tells us about his failures—four women in a row. Now, we have a new initial incident: Allan realizes that he is in love with Linda. This leads to a climax in which he kisses her and she returns his feelings. At last, Allan is a success. But something happens that upsets this happiness. In what could be described either as a new initial incident or complication, Allan's best friend—Linda's husband—requests Allan's help in saving his marriage. This event leads to a third climax in which Allan makes the noble gesture by breaking off the relationship with the woman he loves, just as Bogart did at the close of the film *Casablanca*. Finally, we come to the conclusion. How has Allan changed? Is he better or worse? Has he won or lost? Clearly, Allan has won. When he decides to forget his ex-wife, she disappears, because only his memory of her makes her real. Bogart says that Allan doesn't need his help anymore; he can make it on his own. And, as proof of this, a potential new romance appears in Allan's life. The conclusion tells us that Allan has defeated his antagonist—that part of himself that was afraid of life—by becoming a stronger and more confident human being.

Play It Again, Sam is structured in three major episodes, each leading to its own climax. And this structure is made more complex by the addition of a series of short, humorous dream sequences. A clear indication of the protagonist's final success comes when the character who appears as a potential new romance at the end of the play turns out to be played by the same actress who, earlier in the script, represented Allan's ideal dream girl, Dream Sharon.

This form of simple structural analysis gives the director an overview of the way the action of the play works. And it leads to an understanding of the purpose and meaning of that action. How does this relate to the type of analysis we did earlier when we studied the beats within a scene? When the director understands the way the large units of the play work, he or she will also understand the way any individual scene fits into that overall action. Each scene accomplishes some specific goal that is necessary for the overall action, moving that action along in a specific way. Just as each beat leads to the development of the overall scene, each scene helps to develop the action of the play as a whole.

External Analysis

In this chapter, we have concentrated on internal analysis of the plot structure of a script. This emphasis does not imply that external analysis is not a valuable tool for the director as well. Research—concerning the play, of other productions, of other scripts by the same author, and for a period piece, of the theatre and society for which the play was written—is essential. For example, a director contemplating a production of *Hamlet* would be wise to consult David Bevington's anthology of *Twentieth Century Interpretations of Hamlet* (1968), among numerous other sources. Even for a contemporary play, a study of the critical commentary about the original production may aid the director in discovering the particular strengths and weaknesses of that script. Outside research may well expand the director's vision of the possible interpretations appropriate for a particular script. If directors can learn about the playwright and immerse themselves in the period of the play, they can gain knowledge and inspiration for their production.

Summary

In this chapter, we have looked at the ways in which the plots of drama are structured. We have examined types of conflicts, the structure known as the *classical paradigm,* and some common variations of that simple pattern. Then a lengthy application of this type of structural analysis was made on our example play, *Play It Again, Sam.* Finally, the information developed in our analysis was synthesized into an explanation of the entire play. Although little time was spent on the discussion of script research, this does not mean that such external analysis is unimportant. However, the author does believe that internal analysis of the script is most essential for directors in their attempt to understand the script of the play.

CHAPTER 6

SCRIPT ANALYSIS Possibilities

In earlier chapters, we looked at a specific method of play analysis by means of structural analysis of the drama's conflict, as well as detailed study of the beats in a single scene. In this chapter, we will discuss play analysis in a broad, general sense, including the goals, possibilities, and limitations of the process. Much of this discussion is based on the work of Roger Gross in his excellent book, *Understanding Playscripts* (1974).

Definitions and Goals

A drama or play is an event that takes place on a stage. For the audience, it is a communication event, an experience that they filter through their own backgrounds and perceptions in order to come to an understanding of its meaning. A drama or play exists as a **playscript,** as well. Oscar Brockett used to say that the script is related to the finished play production in the same way that the blueprints of an architect are related to the finished skyscraper. In this sense, the script is a plan that will lead to the finished production. The director's job is to interpret or explain the script—as opposed to evaluating or criticizing it—with a particular goal in mind, turning the script into a finished play—a fully staged production.

The Commanding Form

The script sets up what Roger Gross calls a **commanding form,** an organized pattern of events in the lives of certain characters that sets controls on what the directors and actors can do, provides them with some absolute requirements along with a range of options and choices. The commanding form sets limits, as well—a range of options that seems to be improper, unsuitable, or wrong for the play. What the script does not do is require, explain, or dictate the precise details needed to accomplish its goals. The choice of details is left to the directors and actors as long as that choice remains within the commanding form of the script. Directors and actors will find that there are many different ways to stage any particular moment in a script that will seem proper and that will work well within the commanding form of the script. When the script provides a moment in which one character would move away from another, both the location of the actors onstage and the direction of that movement may be a matter of choice. Only the negative movement is implied by the script. However, a positive movement toward the other character onstage would seem improper because this movement is outside the commanding form.

The director attempts to discover this commanding form, to find his or her **interpretation** of the script. The result will always be an interpretation rather than an absolute conclusion, because meaning derives from the process taking place between the script and the interpreter. The words in the script vary in meaning. One director reads them, and because of his background and experiences in life, his conclusions will differ from those of another reader. Ever so slightly, each interpretation will differ from the next, none absolutely true in a mathematical sense. Although the commanding form clearly limits the range of interpreted conclusions, it allows variation from one interpreter to another.

Drawing on the creativity of the actors, the director tries to keep their contributions to characterization and movement within the commanding form of the script, according to the director's interpretation of that form. Together, the actors and director attempt to discover a subtext of the characters' thoughts and desires that will explain the dialogue in the script. Each beat is studied to discover the characters' purpose and desires, and the way in which these change from one beat to the next. For example, the actor says to the actress, "You are beautiful." The subtext—which may imply that he has meant this sincerely, ironically, or in a manipulative manner—will provide the actor with motivation for both sensible movement and line delivery. Depending on what the character is thinking, the actor will read the line and move differently. Ultimately, script analysis leads the director and actors to an understanding of the subtext throughout the play.

Interpretation

The directorial interpretation amounts to all that the director knows about the script: both the rational aspects, which can be explained and discussed, and the subliminal responses, which remain on an instinctive level. Artists rely on much unspoken knowledge of the script, and continuing experience with that script throughout rehearsals promotes constant growth of this knowledge.

In a general sense, interpretation is a matter of analysis, breaking down something for the purpose of explaining how it works. The goal of this analysis is to create a new synthesis—an explanation for the whole artwork when it is put back together again. Each part of the artwork must be understood in terms of why it is there and what it accomplishes in relation to the parts that surround it. Take, for example, the play *Egmont* by the classical German writer Goethe, in which the title character faces a mortal conflict with the Duke of Alba. An analysis of this conflict fails to explain the presence of many scenes in the play; they seem irrelevant to the major conflict. What other purpose could these scenes have? As it turns out, their purpose is to show different aspects of Egmont's character. A series of scenes show that he is willing to break the codes of his noble birth by marrying a commoner with whom he is in love. Another scene shows him as a benevolent ruler, wisely solving the problems of the peasants who come to him. Each of these scenes develop the nobility of Egmont as a human being, strengthening the emotional commitment of the audience to him in his conflict.

Each part of the artwork must be understood, given some interpretation, because the actors must have something concrete to play. This author directed a production of Samuel Beckett's *Waiting for Godot* some years ago. In the play, two characters are waiting in a desolate, unspecified place for someone named Godot, but Godot, who sends occasional messages saying he will come tomorrow, never does arrive. Analysis reveals that Godot is a symbolic concept representing whatever it is in life that people wait and hope for. People wait for their ship to come in, or for good things to happen in their lives, but they take no positive action to improve their lot. They just wait for outside help—help that never arrives. Beckett maintains the symbolic quality of Godot by never allowing the audience to get a handle on his identity. Some dialogue hints that Godot is God, but later dialogue makes it clear that Godot cannot be God. Thus, as a symbol, the identity and meaning of Godot remains deliberately vague. However, actors cannot play vague symbols. In order to be seen as real human beings, the characters had to know how they arrived in this desolate place, where they thought this place was, and who they thought they were waiting for. So, although we avoided giving simple answers to the audience, the actors made up an elaborate subtext—a story which involved an airplane crash—reasons why they had come and why they were waiting. None of this is contained in the script; still, the actors needed concrete answers because they could not play characters with no past life, waiting for no reason for an entity without meaning called Godot. Actors must have a reality to play, a concrete interpretation. If the director does not supply an interpretation, the actors must make one up on their own.

Gross describes the goal of interpretation as **synallaxis.** Synallaxis means that the director has settled on an interpretation that explains the placement and value of each moment in the play, justifying each scene and each character in terms of what they accomplish for the play as a whole. An acceptable interpretation must integrate every part of the script. Take, for example, a particular production of a play called *Indians* by Arthur Kopit. The protagonist is Buffalo Bill, who tends to represent the white man in his relationship with the American Indians. As he relives or reviews his life, Buffalo Bill (who always thought of himself as a friend of the Indians), realizes that he was responsible for their destruction. The play is not realistic; it jumps from one strange location to another with seemingly realistic scenes intermixed with mystical, dreamlike moments. The set designer's interpretation was that the whole play took place in Hell. When the director pointed out that there were some scenes that could not possibly be taking place in Hell, the designer's response was to claim that the playwright had made some mistakes. Obviously, the mistake was in the designer's interpretation. Hell is an acceptable location only when it makes sense for every scene in the play. The acceptable interpretation must achieve synallaxis; in other words, there must be a satisfactory explanation for all of the elements of the script.

The interpretation that makes the most sense to a particular director is the best one, but not necessarily the right one in any absolute sense. The real question is whether the interpretation is reasonable and fitting, one that makes good sense within the script's commanding form. Because conclusions are probable or sensible or practical, the director should be wary of snap judgments, must constantly be suspicious of first impressions, and be willing to revise the interpretation when new evidence or inspiration appears. The object is to discover all of the possibilities, while avoiding those interpretations not justified by the script. This author had an experience during rehearsals for Tennessee Williams' *Night of the Iguana* that illustrates this idea. From early analysis we were aware that the play was structured in an unusual fashion. All of the major scenes of physical action—fight scenes and the like—were found in the middle of the play. What remained were long, quiet discussions, very little of which could be described as climactic action. We were aware that some effort would be needed to hold the interest of the audience during these final scenes, but we did not understand why Williams had arranged the play with this atypical structure. The answer finally came to us one evening well along in the rehearsal period, while listening to the protagonist deliver a particular speech. The protagonist describes the typical sequence of events that takes place in every one of his relationships with women. The remainder of the play is an illustration of this speech in action as the relationship between the protagonist and the leading lady goes through this sequence of events, step by step. The point is that directors should be flexible in their interpretation, remaining open to new discoveries about the script even late into the rehearsal period.

Script Alteration

An artwork causes an experience to take place between the stage and the audience—an intense and immediate psychological and emotional experience. That experience is probably built into the commanding form of the script. The director's production will have to be faithful to that commanding form if it is to create that experience for the audience. However, being faithful to the commanding form might require the director to deviate from the surface script. Shakespeare's *Midsummer Night's Dream* had a celebrated modernist production on Broadway with all-white sets and characters swinging overhead on trapezes, looking a bit like circus performers or people from outer space.

Much Ado About Nothing was reset into the 1890s. War plays, historically belonging to the sixteenth century, have been done in Civil War uniforms, looking much like *Gone With the Wind*. But these are changes in the surface aspects of the artwork; each of these productions was faithful to the author's original intent and to the commanding form of the script. However, a famous production of *Julius Caesar* done by Orson Welles in the late 1930s clearly went beyond the commanding form of the original script. Welles modernized the play, rewrote it and rearranged the scenes in order to turn it into a commentary on

Hitler and his Nazis, poised for conquest just before the Second World War. In effect, Welles created a new version of *Julius Caesar,* a version with a different commanding form.

An excellent chapter in Cohen and Harrop's *Creative Play Directing* (1984, pp. 241–77) contains multiple examples of the different styles in which plays have been done, particularly those of Shakespeare. In *The Director at Work* (1985, pp. 12–16), Benedetti describes the director's possible approach to a play as either conservative (as it was done in the original production), liberal (treating the play to bring out its relevance for the contemporary audience), or radical (recreating the play as in the example of Welles' *Julius Caesar*). To some extent, the reader of a playscript is always in the liberal mode, applying his or her own contemporary sensibilities when determining the meaning of the events.

In the late 1970s and throughout the 1980s, a trend toward radical innovative productions appeared in which directors often drastically altered the commanding form originally intended by the playwright. This trend, usually labeled **postmodernism**, allowed the mixing of seemingly incompatible styles and justified radical, new interpretations of playscripts on the basis of poststructuralist ideas; that is, the meanings implied by the playwright's language are open to a much wider range of interpretation than was previously thought acceptable. For example, in Peter Sellars' production of *Orlando* at the American Repertory Theatre, the main characters in Handel's opera were played as astronauts, while his Chicago production of *Mikado* was played in the corporate boardroom of a modern Japanese company. The fact that Samuel Beckett threatened legal action when his *Endgame* was reset in an abandoned subway tunnel by director JoAnne Akalaitis focused attention on the debate concerning the rights of the script's author versus the director's right to interpret the script in new and unusual ways.

For our staging of *Play It Again, Sam,* the director altered a few lines in the script, either because the line had become dated since the original writing or because the line referred to something specific in New York City that our audience would not understand. For example, while desperately searching for a girlfriend, the protagonist says that he will have to find some nymphomaniacs, or at least some salesgirls from Paraphernalia. Clearly, the line is intended to get a laugh, but our audiences had never heard of "Paraphernalia." We substituted "Penneys"—not a perfect parallel but it always got the laugh. In another instance, the protagonist wishes he were as attractive to women as the movie star Rock Hudson. Because time has altered the image of Rock Hudson, we substituted the name of another film star, Robert Redford. With each of these line changes, we were attempting to preserve the audience reaction originally intended by the author, while remaining within the commanding form of the script.

At what point does such alteration or cutting of lines in a script become illegitimate—a disservice to the script and an insult to the playwright? Opinions differ. Purists contend that altering Shakespeare, for example, is tantamount to rewriting the Bible—it just isn't done! Yet Shakespeare was a

In the Director's Chair

Augustin Daly (1838–1899)

One of the most important early producers and directors of the American stage, Daly began as a drama critic in New York before trying his hand at playwriting, producing such melodramas as *Under the Gaslight* (1867) and *The Red Scarf* (1869). Daly directed his own resident acting troupe in New York City from 1874 until his death in 1899. Daly's goal as a director was to achieve an ensemble interpretation of a play in which the actor playing the leading role was no more valuable or essential in the production than an actor in a minor role. To Daly, all actors were equally important in achieving the artistic and social unity of effect envisioned and overseen by the director. Thus, Daly's company was famous for the ensemble realism of its acting style. Guest actors were often unable to perform comfortably with Daly's group because their traditional style of acting would not blend in. Daly was known as a star-maker, but only because he would part ways with any actor who expected special treatment because he or she had been made famous by one of his productions.

sensible, practical artist of the theatre. Knowing that modern audiences could not relate to the full four-hour version of *Hamlet,* he would shorten the play, just as any sensible, contemporary director should. If there is no possibility that the actors can make sense of a particular phrase for the audience because the language is archaic and obscure, that phrase should be cut. Why bother to say something that the audience cannot understand? On the other hand, this author does not believe that off-color language should be cut from plays for conservative or moralistic reasons. Taking the harshness out of a play, making it nice and sweet, can seriously alter the commanding form. For example, cleaning up the language in the musical, *The Robber Bridegroom,* destroys the earthiness of the script, robs it of its pizzazz, and turns it into a cute piece of children's theatre. Clearly, the whole issue of altering or cutting a script for a particular production is controversial. In this author's opinion, any alteration in the script should be made with the intention of preserving or enhancing the original goals of the playwright, remaining within the commanding form of the script.

First Impressions

The first experience, or first impression of a script, causes a reaction called the **synoptic response.** Whether one reads the script or attends a production of the play, the first emotional experience—the first reaction to the commanding form before any detailed analysis takes place—is the synoptic response. The director must be able to recall the synoptic response because that defines the audience experience that the director wants his or her own production to elicit. In all likelihood, the play was chosen because the director's own synoptic response was positive. Whether the play was exciting or emotionally touching or wonderfully funny, the director liked the play and wants to give the audience that same experience. Therefore, the synoptic experience is the ultimate goal of the director's production. The big picture must not become lost in the details of analysis and rehearsals. The goal of script analysis is to discover how the script causes this synoptic response.

Artistic Synthesis

The actors look at the play as if the characters were real human beings in a real life, while the director studies the play in order to discover the way in which these characters and scenes fit together to create the commanding form. The actors are looking for the characters' purposes and strategies; the director is looking for the playwright's purposes and strategies. Once the director has a clear interpretation of the script's commanding form—and the way in which each part of the script supports that form—the director and actors will base their decisions, moment-to-moment in the rehearsal process, on that interpretation. Therefore, the interpretation must make sense both fictionally and functionally: for the characters as real human beings living in a fictional life and for the manner in which the script functions as a dramatic structure intended to create a specific audience response.

Summary

In this chapter, we have discussed the goals, possibilities, and limitations of script analysis. Interpretations of a script will vary from one director to the next; each of these different interpretations will be valid as long as they are within the commanding form of the script. Clearly, the script limits interpretation in some areas and leaves a range of options in others. Early responses to the script establish the synoptic response, a holistic reaction to the work of art prior to the analysis of its details. The director attempts to understand the way in which the script, both as a vision of human life and as an artistic construction, causes this synoptic response in its audience. This process might be described as the artistic, or aesthetic, analysis of the playscript. In the following chapter, we shall see that the director must study the script for its many practical problems as well.

CHAPTER 7

SCRIPT ANALYSIS
Practical Challenges

Once the director has chosen the play, he or she must read it, study it, understand it. Even for a fairly simple script like *Play It Again, Sam,* the director read the play three times prior to auditions. The first reading was for pleasure and to discover the synoptic response. When the designer began pressing for details of the set some weeks later, the play was reread with that purpose in mind. Finally, the script was read a third time in order to find out more about the characters and to choose audition scenes.

Audition Scenes

The following is the director's list of scenes for audition:

Audition Scenes

Characters	Pages
Nancy/Allan	6–7, 8–9, 15, 48
Bogart/Allan	7–8, 18–19, 38
Bogart/Allan/Linda (Nancy)	40–45
Bogart/Allan/Dream Linda	52–54
Dick/Linda/Allan	9–17
Allan/Linda/Dick/Sharon	20–26
Allan/Dick	33–34
Allan/Linda	34–36
Dream Allan & Linda	37–38
Allan & Dick (in roles)	49–51
Dream Sharon & Allan	19–20
Gina (dumped at door)	28
Vanessa (the lover)	28
Go-Go Girl (dances & says little)	
Intellectual Girl (at museum)	31
Barbara (final entrance)	56

Not knowing how many people might appear at tryouts, the director made careful calculations about the size of the cast. The script calls for three men and nine women; however, with some actresses playing more than one role, the play could be done with three men and six women.

Properties

At one point, the director reread the script in order to make a list of necessary **properties**—those items used by the actors and specifically mentioned in the script. Usually, this procedure is forgotten until the designer requests a list in the midst of rehearsals when the director's time is limited. In this case, when looking for technical problems, the director made an early list of props. Each time some object was mentioned in the script—if there was a magazine on the set or someone picked up a glass—the director wrote it down.

Props—Sound Effects

Maltese Falcon movie
Aspirin bottle
Books, magazines, coffee mug, sweater, TV trays
Newspapers, paper towels, wastebasket, robe, towels, T-shirt
Coke, Fresca, pills (Darvon)
4 clean glasses
Mirror & Bar
*Piano version of song: "As Time Goes By"
Jar of cocktail nuts in a bag (p. 20)
2 bowls for the nuts
100-yard dash medal
*Bartok & Thelonious Monk albums & others
Booze bottles at bar. J & B—Harveys Sherry & Bristol Cream
Ice from kitchen (ice bucket)
Water pitcher
Glass of sherry
*Music Build & Record Scratch (Thelonious Monk) pp. 23–24
Photography magazine
Phone
Old address book
*Go-Go music at disco—segue into slower number & suddenly back to fast
*Birds, etc. sound track with Linda at the park
Plastic skunk birthday present
*Jet-spray sound
Bag of groceries—candles & candlestick
Gun & blanks for Nancy
Door buzzer
Dagger to stab Allan
Dick's suitcase & coat
A separate gun for Linda

The properties began to appear earlier than they do for most shows, probably because the prop crew was able to begin work at least two weeks earlier than usual.

Designing the Set

According to Louis Giannetti (1993, pp. 292–93), "A systematic analysis of a set involves a consideration of the following characteristics:

1. *"Exterior or interior.* If the set is an exterior, how much does nature function as a symbolic analogue to the mood, theme or characterization?

2. *"Style.* Is the set realistic and life like, or is it stylized and deliberately distorted? Is it in a particular style, such as colonial American, art deco, sleek contemporary, etc.?

3. *"Studio or location.* If the set is an actual location, why was it chosen? What does it say about the characters?

4. *"Period.* What era does the set represent?

5. *"Class.* What is the apparent income level of the owners?

6. *"Size.* How large is the set? Rich people tend to take up more space than the poor, who are usually crowded in their living area.

7. *"Decoration.* How is the set furnished? Are there any status symbols, oddities of taste, etc.?

8. *"Symbolic function.* What kind of overall image does the set and its furnishings project?"

Of course, item 3 relates only to the cinema. Nevertheless, the list is thorough in its description of the different aspects of a setting that the director ought to think about. Clearly, a good director is aware of the powerful symbolic import of scenery, costumes, and lighting.

Directors must be prepared to work with their designers and have design meetings at which they can discuss the play in an intelligent manner, having thought about the necessary qualities of the play's setting. Both director and designer will usually discuss their ideas at a preliminary meeting. At a second meeting, the designer will return with some sketches of a potential set. At this point, the director may suggest some alterations, if necessary. For example, the set for a production of Arthur Miller's *A View From the Bridge* consisted of a city street on stage level with the interior rooms of a house visible further upstage on a platform. But the designer had put the entryway to the house at stage center, and even though the hallway had no solid walls, the framework and pillars would have blocked the view of the audience. Therefore, the director suggested that the entryway be moved to the stage left edge of the house platform. The designer complied, and the finished set was most satisfactory.

The director's relationship with the designer is not always so smooth. Designers can range from those who appear at the first meeting with a completed set in mind, unwilling to accept any directorial suggestions, to those who expect the director to simply tell them what he or she wants for a set. The director may find it difficult to discover a working relationship that encourages the designer to be creative, but only within the director's interpretation of the commanding form of the script. In one production of Shakespeare's *As You Like It,* the director wanted

In the Director's Chair

David Belasco (1853–1931)

David Belasco got his training in the remote frontier of California theatre, where he was an actor, a playwright who dramatized or adapted novels and old plays, and a stage manager known for devising spectacular melodramas with live animals, fires, and battle scenes. As an all-around man of the theatre, Belasco was one of the first stage managers to elevate and develop that position into that of the new director in the theatre. In 1880, he became stage manager for Daniel Frohman, staging Bronson Howard's *Young Mrs. Winthrop* at the pristine Madison Square Theatre, a theatre specifically designed for the new realistic scenery. Belasco later became stage manager for Steele MacKaye at the Lyceum until the 1890s, when his playwrighting and managerial career began. As a playwright, his work was romantic, as his famous *Madame Butterfly* demonstrates. But as a producer and director at his own Belasco Theatre, he was renowned for the realism of his acting ensemble, his stage settings, and his lighting effects.

a modern set with many platforms and levels that could represent all the various locales of the play, such as the castle and the different parts of the forest. However, the designer arrived at the first meeting with his mind fixed on reproducing the look of an Elizabethan theatre, much like Shakespeare's Globe Theatre. Although he acquiesced to the director's wishes, the designer was never happy with the resulting set. In another example, a director tried every possible approach with a particular designer through a series of shows, none of which were successful. Finally, he simply gave that designer a sketch of the set he wanted at the first meeting for a production, a working method that the designer seemed to find quite acceptable.

In general, the director who is not trained in the art of set design should seek a working relationship that fosters the artistic creativity of the person who is a trained expert—the designer. At the first production meeting, the director should describe the goals, the effects, what the audience should feel, the dominant quality of the play, and the entire production approach. Directors should tell their designers what they plan to do with the show rather than what the designers should do. Directors should see designers as an extension of their own creativity rather than as a threat to it. Designers give directors room to do more than the directors themselves could do.

The director may choose from a number of styles of set design. A set can represent a realistic environment in great detail or in a very simplified way. For example, a streetlight on an empty stage will serve to define the street corner. A set can be totally abstract—for example, consisting of platforms and levels that are not intended to stand for a lifelike environment. There can be multiple sets on the stage at the same time, as in our example from *The Rainmaker,* or the director could choose to work with a bare stage. In his book *Play Direction,* Dietrich says that a set should be attractive, practical (useful for the actors and directors in terms of staging the play), and meaningful (capturing the aesthetic qualities and mood of the play). In general, the technical aspects of a play—the scenery, costumes, lighting, and sound—must be strong, without overwhelming the other elements of the play. The director must be careful not to approve a set design that clashes with the basic style of the play. In an original script dealing with the issue of mercy killing and the awful decision faced by the family members of a man in a permanent coma, the designer produced an expressionistic interior for the home—the distorted, leaning walls were intended to represent the internal turmoil of the characters. However, reputable professional designers criticized that choice because an expressionistic setting seemed out of place with the realistic style of the playscript.

The designer provides the director with a sketch or a more elaborate rendering of the potential set, sometimes with a full-scale model much like a doll house, and a floor plan. Often, a simple pen or pencil sketch is preferable to something more elaborate because the designer usually captures a sense of the mood and lighting of the set—a quality that the scale model lacks. Unless the director can read a floor plan well, it is advisable to lay the plan out on a floor in full scale, placing some makeshift furniture in it, in order to determine whether there is enough space for actor movement. This author learned this lesson when he asked a designer to enlarge a room after the set was under construction. The play was *Philadelphia, Here I Come,* and the set consisted of a kitchen and a bedroom. As it turned out, when the actors were sitting in the chairs at the kitchen table, there was not enough room to move around the table. The blocking was stifled; therefore, enlarging the room became a necessity. But the director should have foreseen this problem before set construction had begun.

Thus far, our description of the director/designer relationship has assumed a small theatrical operation with a single designer. However, directors usually work with costume designers as well, and a larger operation might have a separate lighting designer and sound designer. In most cases, the set designer is the chief officer of the design team, working with the other designers to create a unified production style. Obviously, the set must be planned before the lighting designer can begin work, and the costumer must be aware of color contrasts between costumes and the walls of the setting. Early production meetings between the director and the design team should set the tone and style of the production, assuring the director that everyone is headed toward the same goals. Private conferences with the costumer and the sound designer will be useful when each comes up with specific ideas for the show. The wise director will maintain some communication with his or her designers throughout the rehearsal schedule in order to be cognizant of the direction their work is taking.

The set designed for *Play It Again, Sam* consisted of a living room at center and right and a raised platform at left that contained the main entrance to the apartment through an archway upstage. The stage left wall contained an exit to the kitchen; the stage right wall, a fireplace upstage and an exit to the bedroom below. A secret entrance for characters in the dream scenes was situated behind the fireplace, up right. (See Figures 7.1 and 7.2.) Once he had a sketch of the set, the director began to plan the entrances of the dream characters, spreading them among the various possible exits, and marking them in the margin of his summary of the play. Only one exit clearly defined a dream character because normal characters never used it.

The director discovered that the script implied the use of two more exits, off the set and near the proscenium, downstage left and right. At the opening of the second act, which begins with a series of brief dream scenes, the director felt the need for these exits which would create three exits used only by the dream characters.

The scene in which the protagonist meets a girl at the art gallery was clearly intended to be played on the forestage in front of the main set. Therefore, the director asked the designer to move the entire set two or three feet upstage, leaving room for exits at the proscenium. The director also asked that a low railing be added at the downstage edge of the platform at stage left because he thought it would be a useful object for the actors.

Another problem was presented by the position of the apartment entrance in an alcove upstage left. A crucial, climactic moment in the play takes place in that doorway when Linda returns to kiss Allan at the end of the second act. On this set, half of the audience would not be able to see the kiss. Rather than alter the set, the director solved this problem by staging the kiss not in the doorway, but further onstage in the archway of the alcove.

Unlike the aforementioned process used for *Sam,* the director must often be responsible for planning his or her own setting. An obvious example is the

Figure 7.1

A sketch of the proposed setting for *Play It Again, Sam* based on designer Shawn Stewart-Larson's preliminary sketch.

Figure 7.2

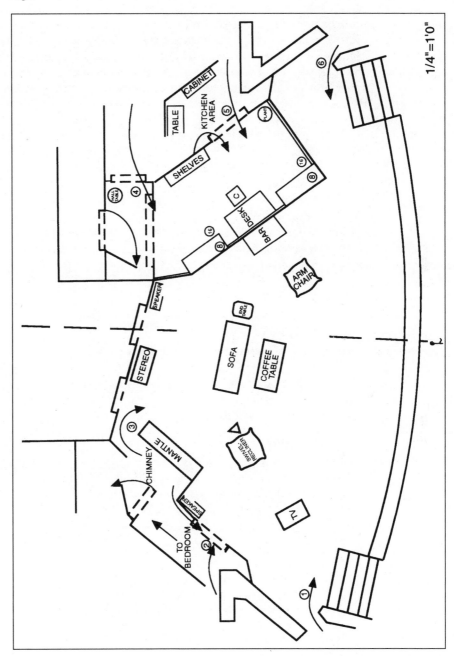

Designer Shawn Stewart-Larson's floor plan for the proposed setting for *Play It Again, Sam.*

student-directed classroom scene. Decisions must be made about the setting, exactly as we made them for our staging of the scene from *The Rainmaker*. A setting should be arranged to facilitate the movement of the actors. Unlike an ordinary room, in which the furniture is placed against the walls, the stage is like a large room in a mansion in which the major units of furniture, such as sofas and chairs, are arranged so that the actors can circle around the furniture. For example, if an actor is standing while in conversation with someone seated on a sofa against the upstage wall, the standing actor would have to face away from the audience a large part of the time. But if the sofa was placed out in the open space, the actor could stand beside it or behind it during the conversation, thus opening up to the audience view. All of the standard concepts of balance and symmetry should be applied to the arrangement of scenery on the stage as well. These concepts will be discussed in detail in Chapter 12, "Principles of Arrangement."

One final point: Placing furniture such as a sofa face-on to the audience creates a sense of cold formality one might associate with an office, whereas placing that same sofa on a slight diagonal seems more informal and warm. These few principles should help the director arrange his or her set pieces in a practical and useful manner.

Locating the Problems

When directors are analyzing the script for practical purposes, they look for problems that might prove difficult to solve. The following is the director's problem list for *Play It Again, Sam:*

Problems

Alter things on pp.: 10-11-18-29-39 (Rock Hudson, etc.)
Music build on p. 23 (record scratch-Thelonious Monk)
Go-Go music—segue to slow—and then back
Piano version of "As Time Goes By"
Park sound effects (Birds, etc.)
Use music behind all dream scenes?
Bar & Mirror?
Where do they sit when they are at the disco?
What is a hassock?
They kiss in the doorway—can we see it?
People talk Italian on p. 50
Sharon & dream Sharon different actresses.

The first item reminds the director to make slight alterations in lines that have become dated. There follows a series of comments on music and sound effects. For example, one would not want to scratch a real record every night; therefore, a recording of a scratch must be made that can be played on cue. The question of whether to use music during all the dream scenes requires a major choice in terms of the style of the show. Looking for ways to make the dreams clearly different from the scenes of reality, the director finally decided to use various appropriate musical backgrounds for all the dream sequences.

The second group of comments is related to the setting. The characters serve drinks; therefore, should we have a bar on the set? The designer preferred a small cart on wheels for the drinks. A hassock is mentioned as part of the furniture, but once he discovered what a hassock was, the director decided not to use one. Because there was no table on the set, the director wondered where he would seat the patrons in the disco dream scene. Finally, noting that the characters spoke Italian in the gangster dream scene, the director reminded himself that he must learn what those phrases meant and how they should be pronounced.

For the same reason that the director chose to use background music in the dream sequences, he realized that the lighting should change for each dream scene, as well. The director decided to stage as many of those dreams as possible in limited areas of the stage so that the lighting would go from full stage area to a distinctly smaller stage area, then back to full stage after the dream. The most difficult dream scenes would be the ones involving Bogart. Because those scenes are lengthy and Bogart must have the use of the full set, an entirely new pattern of lights would be needed to differentiate between his scenes and reality.

Questions of Style

Other choices had to be made that might be described as matters of style. For example, the protagonist has many solo speeches during the play. Should he address these monologues directly to the audience in a frank, presentational style? Woody Allen is known for his use of this style in such films as *Annie Hall,* in which his character speaks into the camera, privately talking to the audience about his problems. Regarding our production, the director and leading actor made the decision together; based upon our interpretation of the script's intentions, we chose to play the scenes realistically, in a representational style, as if the character was speaking his thoughts aloud in private—just talking to himself. However, either style clearly would be an acceptable interpretation of this script.

Whereas some of the dream scenes obviously are intended to be played melodramatically—in a broader acting style than in the real-life scenes—the director chose to play one particular dream scene in a directly opposite manner. After Linda has gone off to the grocery store, she reappears as a dream character while Allan contemplates how she might react to his advances. The director's choice was to have her return in such a normal manner that the audience would be tricked briefly into thinking that this was the real Linda rather than a dream character. Of course, the audience soon would figure out the truth from the outlandish things that Linda does. Again, this decision was a matter of style; playing dream Linda more melodramatically would be well within the commanding form of the script.

Censorship

Although it is implied that Allan sleeps with the wife of his best friend between the second and third acts of the play, *Play It Again, Sam* is unlikely to provoke negative comments from the audience. The play has no violence, no overt sexual activity or nudity, and minimal off-color language. In general, violence is not a problem area for the stage; movies are much more gruesome and graphic. Nor do many plays deal with any form of nudity. Strong language, however, may draw some flak in the form of letters of complaint.

As a matter of fact, off-color language will provoke more complaints than will lurid events in the plot. *California Suite,* a series of four 1-act comedies, provides an example. No one seemed bothered by the issue of homosexuality in one of the stories, but the profanity in another story—especially by the female characters—evoked letters of complaint. Because people in the Midwest swear less often in ordinary conversation, language that seems fairly normal in some parts of the country may draw attention to itself in others. While some language may be thought of as tacky or tasteless, other phrases may be offensive to some audiences, because they take the Lord's name in vain. To one person, these types of words or phrases may be a means of expressing emphasis or anger. However, another person might be offended.

The ability that off-color language has to offend depends upon the context in which it is used in the play and upon the way in which the actors deliver the lines. Scenes of high emotion will seem to justify stronger language. At the same time, young actors tend to place great emphasis on swearwords, words that may be underplayed or thrown away in ordinary conversation. For example, in the play *Noises Off,* one of the characters uses the "F-word," one of the most powerful of swearwords and most likely to offend. In the first act of this backstage comedy, the director is sitting out in the audience while his actors rehearse a play-within-the-play onstage. After one of his actors has interrupted the rehearsal one time too many, the director's response is, "Thank you, Gary. Now get the f--- off the stage." Even though the actor delivered this line with low-key irony by underplaying the strong word, the director decided to alter it. Because the word seemed unnecessary and a negative reaction to it would harm the play at this point, the director substituted the milder word, "hell." In the second act of *Noises Off,* the set has spun around and the audience watches the activity backstage during an actual performance of the play-within-the-play. Actors are beating one another up and the scene is sheer comic pandemonium when the director suddenly appears and says, "What the f--- is going on here?" The strong word was underplayed properly, and the audience laughed heartily. In this situation, even the "F-word" seemed appropriate and inoffensive.

On the whole, this author does not believe in cutting off-color language for moralistic purposes. Altering or cutting language in order to sustain the audience reaction originally intended by the playwright is acceptable. However, strong language that is appropriate to the story and required by the commanding form should never be altered. An example is provided in the play *Same Time, Next Year,* which deals with the relationship of a couple over a period of twenty-five years. The couple meet once every year at a resort; each scene in the play shows their meeting every fifth year. In this way, the play reveals the two characters' reactions to changing lifestyles in America; for example, the woman begins as a meek housewife, becomes a hippie in the sixties and a successful businesswoman in the era of women's liberation. Early in the play, we have come to know this character as mild-mannered and conservative. Suddenly, she appears at the opening of a new scene dressed outrageously as a hippie, and her first words are, "Ya wan'a f---?". There is no doubt that the audience will be shocked and perhaps offended at this moment; however, that clearly is the playwright's intention. Therefore, alteration of this phrase would be inappropriate.

A few dramas present the director with the problem of nudity onstage. In *Butterflies Are Free,* the leading lady is onstage in her underwear a good deal of the time. Although such clothing is no more revealing than a bathing suit, underwear creates a more sensual illusion. *Equus*—a play about a psychiatrist treating a young man who inexplicably has blinded all the horses in a stable—contains a scene intended to be done completely in the nude. The young man has his first intimate experience with a girl late at night in the stable. Nothing overtly sexual takes place, but both characters are nude. Careful study of the script does provide an alternative to the nudity, however. In an earlier scene, the young man takes off his clothes in pantomime, then rides one of the horses at the stable. Therefore, the pantomime of the nudity in the later scene between the boy and girl is consistent with the style established earlier in the script. However, partial nudity would seem to be a cop-out. Only the two extremes are appropriate to the commanding form of the script.

The Elephant Man contains a nude scene that is absolutely required by the script. In a gesture of loving friendship, the leading lady shows her breasts to this terribly deformed man who has never known a woman. The actress disrobes to the waist with her back to the audience. When the doctor suddenly enters the room, she turns away from him, toward the audience, covering herself with her arms. Little is revealed to the audience, but the sensual illusion is very powerful. This scene is a major climax of the play, a scene that must be done as written. If the director cannot stage this scene properly, he or she should choose another play.

From the time of Plato and Aristotle, theatre has faced the controversy of whether it should show life as it ought to be—setting good examples—or whether it should show life as it is, with all its foul words and evil deeds intact. Great theatre has demonstrated both the ideal and the real, from *Cyrano de Bergerac* to *The Lower Depths*. The director may choose the type of play he or she likes. Once the play is chosen, controversial issues should always be treated with tact, never with cowardice.

Rehearsal Schedule

The final step in the director's preplanning of a production is to set up a rehearsal schedule. If possible, the show should rehearse at the same time and in the same place every day to minimize absences caused by forgetfulness. Even the director of a classroom scene is well advised to fix a written rehearsal schedule so that everyone knows where and when to meet. Nothing is more frustrating for the director than trying to stage a play with some of the cast members absent from rehearsal. The following is the rehearsal schedule for *Play It Again, Sam:*

Play It Again, Sam Rehearsal Schedule

October	13	1st read through	(READING AND ANALYSIS)
	14	No Rehearsal	
	15	Character Discussion & Rehearsal Goals	
	16	(MH106) 2nd read through	
	19	Blocking Act I, Scene I (pp. 6–17)	(BLOCKING)
	20	(MH106) Blocking I 2 (pp. 18–26)	
	21	No Rehearsal	
	22	Blocking II (pp. 27–36)	
	23	Blocking II (pp. 37–46)	
	26	Blocking III (pp. 47–56)	
	27	Run Act II	
	28	Run Act III	
	29	Run Act I	
	30	Run through entire play	
November	2	(MH106) Lines I 1	(LINE LEARNING)
	3	(MH106) Lines I 2	
	4	Lines II	

5	Lines III	
6	Run through entire play	
9	Act I	(POLISHING)
10	Act II	
11	Act III	
12	Run through	
13	Run through	
16	Technical Rehearsal	(DRESS REHEARSALS)
17	Dress Rehearsal	
18	Dress Rehearsal	
19	Dress Rehearsal	
20	Performance	
21	Performance	
22	Performance	
23	Performance	

Unlike the usual schedule, *Sam* had a portion of a sixth week for rehearsal. However, we were forced to relinquish the theatre to other events rather often, indicated on the schedule either by the phrase "No Rehearsal" or by "(MH106)," which means that we moved the rehearsal to a classroom. Only once during blocking did the classroom location cause a problem. We gained two nights of rehearsal which were used for blocking and a run-through of the play with script in hand between blocking and line learning.

In order to plan the rehearsal schedule, the director must divide the script into units of reasonable size for blocking and take into consideration any conflicts or problems such as the need for some cast member to be absent from rehearsal to attend her sister's wedding or some other event. An effort should be made to schedule scenes so that actors do not spend the whole evening sitting around waiting for their entrance. If an actor has a brief entrance at the close of a scene, the director might be able to stage that moment at a later rehearsal in which that actor plays a larger role. When possible, the director should avoid wasting the actors' time. A brief calculation will show that *Play It Again, Sam* had twenty-six rehearsals, each three hours long, for a total of seventy-eight hours of rehearsal before the opening night. This is a minimal number of hours for a thorough rehearsal. The majority of university productions use a six-week rehearsal period, and more elaborate productions such as musicals will probably need even more rehearsal time. Professional productions tend to rehearse for three or four weeks, forty hours per week, or at approximately the ratio of sixty to one: 120 hours of rehearsal for a production that lasts two hours on stage.

Summary

In this chapter, we have talked about the practical problems that the director must discover and solve and the practical tasks that the director must complete when analyzing the playscript and preparing for the production. We have dealt with audition scenes, properties, design of the scenery, special problems, matters of style, censorship, and rehearsal schedules. Organizational ability and common sense will serve the director well at this stage of the game.

CHAPTER 8

SCRIPT
ANALYSIS
Examples

In the previous chapters, we looked at script analysis in a theoretical sense, at the goals, possibilities, and limitations in general. In this chapter we will discuss the analysis of two scripts in specific detail. Both plays are famous and difficult works of art: *Night of the Iguana,* by Tennessee Williams, and *Uncle Vanya,* by Anton Chekhov. These examples should help make the process of script analysis more concrete to the reader.

The First Story

The protagonist in *Night of the Iguana* is a man called Shannon, a former minister who was tossed out of the church because he made a habit of seducing his young teenage parishioners. Shannon's continuing desire to be a spiritual person clashes with his continuing sexual desires. He has fallen so low that he now acts as a bus guide for religious women on tour in Mexico. In the first scene of act 1, Shannon—on the verge of a nervous breakdown—has brought a busload of women to a shabby, decaying hotel run by an old friend, Maxine. Maxine, who has always had an interest in Shannon, is a tough, sexy lady, recently widowed. As usual, Shannon is in trouble. He has seduced a young lady on the tour named Charlotte, and the boss-lady of the tour group, Miss Fellows, threatens to have him fired. During all of this confusion, two penniless travelers arrive: Hannah and her ancient grandfather, Nonno. They usually make a living traveling from one hotel to the next, selling their wares—the woman doing artistic sketches of the guests while the old man recites his poetry when his memory does not fail him. Just as Maxine is about to kick them out, Shannon intervenes and prevails upon Maxine to give them shelter. Maxine is clearly jealous of this new, potential rival for Shannon's affections.

In the second scene of act 1, Charlotte pursues Shannon, and he faces down his teenage conquest who, like all the other young ladies, brings him nothing but trouble. Shannon tells Hannah the story of his lost ministry and of his belief that God is fierce, like thunder and lightning. Hannah believes that people just need simple comfort; she gently describes Shannon as a man of God on vacation. Maxine pursues Shannon, who is a haunted man more in need of rest and escape than the physical activity Maxine has in mind. The jealous Maxine warns Hannah to stay away from Shannon. At the close of the act, Shannon's God arrives in the guise of a violent tropical thunderstorm.

In the second act, the level-headed Maxine continues to work on Shannon: "We've both reached the point where we've got to settle for something that works for us in our lives—even if it isn't on the highest level." Miss Fellows has brought in some company men; a big fight ensues, and Shannon is fired from his job as a tour guide. Left behind by his tour group, Shannon has a breakdown and is tied into a hammock for his own protection. The women face off again, Maxine still jealous of Hannah.

A strong sympathy exists between Hannah and Shannon because both are travelers, lost and alone. After he calms down, she frees him. When he asked about her relationships with men, Hannah tells a long story which indicates that she remains a virgin. Shannon wonders if they might not travel together, but he soon discovers that Hannah cannot stand to be touched by a man. They have become close, but their relationship can go no further. Earlier in the play, some native boys had captured an iguana and tied it under the porch, planning to make a meal of the lizard. At Hannah's request, Shannon now frees the iguana, which is symbolically at the end of its rope, as are many of the play's characters.

Hannah's grandfather completes the poem on which he has been working for years, a poem about finding the pride and courage to face the inevitable decay and death of all living things. Shannon finally accepts Maxine's offer of shelter and support. Sitting in his chair, the old man quietly dies. At the final curtain, Hannah is truly alone.

Analysis of the Conflict

An analysis of the conflict in the script of *Night of the Iguana* should lead us to an understanding of the structure of the action and its purpose. Shannon is the main character—the protagonist—because the script clearly is telling his story. Who or what is Shannon's antagonist? Most obviously, Miss Fellows is the opponent in his struggle to keep his job as tour guide. However, this conflict ends halfway through the play when Shannon loses his job and Miss Fellows disappears from the script. What is the rest of the play about? Does a new episode begin, a new conflict? The end of the play deals with Shannon, Maxine, and Hannah—a second conflict which has been going on from the play's beginning. Maxine wants Shannon to be her husband, a fate he resists throughout the story. How should this be described? Perhaps Shannon is his own antagonist in this case, faced with a choice between Maxine and Hannah. The more action-packed conflict with Miss Fellows is clearly less important because it does not carry through to the end of the story; nor does the play seem to be a simple romance—a boy-meets-girl tale about Shannon and Hannah.

The whole question of the antagonist in *Night of the Iguana* must be considered carefully. What is Shannon's overall problem as a human being? What is wrong with his life? What has brought him to the verge of a nervous breakdown? His affair with young Charlotte, which creates the conflict with Miss Fellows and leads to his downfall, is typical of the problems that always have destroyed his life. Shannon is his own worst enemy. Now, we have discovered the key. The conflict with Miss Fellows is merely an illustration of the inner conflict between Shannon the minister and Shannon the seducer. Even the choice posed by the second conflict supports this idea, because Hannah seems virginal and spiritual while Maxine is sensual and physical. Thus, our expectations are aroused by two dramatic questions: Will Shannon lose his job? Will Shannon go with Hannah or stay with Maxine? But the underlying dramatic question, hidden within the two surface actions, deals with whether Shannon can solve his internal battle, get his life together, and stop torturing himself. If this is true, the events of the story should support this conclusion.

The first act contains two initial incidents: Miss Fellows threatens to have Shannon fired; Hannah arrives and Shannon helps her, despite Maxine's jealousy. Thus, act 1 sets up the exposition of Shannon's life of failure and a possible love triangle with Hannah and Maxine. In the second act, both actions reach a climax: Shannon is fired and has an emotional breakdown; Shannon and Hannah are sympathetic but unable to save one another. Thus, act 2 contains the action-packed climax of Shannon's struggle with the tour group and the quiet climax of the love triangle, as sympathy between Shannon and Hannah is found impossible to consummate.

In the conclusion of the script, the old man completes his poem and dies. Shannon finally accepts Maxine's offer of love and support. What does this conclusion tell us? Has the protagonist won or lost his inner battle? At best, he has compromised, giving himself a chance to live a normal life. Surely he has won as much as it is possible for him to win at this time in his life. In *Night of the Iguana,* a tortured man finds some stability—a haven from his perpetual inner storm. Fighting to maintain his dignity, not giving up the tour group, not giving in to drink or to Maxine, he finally realizes that he is incapable of standing alone, and he accepts help.

Note that the conclusion contains the completion of the poem and the death of Hannah's ancient grandfather. In what way is this event relevant to Shannon's problem? Remember, all of the parts must fit together in order for the interpretation to be acceptable. The answer is in the content of the poem which deals with old age, decay, and death. Seeing that trees and other living things seem to face the oncoming winter and the decay of their leaves in this symbolic death with a calm lack of fear, the old man pleads for this kind of courage so that he too can face death without fear. Shannon must have the courage to face reality in the same sense. Despite the decay of all his hopes and dreams, he must have the courage to find a new life. Therefore, the old man's poem is a statement of one theme of the play.

Analysis of the Image

Another approach to script analysis can be found in the search for an **image,** or metaphor, that describes the whole play. Such images are often more useful for set and costume designers because images are usually visual in nature. For example, one production of Shakespeare's battle of the sexes, *The Taming of the Shrew,* used the image of a boxing match. The action of the script seemed like a boxing match to the director; therefore, the setting was designed to look like a

In the Director's Chair

Andre Antoine (1858–1943)

Andre Antoine founded the first theatre in Europe dedicated to the new concepts of Naturalism, the Théâtre-Libre, which lasted from 1887 to 1894. Naturalism was a form of realism based upon the concept of bringing a scientifically accurate vision of real life into the theatre, which had been dominated previously by romantic melodrama. Antoine formed his private theatre in order to produce banned works by such major new playwrights as Henrik Ibsen and August Strindberg. Because the new science asserted that people are controlled by their heredity and their environment, Antoine did away with painted backgrounds, staged his actors within sets filled with three-dimensional objects (the furniture from his own home, for example), and retreated behind the fourth wall in order to perform in a life-like manner, as if the audience were not present. The setting had become the environment that shaped the characters' lives. The characters had become three-dimensional human beings with a complex psychology, and the director worked with his actors to create an ensemble interpretation of the world of the play. In later years, Antoine became the grand old man of French theatre.

boxing ring. Each scene was treated as if it was a round in the fight, complete with the ringing of a bell and a character carrying a large poster that announced the number of the round.

Image analysis can often provide useful information and, once in a while, lead to an unusual and exciting production. The image for *Night of the Iguana* is one of life's decay, as pointed out in the grandfather's poem. The play is set in the jungle where everything is damp and rotting. The old hotel is rotting and falling apart. The lives of all of the major characters are falling apart as well. In this author's production of *Iguana,* derived from the present interpretation, this image of decay led to a brilliant set design—a building of weathered wood, like a dilapidated old barn, with the boards spaced so that the audience could see into the hotel rooms when they were lighted.

Psychological Analysis

Another general approach to analysis is based upon the work of Sigmund Freud. Freud described the human psyche in terms of the id, ego, and superego. Deep in the subconscious, the id represents the uncontrolled drive to fulfill our needs, particularly our sexual needs, but also anything vital to our survival. For example, many drug addicts are id-driven; their need is so great that they will do anything—steal or kill—in order to fulfill it. A second level of the psyche is called the ego. The ego provides a form of realistic thinking that puts some control on the id. For example, a man looks at a beautiful woman walking down the street. His id might tell him to grab her and make love to her on the spot. But his ego would warn him of the practical dangers of such an action; he might be arrested and spend the rest of his life in prison. The third level of the psyche, the superego, would also discourage such a foolish action, but for an entirely different reason. As the moral and spiritual aspect of the mind, the superego would tell the man that such an action is wrong and immoral. Thus, the id represents basic drives, the ego provides realistic controls on the id, and the superego provides moralistic controls.

This pattern of id, ego, and superego is often used as a device for script analysis. Such Freudian analysis may be useful in explaining the action of a script, but just as often, it fails to fit a story in any way. The question to ask is if the major characters fall into one of the three categories. Is one character id-driven? Is another particularly moralistic and superior? If the categories represent the characters, this fact may help to explain the script's overall action.

In the Freudian analysis of *Iguana,* Shannon is torn between the id and superego aspects of his character, between sexuality and earthiness and the spirituality of his calling as a man of God. He seems to have no ego qualities, no practical common sense to help him survive in the real world. At first thought, the sexy Maxine seems to represent the id; the spiritual Hannah, the superego. But further consideration leads to the conclusion that the women in the play fulfill all three positions: Charlotte as id, Maxine as ego, and Hannah as superego. Shannon is torn between his id drive for young girls like Charlotte and the total spirituality to which he aspires. Hannah is clearly an extreme representative of the superego, for she is pure, loving, spiritual, and totally nonsexual. Shannon must be both spiritual and sexual; neither Charlotte nor Hannah could fill both of these needs. On the other hand, Maxine is a strong, practical, sexy woman. She can provide the solid basis in reality that Shannon lacks. Maxine lacks the spirituality that might make her the perfect solution to Shannon's problems, but she will be able to guide this weak man through his troubled times. For Shannon, Charlotte is the wrong choice, Hannah is an ideal but impossible choice, and Maxine is the realistic choice. Thus, a Freudian analysis is effective in describing the major conflict and action of *Night of the Iguana*. Torn between warring id and superego aspects, the protagonist finally moves toward the discovery of an ego position by choosing Maxine. The Freudian analysis also corroborates the conclusions drawn from the earlier structural analysis of the script's conflicts.

The reader should recognize that the preceding example is a simple and specific use of the ideas of Freud. Much more complex analysis can be done, using the ideas of Freud and his followers, particularly Jung. One is reminded of Freud's Oedipus complex, used by Laurence Olivier in his famous production of *Hamlet,* to explain the relationship between the title character and his mother. Both psychology and mythology provide sophisticated points of view and tools which can often be useful in the analysis and interpretation of playscripts.

A New Playscript

Our second major example of script analysis—that of *Uncle Vanya*—will consist of the director's notes used in preparation for a production of the play.

Vanya and his family own a small estate and farm in rural Russia. Years ago, Vanya's sister married a university professor and had a daughter named Sonya. Sonya and her Uncle Vanya have been running the farm and sending most of the profits to support the work of the Professor. When Sonya's mother died, the Professor married Yelena, a beautiful and sophisticated woman from the big city, who is thirty years younger than her husband. When the play opens, the Professor, who is planning to retire, has returned to the family estate with his new wife. Vanya's mother and the elderly family nurse maid also live at the farm, but they are minor characters. The other important character is Vanya's best friend, the handsome local physician, Dr. Astrov.

The following director's notes consist of a major first summary of the script succeeded by a series of three reductions, or commentaries, in which the director attempted to discover the key events and meanings of the script. Finally, based upon this plot summary and the commentaries, the director analyzed the script using as tools structural analysis of the conflict, Freudian analysis, and image analysis.

Analysis of Symbols and Pattern in *Uncle Vanya*

<u>Act 1:</u>   Garden chairs, swing, openness, sunny afternoon—Dr. Astrov defensive about his drinking—The life and the people are tedious and

uninteresting—a recent epidemic and the death of a patient have set him on edge—but life has blunted his emotions for he has no strong feelings for anyone anymore.

The coming of the Prof. has upset their lives & schedules—Vanya particularly finds himself unable to work.

Prof.'s eccentricities show in that he wears coat, galoshes and umbrella for afternoon walk in good weather.

Vanya is extremely jealous of and angry at the Professor—jealous of his success in life, angry at his real lack of accomplishment—he doesn't deserve all this praise, care, and the beautiful Yelena.

Vanya petulantly attacks Mom's politics—blaming himself for wasting his life on such matters—now it's too late for him and he feels left with nothing. (Dr. Astrov in his late 30's, Yelena late 20's and Vanya late 40's).

Astrov shows his one passion as he dramatically talks of the forests and conservation.

Yelena has noticed the Dr. and realizes Sonya's interest in him as well—Yelena is open with Vanya as with no one else—she takes Vanya's love for her as she would from a friend—she discourages him but causes no scandal.

Act 2:   Dining Room—Nighttime—Watchman tapping outside. A major thunderstorm comes in almost immediately. The Professor is cranky, in pain, feels like everyone is against him. Trapped in the country, he longs for his former position—the prestige, the intellectual conversation. Here, he seems only to want and dread death. He also feels he is losing Yelena's love.

Vanya makes another pass at Yelena, with great sensitivity, passion and need—he is slightly drunk. He has a self revelation that life has truly cheated him. Astrov enters, making excuses, but truly hoping to find Yelena. Vanya is in such a state of emotion that he breaks down in tears.

Astrov & Sonya talk. He is bitter about life because he sees no light at the end of the tunnel—no goals—no possible real success of some kind. He repeats that he has no emotional attachment to anyone. He promises her that he will give up drinking. She shows clearly that she is enamored with him but he does not understand. He mentions that only beauty affects him, indirectly telling us of his growing feelings for Yelena, but he does not consider this love, only an unspoken lust. She speaks of a hypothetical younger sister loving him—he says no. In soliloquy, she tells us of her love and how terrible it is not to be pretty.

Yelena enters, possibly looking for Astrov. Sonya has always believed Yelena married the Professor for his money. Yelena reassures her—they exchange confidences and become friends. Yelena sees Astrov as having a spark of genius. Music has been Yelena's ambition—she now sees herself as a secondary character, a failure in both music, marriage, and love affairs. She has a sudden and clear revelation that she is truly unhappy and will probably continue so.

Prof. refuses to allow them to play music. Music becomes a symbol of freedom in this act. The girls want to play in their moment of happiness only to be stifled by the Professor.

Act 3:   The drawing room—Daytime—Autumn—September—Notice that Yelena is always on the move—setting herself apart from the others—roaming about when most are sitting down.

Sonya is now neglecting her work. She sees Vanya and Astrov changing as well and wonders if Yelena is not a witch. With great passion, she tells Yelena how much she loves Astrov, and how painful it is that he doesn't notice her. Yelena promises to intervene. If he doesn't love Sonya, he shouldn't come there anymore.

Alone, Yelena is torn between her own feelings and guilt—She knows why Astrov comes—yet she would like to arrange things for Sonya—she too is moved by Astrov, but too cowardly to do anything about her feelings.

With Astrov, Yelena raises the Sonya issue—both are under great tension because of their own feelings for one another. He might have considered Sonya, but not as he feels now. He makes a pass at her— She resists, lest he think she had that in mind all along rather than Sonya's welfare—He persists—They kiss and Vanya sees them. CLIMAX

The Professor proposes to sell the estate—Vanya freaks out: All his pain and bitterness are lavished on the unsuspecting Professor. Sonya, now aware of Astrov's refusal, is in agony when she begs the Professor to understand and forgive Vanya—Only the nurse is calm.

Vanya attempts to shoot the Professor, but misses.

Act 4:   Vanya's Room—Bedroom and office—Vanya's and Astrov's worktables—Birdcage—A wall map of Africa—Big sofa—More like a private office and den because beds are in other rooms. A still autumn evening of the same day as the shooting.

Vanya frustrated and ashamed—Astrov consoles him in that they are alike and suffer the same fate—wants Vanya to return morphine which he has stolen. Sonya makes Vanya return it. She too is in pain and must drown it in work.

Astrov jokes about Yelena bringing destruction wherever she goes—They kiss goodbye (actually she kisses him).

The Professor and Vanya have made up—Things will remain as they were before—He says goodbye and they all leave—The doctor soon follows.

Sonya comforts Vanya as they work—The watchman taps.

First Summary

Thunderstorm in act 2 parallel to arguments with Professor—it passes but Vanya remarks it has brought him no relief. If there is a symbol here, it is a storm in the relations between the Professor and his wife. With Nurse comes the rain, but the thunderstorm continues for Yelena. The act ends with her revelations.

Pattern of settings closing in from open gardens to tiny workspace.

Symbol of music being parallel with personal freedom and happiness (in act 2).

Contrast of Vanya's emotionalism with Astrov's closing off of all emotions as a reaction to the same stifling lives, lost hopes, midlife crisis. Both are electrified by Yelena who brings to their lives beauty and the ability to feel passion once again (Yelena as life force, as *witch,* reassertion of ID).

Does Vanya's map of Africa represent his longings and fantasies just as Astrov's conservation charts?

Time span of the play is from summer to autumn, perhaps symbolic of the stage of life of the main characters.

Growing interest and love for both Yelena and Astrov from the very beginning—unconscious at first—resisted (Astrov assures us it's lust—she recognizes her own unhappiness, both now and in the future)—and finally consummated only in the admission of the fact.

Tomb or prison images for the set—a trap for the characters? It is Astrov's passion for ecology which attracts Yelena and Sonya.—Resignation: Is lack of passion better?—is passion a positive virtue? Where is Yelena's passion? Passion and pain go hand in hand.

Yelena relates openly only to Vanya at first—later to Sonya, and finally to Astrov.

Yelena is always on the move—setting herself apart from the others, roaming about when most are sitting.

Tapping of the watchman—opening and closing of act 2 and close of play—can't see any symbolic import in this at this point.

Contrast of Yelena and Sonya—Beauty vs. plainness / withdrawn and thoughtful vs. open, loving, naive, duty bound / incapable of action vs. an active accomplisher / passive vs. active.

Second Summary

For Yelena, the storm symbolizes the turmoil within her marriage and herself—her music symbolizes her lost happiness and freedom.

Yelena as life force, as witch, as storm. Settings of the play, closing in—life closing in on them—limiting their potential, their possibilities—fixing them, trapping them in the same routine forever.

Vanya and Astrov's maps and charts represent longings and fantasies—Yelena's music, as well.

Play is about the unconscious growth of love between Astrov and Yelena.

Play is about the need for passion and lost passions (both romantic and ecological). But passion is always coupled with pain. About the reawakening of passion.

Play is about Yelena's growing relationships—with Vanya, then Sonya and finally Astrov.

Yelena is always on the move—setting herself apart from others, roaming about when most are seated.

Contrasts of Yelena and Sonya, Astrov and Vanya. Astrov and Sonya are people of repressed emotions; Yelena and Vanya wear their hearts on their sleeves (that is why they relate so well).

Conclusions

The play is about lost passions and the need to feel passion. It is about the reawakening of passion, which is always coupled with pain. The beautiful Yelena appears on the scene—a life force—a witch—a storm breaking in the lives of all the characters. The settings of the play close in on them, just as life is closing in on them, limiting their potential, their possibilities—fixing them, trapping them in the same routine forever.

Vanya and Astrov's maps and charts and Yelena's piano represent their longings and fantasies.

Time span of the play, from summer to autumn, is symbolic of the stage of life of the major characters.

The Analysis

Having done a lengthy summary of the play and drawn some conclusions in the brief commentaries, the director was prepared to analyze the conflicts. More than one conflict exists, but each is clearly interlaced with each other. Astrov is Vanya's best friend and confidante; yet he is Vanya's rival for the affections of Yelena. Yelena becomes Sonya's friend and confidante; yet she is Sonya's rival for the affections of Astrov. The protagonist of the main plot is Uncle Vanya: Uncle Vanya versus the Professor or perhaps, simply, Uncle Vanya versus himself because his problems are not truly caused by the Professor. The second plot, or subplot, involves the love triangle of Astrov, Yelena, and Sonya. This plot is difficult to categorize, because both Astrov and Sonya seem to be protagonists, and neither Yelena nor the Professor are deliberately antagonistic to the other characters. There are no simple villains in Chekhov's world.

Following are the director's notes which attempt to describe the action in which the two conflicts are brought to a climax and concluded in the story.

Initial Incident

Somewhere in act 2—Vanya feels he has wasted his life on the worthless Professor and is in love with Prof's wife.

(*Sub Plot*) Sonya in love with Dr. but he doesn't know it.

Climax

Vanya sees his love kissing Doctor. Professor plans to sell the estate. Vanya goes berserk and tries to shoot the Professor.

(*Sub P*) Yelena acts as go between for Sonya, but Dr. loves Yelena instead and Sonya's hopes are crushed.

Conclusion

All the intruders depart, leaving Vanya and Sonya alone to comfort one another.

(*Sub P*) Dr. and Yelena have poignant parting scene.

All their fondest hopes are dashed at the end—the characters part, each facing the harsh reality of the dreariness of their existence.

An intruder play—Yelena brings beauty and hope into their world—destroys their peace of mind—and everything is left as it was before only on the surface—great sorrow and suffering is the real legacy of Yelena's visit. (Perhaps some new recognition of who they are and what they are capable of as persons, as well.)

Psychological Analysis

Id—Yelena	This analysis does not work well, but it
Ego—Vanya, Sonya	points out Yelena's deep sexual, life-force
Superego—Astrov	which is exerted on Vanya & Astrov, causing Sonya's ultimate unhappiness.

Image Analysis

Like a placid pool of water into which a stone is thrown, making waves and stirring up the hidden things in the bottom of the pool.

Like a mortuary or tomb or prison into which comes, not a savior, but a life force which makes all the inmates aware of their fallen condition. She brings them back to life, but only for an instant, and then disappears leaving them sadder, wiser, but less content and happy.

Based upon the above analysis, a number of decisions were made concerning both the style of the production and the director's approach. Although the play is set in rural Russia, the translation was distinctly British English, one that was used for a production by Laurence Olivier. The director decided to translate the play into American English with the aid of a bright student **dramaturg,** purging it of typically British phrases. During rehearsals, a slight, upper-class British dialect was added for the Professor and Yelena, helping to distinguish them as the outsiders from the big city.

The pervasive mood of the play is downbeat and a bit dreary, concerning as it does people who are unhappy with their lives but are unable to change their condition. Whereas most readers see the play as dramatic and tragic, Chekhov always described his plays as comedies. The director decided to take the author at his word, to search for the comedy in the script as a means of playing against the pervasive sadness. The way the character of Uncle Vanya was approached was the key, and scenes such as the one in which Vanya and Astrov get drunk together could be played in a comic tone. Clearly, Vanya is a bit of a buffoon, a character both comic and tragic. The director's decision to search for the comedy—the moments of happiness in the characters' lives—in order to play against the general tone of sadness in the play became a controlling factor in this production of *Uncle Vanya*.

Summary

In this chapter, we have looked at a particular method of script analysis used by one director in order to arrive at his interpretation of a playscript, for the purpose of translating that script into a full production of the play. Other approaches to analysis are equally valid as long as they lead the director to his or her ultimate goal: A sensible and useful interpretation of the playscript on which the director and actors can base their work. Because that work is directed toward an audience, the ultimate result of all the efforts by both directors and actors is the final production of the play. In reality, that event is an interaction between the production and its audience. As a result, directors should be knowledgeable about audiences and should attempt to understand their reactions to the dramatic event. In view of that fact, we take up the study of audiences in the following chapter.

CHAPTER 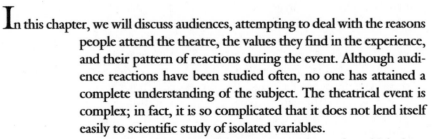 9

AUDIENCE REACTION

In this chapter, we will discuss audiences, attempting to deal with the reasons people attend the theatre, the values they find in the experience, and their pattern of reactions during the event. Although audience reactions have been studied often, no one has attained a complete understanding of the subject. The theatrical event is complex; in fact, it is so complicated that it does not lend itself easily to scientific study of isolated variables.

Motion pictures and theatre are art forms for which there exists no single correct method of creation. There are many methods, but there is no formula for success. With all of their expertise and years of experience, some Hollywood movie moguls make a $30,000,000 movie that is a great success and immediately follow it up with a $30,000,000 flop. Obviously, they do not know what pushes the right buttons in the audience. Usually, after they have spent millions making a film, having it put together by some of the world's finest experts, they show it to some preview audiences and, based upon the reactions, make significant alterations in their work. No one knows exactly how an audience is going to react; so, in the long run, they look for comments from the true experts, the audience members themselves.

Reality and the Theatre

An understanding of the audience is vital to the director because that moment of interaction between the artwork and the audience is the culmination of all of the director's efforts. For the most part, directors try to create an illusion of reality on the stage, an illusion that they want the audience to accept as real life. Yet, the stage does not present reality, and the audience seldom confuses the reality presented on the stage with their own lives.

The playwright alters reality. Characters are not shown eating their meals unless that action is important to the story. Seldom are actors seen going to the bathroom or doing many of the things normal human beings do. Instead, we see certain scenes in the characters' lives that are important to the particular story. The play is a carefully selected and rearranged vision of reality, a reality that is intensified and emotionally heightened. The characters are in some crisis because that is dramatic. Only selected parts of reality are shown, and they are rearranged for dramatic effectiveness, leading to the play's climax.

In some way, the audience accepts this illusion of reality, knowing at the same time that these are actors in a play or movie. The common phrase used to describe this game that the audience plays is the willing suspension of disbelief. This phrase was invented by the famous British poet, Samuel Taylor Coleridge (1817), who drew on the work of the German philosopher Immanuel Kant as popularized by August and Friedrich Schlegel near the turn of the nineteenth century. Coleridge is saying that the audience chooses not to be critical and disbelieve the events on stage. In other words, they choose to allow themselves to be taken in—thus, the willing suspension of disbelief. The audience agrees to put themselves in this peculiar psychological position as if they had a contract with the actors. Standing outside the event and being critical would be easy; they know this is a theatrical production, a fake reality, and they know these are actors pretending to be someone else. However, despite this knowledge, they agree to allow themselves to believe in the illusion.

The willing suspension of disbelief is more easily attained by some than others. Children often become so involved in plays that they lose all critical distance. When a murder is about to take place onstage, they leap up in the audience and shout to the actors, "Watch out, watch out!" For those children, the play has become reality. Some adults on the other hand, have become so cynical and critical that allowing themselves to become involved in a show is no longer possible. For example, professional critics may no longer be able to see a play or film from an ordinary audience viewpoint. Critics may not allow themselves to suspend disbelief because it is their job to disbelieve, to be analytical rather than emotionally involved.

Values of the Theatre

Why do audiences come to the theatre? Why do they want to suspend disbelief? Experts often assume that audiences come to fulfill some personal need of their own—basic drives such as the human need for adventure, romance, love, and the like. As an extreme example, why do people attend sexually explicit stag films or triple-X movies? Sheer curiosity might bring a viewer the first time, but for a person who regularly attended such films, the beginner's reaction—that "surprise" value—would fade rapidly. The sexual activity on the screen may be fulfilling a basic need in the viewer, a need for sexual fantasy not fulfilled in that person's real life.

Freud believed that audiences utilize art to vicariously fulfill their desires and longings, particularly on a subconscious level. Romance novels and soap operas are enormously popular because through such stories, audiences can experience a romantic liaison with an exotic, beautiful partner, without the dramatic experiences intruding into the viewer's real life. Theatre and motion pictures provide a means for the audience to have imaginative experiences, to understand what these experiences feel like without actually participating in them. We may enjoy watching a film such as *Rambo,* but how many of us would like to be tortured and shot at in reality? It is much better and safer to have that experience vicariously in a theatre.

The theatre is often said to offer a combination of values—intellectual values, artistic values, educational values, and psychological values. Obviously, drama takes us to exotic places—Paris, London, Buenos Aries—so that we can experience being in those places. Drama also takes us to different worlds so that we can experience the past, as in a film about Napoleon or a film that takes place in the future, such as *Star Wars.* We may well be enchanted by the color, the style, the beauty of a play or musical; but while we're being entertained by the story, our thinking is expanded by new information and ideas. Nevertheless, this author believes that the vast majority of people attend dramatic events for the psychological and emotional values. If artistic, intellectual, and educational values are also present, some will appreciate those values and others will pay little attention to them. Other values make it a more sophisticated experience, but without the emotional values, few will find the drama satisfying.

Polarization

One concept that deals with the psychological reaction of the audience is called **polarization,** commonly known as "mob psychology." People, when they come together in groups, operate in different ways, often taking actions as part of that group that they would never take as individuals. Under the influence of polarization, people participate in such events as riots, hangings, lootings, and the like, events that they would never undertake alone. A person can act as a group member in a way he or she normally would not act, because there is an anonymity in the group that frees him or her from individual responsibility.

In the theatre, polarization affects the audience most obviously in comedy. One can probably watch a serious play alone and have much the same reaction as if he or she were in a group. However, with comedy, one gets caught up in the laughter of other people. From a director's point of view, we see this all the time; nothing helps a comedy more than a full house. A full house, as opposed to a half-filled auditorium, will produce four or five times as much laughter, not just double the amount. When people are crowded together, the laughter increases geometrically, and those few isolated viewers on the periphery of the crowd will not be laughing as often as those in the middle of the group.

For many years, producers of situation comedy for television added to their shows a soundtrack of people laughing—commonly called "canned laughter." They were trying to create the polarization effect, to give the home audience the feeling that they were part of a larger laughing audience. However, canned laughter often became an ego trip, a method to hype a show that was not really funny. Television comedies are now performed before live audiences, much like a theatrical production, so that the laughter one hears at home is authentic—actually elicited by the humorous events of the show.

Aesthetic Distance

Once the audience has agreed to suspend their disbelief and to participate vicariously in the dramatic event, two concepts are traditionally used to describe the psychological reaction of the audience. The first of these concepts is called

In the Director's Chair

Konstantin Stanislavsky (1863–1938)

For many years, Konstantin Stanislavsky was simply a gifted actor. He came under the influence of George II and his Meininger Company. From them, he adopted the efforts to achieve historical accuracy and the superb staging of crowd scenes. However, he found their acting to be false and declamatory. In 1897, he cofounded the Moscow Art Theatre, which became the home of theatrical naturalism, discovering and giving premiere performances of the plays of both Anton Chekhov (*The Seagull,* 1898) and Maxim Gorky (*Lower Depths,* 1902). At first, Stanislavsky imitated the work of the Meininger director, Ludwig Chronegk, who operated as a producer-autocrat, preplanning and preblocking the entire production, treating his actors as mere pawns to be moved about. But in later years, Stanislavsky rejected this kind of surface realism for a deeper psychological realism that located the heart of the theatre in the actors. He discarded preblocking in order to approach the play along with the actors, going through all the phases of the work and growing together with his actors. Stanislavsky is probably best known for developing the so-called "method" system of acting.

aesthetic distance, an idea that describes the ability of the audience to recognize that the theatrical event is not reality and their ability to remain distanced from it in some fashion. As we mentioned earlier, children often become too involved in a show because they think it is real. They are not distanced enough to understand that the show is just a movie in a world of make-believe. The concept of aesthetic distance seems to describe that agreement to suspend disbelief which takes place between the drama and the audience as a sophisticated psychological position that allows the audience to accept the play on one level of reality—to enjoy and be part of it—while not confusing it with their real life. In the world of the drama, the audience lives vicariously rather than realistically.

Aesthetic distance should not be confused with real distance, the physical distance between the audience member's seat and the stage. Although real distance might decrease one's involvement in a show, aesthetic distance is a mental state, rather than a physical one. When audience members close their eyes or cover their faces during a horror movie in order to avoid seeing some gruesome event on the screen, they are not increasing their aesthetic distance from that film; rather, they are completely cutting off their involvement with the dramatic event for a short period of time. Aesthetic distance allows the audience to remain involved with a drama on a vicarious level.

Emotional Involvement

The second concept traditionally used to describe audience involvement with a dramatic event contains two terms, **empathy** and **identification.** At best, these terms have several different meanings, depending upon the context in which they are used. In an article in the *Educational Theatre Journal* (March 1963), George Gunkle described many different and distinct meanings for the word "empathy" as it was used in the disciplines of psychology, communication, and theatre. In fact, one author may use "empathy" to describe what another means by "identification." Nevertheless, the two terms are commonly used to explain the way that an audience becomes involved and participates in a dramatic event.

For the past few years, this author has been studying the concept of audience involvement. One major assumption of this research is that the audience becomes emotionally involved with the protagonist of the story. They root for that main character, hoping that he or she will be successful and win the conflict. The research differentiated between empathy and identification, giving those terms specific meanings.

The study consisted of a questionnaire in which audience members were asked to record their reactions after viewing different plays and motion pictures. Four different studies were conducted, with the questionnaire evolving and becoming more sophisticated each time. The following is the fourth version of that questionnaire.

This survey asks you to describe your reactions to the main character as you were watching this play or movie.

Your name _____

Name of film or play _____

Who was the main character _____

1. How much did you like and enjoy this film?
    As much as   As little as
    your favorite   7   6   5   4   3   2   1   your least
    movies   favorite movies

2. How much did you like the main character in the film as a human being?
    Very Much   7   6   5   4   3   2   1   Not at all

3. In what way did you relate to the main character:
    A. I sympathized with the main character as if I knew that person and
        cared what happened to him or her.
        Agree   7   6   5   4   3   2   1   Disagree

    B. I had the same feelings as the main character in the story: being angry
        or sad or frustrated or triumphant when the character was feeling that
        way. Like being put in the same situation with the character, sharing
        the same conflicts and problems.
        Agree   7   6   5   4   3   2   1   Disagree

    C. I identified with the main character, almost as if I were living that
        character's life in the story, viewing life through his or her eyes. Living
        vicariously through the character—living out the fantasy, yourself—
        watching the story as if you were the main character.
        Agree   7   6   5   4   3   2   1   Disagree

4. Do you ever relate to the main character of any film or play as in C above?
    Yes _____   No _____

5. In general, how strongly did you relate to the main character in this film or
    play?
    Like the main   Like the main
    character in   7   6   5   4   3   2   1   character in
    your favorite   a movie you
    movie   hated

6. Who or what was the antagonist or opposing force to the main
    character?_____

7. How strong were your feelings about this antagonist?
    The antagonist   The antagonist
    created strong   was weak or
    negative feelings   7   6   5   4   3   2   1   nonexistent
    like frustration,
    dislike, anger

8. If you did not relate to the main character, why not? Other comments or explanations.

_____

_____

_____

First, the viewer is asked to identify the protagonist. Once in a while, some confusion appears over this question. For example, the stage version of Neil Simon's *Barefoot in the Park* has equally strong roles for both the husband and wife, who are in conflict. The majority of viewers identified the man as protagonist, whereas some chose the woman. With most dramas, the audience has little trouble agreeing on a protagonist; however, this play provided both an exception to this rule and an early discovery in the research. Common sense might lead us to expect women in the audience to identify more strongly with the wife as protagonist. This was not the case; of those audience members who chose the man as the protagonist, there was an equal proportion of men and women. In fact, the study has shown that the sex of the protagonist makes no difference to audience identification. Men will identify just as easily with a female protagonist as with a male protagonist, and the same is true of women in the audience. If an audience member becomes involved in the show at all, he or she will do so with little regard for the sex of the protagonist. For example, male and female reactions to the protagonist were exactly alike for such films as *An American Werewolf in London, The Pawnbroker, Paths of Glory,* and *The Times of Harvey Milk*; whereas males were a bit more positive in their reaction to the protagonist in *One Flew Over the Cuckoo's Nest* and a good deal more positive than women toward the protagonist in *Altered States.* The fact that the protagonists in the latter two films treat women with little respect might have influenced this reaction. At any rate, one of the original questions asking if the viewer was male or female soon disappeared from the questionnaire because there was no significant difference in the way the two sexes related to the protagonist.

Question 1 asks the audience to put a value on the film. Question 2 asks them to evaluate the character of the protagonist. Question 3 gets to the heart of the matter—the manner in which the audience relates emotionally to the dramatic event. The categories of these questions were derived experimentally from the audience's own words in early versions of the research. The first is sympathy, the second is empathy, and the third is identification. The author's assumption is that sympathy is the mildest form of emotional involvement, empathy is stronger, and identification is the deepest and strongest. In fact, Question 4 demonstrates the author's doubt that everyone is capable of the strong involvement represented by identification. In all of the studies, an average of 15 to 16 percent of viewers said that they never identified with a protagonist. However, some variation appeared that seemed to depend upon how much they liked the protagonist of a particular film: 25 percent said that they never identified when the films involved protagonists they did not like, 12 percent said that they never identified when dealing with two films that had more positive protagonists, and only 8 percent said that they never identified with any protagonist involving two films with protagonists toward whom they were extremely positive.

Question 3 asked the audience to describe the type of their emotional relationship, and Question 5 asked them to describe the strength of that emotional relationship. Finally, the sixth question, about the antagonist, was a late addition to the research, assuming that a stronger negative reaction to the antagonist might result in a stronger positive reaction to the protagonist.

Only the last of the four versions of this research was put into formal statistical analysis. Three different audiences filled out the questionnaire for eight different motion pictures: *One Flew Over the Cuckoo's Nest, Saturday Night Fever, Paths of Glory, Citizen Kane, The Times of Harvey Milk, Looking For Mr. Goodbar, Altered States,* and *Day for Night.* One mustn't generalize the findings to the whole population, because the audience was comprised of university students, representing a Midwestern upbringing and a very narrow age range. The author wished to discover how well each of the subcategories—character, sympathy, empathy, identification, strength, and antagonist—would predict the audience members' overall evaluation of the film. In the general study, every subcategory had a significant relationship with the overall evaluation. The subcategories predicted 60 percent of the overall reaction; strength of feelings toward the protagonist was the best predictor, followed by sympathy for the protagonist. Whether they liked the character as a human being was occasionally a major factor as well.

For the individual films, the subcategories predicted 70 percent of the overall reaction to *Saturday Night Fever, Harvey Milk, Altered States,* and *Day for Night,* but only 45 percent of the reaction to *Cuckoo's Nest, Citizen Kane,* and *Goodbar.* The reason for this low level of prediction is that audiences liked the overall film more than they liked the protagonist. According to the critics, *Citizen Kane* is the finest movie ever made; yet students have difficulty dealing with this film in the same ways they may deal with other films. The character of Kane is not very sympathetic—at times, one likes him and, at other times during the film, one does not like him at all. We are used to drama in which the protagonist is a truly positive character—the good guy, someone we adore. Even when the protagonists are killers, like Bonnie and Clyde or Butch Cassidy and the Sundance Kid, they are presented as nice people, likable, easy to identify with. Citizen Kane, on the other hand, was at times a villain and at other times a hero, and often just an ordinary human being. Audiences have greater difficulty dealing with such complicated characters, and the protagonists of *Cuckoo's Nest* and *Goodbar* fell into this category as well. However, despite the slightly lower reaction to the protagonist, *Cuckoo's Nest* was everyone's favorite film.

As for the way in which audiences relate to the protagonist, earlier studies clearly indicated that the more they liked a film, the more likely they were to say they related to the protagonist beyond sympathy to empathy and even to identification. In the second study, which dealt with nine films, subjects were split halfway between empathy and identification as their average strongest reaction.

In the third study, which dealt with six films, the average reaction was one of empathy. In the fourth and final study, for all eight films, empathy for the protagonist was almost as pervasive as sympathy.

Conclusions

What conclusions can be drawn from the preceding studies? The emotional relationship between the audience and the protagonist—both the type of relationship and its strength—will be a significant factor in determining whether the audience enjoys and approves of the dramatic experience. The more deeply audience members care for a particular dramatic event, the more likely they are to have a deeper and more intense emotional experience. Women and men are affected equally, and a substantial portion of the audience never goes so far as to identify with a protagonist as if they were that character for a brief period of time.

Finally, the reader should take note that only 60 percent of the overall reaction to a film was predicted by the emotional relationship between the audience members and the protagonist. What factors control the remaining 40 percent? Researchers of audience reaction say that the most important factor is whether the film or play had a good story line. When asked in polls, audience members claim that a "good" story is the most important factor for them. A subsequent study undertaken by the author appears to confirm this idea.

In the current questionnaire, half of the questions related to the protagonist as in the earlier study, but a second half asked about the audience interest, involvement, and satisfaction with the story. Whereas the earlier study concerning the audience relationship with the protagonist predicted only 60 percent of the audience's overall reaction to a film, this new study was able to predict 87 percent of the overall reaction to a series of films. Clearly, the emotional relationship between the audience and the protagonist, combined with their feelings about the expectations raised and resolved by the story, are the most significant factors in determining whether that audience will judge the dramatic event a success or failure.

Audience reaction to the dramatic event is obviously more complicated than the emotional relationship with the protagonist alone. We come to the dramatic event with certain preconceived expectations as to what plays and movies are like, as well as expectations concerning the particular genre, whether it is a murder mystery, a Western, or a love story. For the most part, we expect the drama to operate according to the pattern of the classical paradigm. We constantly interact with the narrative—reacting to it, testing it, questioning it—in order to make sense of it for ourselves. Early scenes in the drama establish the world of the play, perhaps a world like the one we know, or else an exotic world such as is found in *Star Wars*. Once we understand and accept the limitations and possibilities of that world, we expect characters and events to operate in a manner consistent with the rules of that dramatic world. All of this provides a context for our vicarious emotional experience with both the protagonist and the story.

Many writers present the concepts of empathy/identification and aesthetic distance as opposites, each one balancing the other. Yet one could become enormously emotionally involved with a protagonist, desperately hoping that character will win and still not move a bit in the direction of confusing the world of the drama with real life. The first drop-off on a roller-coaster is similar to falling from a cliff. Both experiences terrify us, but the roller-coaster offers exciting pleasure because we are aware that we are safe, that the danger is an illusion, a thrilling and intense experience. The vicarious experience in the theatre also offers exciting pleasure while we maintain our aesthetic distance, knowing that the danger is an illusion.

Summary

In this chapter, we have discussed audiences, attempting to deal with the reasons people attend the theatre, the values they find in the experience, and their pattern of reactions during the event. We have examined such concepts as polarization, willing suspension of disbelief, aesthetic distance, empathy, and identification. An understanding of the audience reaction is vital to the director because that moment of interaction between the artwork and the audience is the culmination of all of the director's efforts.

CHAPTER 10

AUDITIONS AND CASTING

In this chapter, we shall talk about the process of holding auditions and choosing a cast for the production. An often repeated saying in the theatre states that 80 percent of the director's success or failure is determined at the moment he or she casts the play. Although that statistic may be inflated, it emphasizes the fact that casting is crucial to the success of the production. No matter how much artistry directors pour into their shows, if they have made serious errors in casting, they will have limited their ability to reach the level of perfection they had in mind. For this reason, professional directors rely on successful actors, seldom trying anyone new. One way to protect the director's reputation is to cast an actor so skilled that he or she will give an excellent performance no matter what the director does. This same situation holds true in the amateur theatre. College or community theatre directors will feel more secure in casting their most talented and most experienced actors and actresses—those who have proven themselves in prior shows.

Audition Goals

In setting up an audition, the first step is to advertise, making sure that all of the potential performers know when and where the tryouts will be held. Directors want to invent the kind of audition that will help them to discover whatever information they deem necessary to make casting decisions. While auditioning for her master's thesis production of *The Boys in the Band*—a play with an all-male cast—a student director had everyone play improvisational basketball, one-on-one, with an imaginary ball. Perhaps she wanted to discover how well they could move or how imaginative they were in an unusual situation. Any device that makes sense and does not scare the actors is acceptable.

What is the director trying to find out during auditions? The director wants to know if the actor can move with ease, what kind of voice he has, how well he can read and make sense of dialogue, how well he is attuned to the material in the script, if he can read with a sense of emotional key. Using this kind of information, the director measures the actor against his or her concept of what the roles ought to be. The director tries to tune in to the image presented by the actor, the way he or she looks and sounds. And the director will draw tentative conclusions, making such notes as, "could play the role of George," or "too young for George; a possibility as the brother-in-law," or "does not read well enough for any of these roles."

Precasting

Although it is human nature to speculate on the possible players available for a role, the director should avoid **precasting,** because it cheats the actors at auditions and blinds the director to new and possibly better performers. Seldom have the results of auditions confirmed the author's prior speculation about the casting. For example, we did a production of the play *Distilling Spirits* for which a group of former students returned. Having worked with each of these actresses in many different roles and being totally familiar with their skills, the director arranged them into a potential cast before the auditions. Although most of them were members of the final cast, not one actress ended up with the role in which the director had seen her prior to auditions. The director must have confidence in the audition process; it is there that the true cast will reveal itself.

Range of Physical Types

Directors should not picture the characters in greater detail than is necessary prior to tryouts; rather, they should leave themselves open to the widest possible range of actor types allowed by the script. However, the leading role in *Play It Again, Sam* was played by Woody Allen himself. Does the character have to look like Woody Allen—short, nebbish, with glasses? The character constantly makes jokes about his physical appearance. But none of our actors looked the least bit like Woody Allen. In fact, the actor who was ultimately cast in this role was far from being a Woody Allen-type. At first, this actor seemed more suited to play Linda's husband, the protagonist's best friend. He was tall and dark, with a deep, mature vocal quality. But the moment he read the first few lines at auditions, everyone in the auditorium instantly knew that he was right for the leading role. Up to that moment, the director had read one particular actor again and again, convinced that he could play this part. He was small, bright, and articulate, with physical and vocal characteristics comparable to those of Woody Allen. However, he could not read the lines of the character in a funny manner. Intellectually, he understood the humor and laughed when he read the lines, but he was unable to play that humor in his line delivery. But when the tall actor with the deep voice read those same lines, the entire audience broke out in laughter, even though they had heard those lines many times before during the audition. This actor instinctively knew how to play the comedy, an absolutely critical requirement for the role. Only one line—a reference to the character being short and red-headed—had to be altered; otherwise this actor was perfectly suited to the role.

Even a role written by Woody Allen for himself can be played by a wide range of physical types. Therefore, the director should seek out the actor who can play the role well and avoid being overly influenced by the actor's physical appearance.

Specific Limitations

Once in a while, a role will have such specific characteristics that it will prove difficult to cast. For a community theatre production of *The Marriage-Go-Round*—a comedy about a mature couple whose marriage is disrupted by a visiting Swedish bombshell—the director could not find a suitable actress for the role of the young Swedish girl. The part calls for the "perfect girl"—a beautiful, athletic, intelligent Miss America-type. Because the character has 30 percent of the lines in the play, the role requires some acting experience and an ability to play a deliberately flirtatious and sexy character. The director thought of three possible performers; however, two were unavailable because of prior commitments, and the third felt herself to be too conservative and shy for such an overtly sensual role. Finally, in order to complete the cast, the director had to use an entirely inexperienced actress. In this unusual instance, the specific physical appearance of the character was required by the commanding form of the script.

Most roles in the theatre may be acted by a wide range of physical types, but outside limitations do exist, beyond which the director dare not go. For instance, in casting the title role of *Cyrano de Bergerac*—the famous swordsman with the absurdly long nose—a director considered the possibility of using a brilliant young actor who was very heavy—at least 100 pounds overweight. The actor's reading at auditions had been superb. Could Cyrano reasonably be played by a man of this size? The director consulted colleagues and friends. Most of the reactions were negative. The women pictured Cyrano as unattractive only because of his enormous nose; without that nose, he would be a handsome fellow. And those audience expectations set limits on the possible physical appearance of any actor to be considered for the role of Cyrano at auditions.

Audition Procedures

The actual process of auditioning actors requires the director to develop methods for discovering and recording particular information about each performer, information that will be crucial when final decisions must be made.

Actor Questionnaire

In order to gather information about the actors at tryouts, most directors develop a questionnaire for them to fill out. This author prefers three-by-four inch note cards because he can lay the cards out on a table during auditions. What kind of information is needed? Names, addresses, and telephone numbers so that the director can contact the actors. Do they have any known conflicts with the rehearsal schedule, such as a job, an evening class, or a family reunion that they must attend? The director also wants to know about their prior acting experience, especially if he or she has not worked with an actor in another show. Finally, in order to avoid casting someone who will not accept the role, the director should ask if the actors wish to place limits on their audition. Having an actor back out of the cast creates a negative situation for both the director and the actor. In this situation, the director must cast a performer who will know that he or she was second choice, and most directors will never again consider casting the actor who backed out of the show. Therefore, the wise approach is to learn ahead of time which roles the actor is willing to accept. Actors will write such comments as: "I'd like the part of Allan, but I'll play any role," or "I'll play anything but the prostitute," or "I'm only interested in the role of the leading lady." The last comment might be indicative of an ego trip, but that does not matter. Perhaps the actress would have to quit her job in order to be in the play, and she was unwilling to make such a sacrifice for a minor role. The director should consider that actress for the leading role; if she does not fit the part, she will not be cast in the show. Whatever the reason, the director should find out about these things before making casting decisions.

Remembering the Actor

The first note that the director should make regarding an auditioning actor is a brief physical description, something that will differentiate him or her from the others, so that the director will remember the actor when reviewing the notes at a later time. A comment like "the fat one with the long blonde hair" may not be flattering, but it will serve to bring that performer back to mind. If a director cannot recall what the person looked like, he or she will not be able to consider that person for the cast. The actor will have lost his opportunity—a clear failure on the part of the director. At the auditions for *Play It Again, Sam,* four new, young girls tried out. All were blonde and were approximately the same height and weight. On the director's note cards, one became "the girl with the pink headband," another became "the girl with the big bust line," and another, "the girl with the unusual voice quality." Silly notes, perhaps, but they served the key purpose of differentiating these women in the director's memory.

Assessing the Audition

What the director is trying to find out about the actors depends a great deal on the particular play. In general, the director makes notes about the vocal quality of the actors, their ease of movement, and the overall sense of the image—particularly in terms of level of maturity and strength or forcefulness onstage. Such notes as, "seems like a young teenager," or "has a deep, forceful voice quality— could play a mature character," will be particular useful. Most important, the director wants to know if the actor can read lines decently, if he or she talks like

In the Director's Chair

Max Reinhardt (1873–1943)

An actor at the Deutsches Theatre in Berlin in the 1890s, Max Reinhardt replaced his mentor, Otto Brahm, as director. Reinhardt adopted and popularized the New Stagecraft and the antirealistic styles of Symbolism and Expressionism, trying to create a new relationship between audience and actors by thrusting the stage into the midst of the spectators. In his long career, Reinhardt ran the gamut of theatrical innovation, spreading new ideas worldwide because he was a visiting director, traveling from one theatre and country to another. During his life, he was the most famous theatrical director in the world. For Reinhardt, each new play deserved its own new style of production; every new production was a unique world that he created. He is, historically, the best known of producer-autocrats. He preplanned his productions in minute detail on paper before rehearsals began. Rehearsals, then, were a period of adjustment in which the actors, in some manner, adapted to the director's concept of the play. He treated actors as puppets, controlling every gesture, movement, and intonation of voice until they achieved his vision of the characters.

a normal human being when reading lines from a script, and if the actor seems attuned to the meaning and emotion of those lines. "Does not read lines well" is the most negative comment that a director can make.

Assuming that the actor reads the lines well, the next question is, "Does he sound like one or more of the characters in the play?" Answers to these questions may be noted as follows: "a possibility for Linda," or "too young for Linda—possibly Sharon or the girl at the disco." The latter note would lead the director to read that actress in both the roles of Sharon and the disco girl, a process which would produce another note such as, "Yes, a real possibility for Sharon." Thus, step by step during the auditions, the director comes closer to deciding which actors might be able to play each of the roles in the play.

Making Final Decisions

After the auditions, the director will make final decisions. This author's procedure is to make a new note card for each character in the play. On each note card, he will list the name of every performer who could possibly play that particular role. Then, beginning with the largest roles for both men and women, the choices are made. For example, the names of three actors appeared on the card for the role of the protagonist in *Play It Again, Sam*. Once the director had made a decision, he moved the names of the actors who had been eliminated down to other character cards, making sure to consider those actors for the other male roles in the play if they were suitable. Then, the second largest role in the play would be cast and so on.

Types of Auditions

The director should try to distribute copies of the script before auditions. Actors who have read the play will do better at tryouts. The usual procedure is to assign actors to go onstage and read a particular scene aloud. The same scene is read often, allowing the actors to become familiar with it, even if they have not been able to read a copy of the script beforehand.

Tryouts should give everyone a fair chance, an opportunity to read a number of times in different roles. If an actor reads poorly the first time, he should be given the opportunity to improve, to show the director what he can do, to feel that he has been treated fairly. While auditioning for a play, the actors are under considerable tension and stress. Therefore, the director should try to create an atmosphere that is relaxed and friendly, to assure them that no one expects a finished performance, that it is okay to fumble a line or make some other mistake, that everyone will laugh with you because we are all human. A little humor goes a long way toward easing tension. More will be learned about the actors' abilities when they are confident and at ease. Finally, if the director has more than one night of auditions, care should be taken after the first night not to make decisions that would prejudice the director against those who audition the following evening.

At the tryouts, some directors assign readings ahead of time. While they are watching one group on the stage, two more groups have been assigned to a scene and are allowed to go outside with their scripts and read through the scene. Thus, the cold reading is a little more polished because the actors have had time to plan a strategy, even, perhaps, some appropriate blocking.

Auditions for Musicals

Auditions for a musical are more complex than for a nonmusical, because they involve singing and dancing as well as the reading of dialogue. For the roles involving singing, actors will bring a prepared song, and the director must provide an accompanist. At dance auditions, the choreographer will do a simple dance step and ask the actors to imitate that step. The process will then be repeated with a more complicated step or pattern of movement. Those who cannot keep up will be eliminated as each movement pattern becomes more difficult.

Professional dancers are trained to reproduce complex patterns of movement that they have seen demonstrated only one time. The author once attended dance auditions for the movie version of *West Side Story,* tryouts that were exactly like the preceding description. Another form of dance audition was used at the tryouts for a stage version of *Carousel.* The choreographer played a recorded musical number and asked all of the dancers onstage to improvise to that piece of music. After watching for only a few moments, it became clear who were the best dancers, and the director had no trouble picking the young woman for the leading dancer's role—that of the daughter of the protagonist.

Balancing Different Goals

A few years ago, at auditions for a production of *The Elephant Man,* the director was faced with an interesting choice for the title role. A new, fairly inexperienced actor gave a wonderful reading. He obviously had worked so hard on this role that he practically had the lines memorized. At the same audition, an excellent reading was given by the most experienced actor of the group, a young man who had been chosen as best actor of the year by his peers more than once. The role of the Elephant Man is an enormous one and extremely difficult. Casting the experienced actor would have been easy and safe; however, the new actor had not only read well, but he had paid his dues. In a number of minor roles in previous productions, he had proved himself to be both capable and reliable, truly a hard worker. In a professional situation, there would be no question; the director would not hesitate to use the more experienced performer. However, in school or community theater production, the director does not want to cast the same person over and over again. If the director does not train new actors, constantly adding to the pool of experienced performers, where will the experienced actors come from in the future? Of course, the director wants to give the audience the best possible show; at the same time, there exists an obligation to train new people and to provide them with opportunities in which their skills can grow and develop. Therefore, the nonprofessional theatre director must try to balance these two goals in casting productions. In the case of *The Elephant Man,* the director chose to give the young new actor his chance. At the same time, he surrounded that newcomer with a strong group of experienced fellow players. Not only was the resulting production a success, but this young leading man was chosen as best actor of the season for his performance in the play.

Summary

In this chapter, we have discussed different types of auditions, audition procedures, the director's goals for tryouts, and the process of casting the play. For the most part, our examples have been drawn from smaller theatre group situations. When actors number in the hundreds—as they often do at large universities and in wide-open professional auditions—some form of brief preliminary tryouts is held, running the actors through one after the other, in order to eliminate the obviously inappropriate performers. Such a procedure, commonly referred to as a "cattle call," will result in a callback of those likely contenders to a second audition in which they will follow patterns more like those described in this chapter. Whatever the situation may be, there can be little question that a well-organized audition will allow the director the best opportunity to find an excellent cast for the production.

PART 3

Rehearsing the Play

At the beginning of this book, we talked about the scope of the director's job, from choosing and analyzing the script to evaluating the final production. When asked what qualities make up a good director, actor Al Pacino said that "great directors can understand staging in such a way that can make a scene come alive. Other have a certain way of pacing a scene. Others have a way of setting a kind of ambience around the set that makes everybody creative around them" (1979, pp. 356–58).

The following section of this book will take the reader through the process of rehearsals that leads to the performance. Particular emphasis will be placed on staging the action, working with actors, pacing and polishing the production, and developing an ambience that encourages creativity. Setting up a warm and positive environment, building esprit de corps and a sense of community with the actors is an essential element in the creative process.

What is the relationship between the director and the actors? In one essential way, the director acts as the eyes of the actor. Onstage, the actors do not know how they look. They have to be confident that they won't make fools of themselves. And the director wants to build the actors' confidence. "Go ahead. Take a chance! In fact, I'll guarantee that when this play goes into performance, you're going to be great!" That is the kind of confidence the director ought to inspire in the actor. In return for the actors' trust, the director provides guidance and protection.

Whereas the process of directing a play involves skillful use of craft, reasoning, and good common sense, this process must also involve such qualities as emotion, instinct, and intuition. Playwright Robert Anderson (1994) tells of a comment made by a critic concerning an exhibit of the works of a painter. The critic said, "The skill of his hands could not make up for the emptiness of his heart." Contained in this critique is an important reminder to actors and directors as well: As artists, we must have a passion for what we are doing—a deep, emotional involvement with the artwork.

CHAPTER 11

THE RELATIONSHIP BETWEEN DIRECTOR AND ACTORS

Obviously, one of the more important artistic aspects of a director's job is learning about actors and learning to work with actors. Although not absolutely necessary, some experience as an actor is extremely useful for any director. Here we will take the actor's point of view, looking at the tasks that the actor must face and the skills needed to accomplish those tasks.

Actors are trained to be imaginative and creative. Of course, there probably is no such thing as a "creative person." People enter into creative states, some more often and more consciously than others. Nevertheless, in reading *Actors on Acting*, the anthology of comments by famous actors and actresses on their craft, the universal catchword is "imagination"—the one characteristic deemed most necessary for acting.

Yet, in her article, "Interpreters, Dramaturgs, and Process Critics," Rosemarie Bank raised a serious question concerning the purpose of training actors in creative improvisation and script analysis when their task is only to follow explicit directorial instructions in the development of a role (1981, p. 13), although her question may imply a dichotomy too simple to fit the facts of an actor's work.

Actors have to adjust, to accommodate their approach to different directors and different production circumstances to the point where, according to Richard Schechner, there is no coherent set of techniques that relates to every situation—there is no method of acting (1980). Perhaps if we look more closely at the results expected from an actor, we may be able to focus on those specific techniques and areas of knowledge and experience most useful in developing the actor's craft.

What is the job of an actor or actress? In general, the actor's job is to discover what the director wants and what the playwright intends, then add the moment-to-moment details of action that fulfill the general guidelines laid down by the director and playwright. We worked on these moment-to-moment details when blocking our scene from *The Rainmaker*. Taking one beat at a time, we attempted to discover what the actor would do on any particular line of dialogue.

Actors and Directors Working Together

Leaving script analysis until a later time, let us look at the actor-director relationship. According to actor Donald Sutherland, getting inside the director's head—truly understanding the director's vision of the role—is the primary goal of the actor (1978). "I think that the director's first accomplishment, if he ever accomplishes this, is to get the actor to understand the director's vision of the piece," agrees Steven Spielberg (Sherman, 1988, p. 185). However, directors often explain their ideas in an almost mystical, metaphorical fashion. Some see this as a more "artistic" way of working, but it leaves the actor desperately searching for some practical way to translate a vague concept into some concrete activity. On the other hand, directors may have so specific a concept of the character that they will command every vocal inflection and gesture in exact detail. This may be helpful for beginners, but it is painfully stifling for experienced performers.

Some years ago, a production failed for this very reason: too much directing of, or overdirecting, the play. The director was staging a play that she had written. In a way, she acted out the part of every character. She told the actors how to say every line, how to make every movement, how to do every gesture.

The resulting production was not successful. The actors performed mechanically, as if they were robots; they were never able to make their lines or their movements seem natural.

At the other extreme was a community theatre production of *My Three Angels,* done in the round. The director, a local businessman, built the set, developed the lighting, and organized the production well; however, he never gave the actors any instructions. They did the play differently each night at rehearsals. Because the blocking was never fixed, an actor could not be sure where the other actors would be located onstage at any particular moment. It became obvious to the actors that some way must be found to fix a permanent pattern of blocking. The decision was made to stick with whatever blocking was used that night at rehearsal. Everything worked out well, and the show was a hit. But prior to that rehearsal, the show had remained in flux, a total improvisation from night to night and a clear example of insufficient directing—also known as underdirecting the play.

To Preblock or Not to Preblock

If the preceding examples seem extreme, the more common middle ground is just as precarious. Young directors are taught to plan ahead, carefully and in great detail. Many will **preblock** the actor's physical movement, planning each movement out and writing it into their scripts. Then, they will read these movement directions to the actors at an early rehearsal so that the actors can copy them into their scripts.

Many other directors choose to work out the blocking during rehearsals as a creative activity, involving input from both actors and director. Some years ago at UCLA, Broadway director Josh Logan was asked if he preblocked. Logan did not know the meaning of the term, explaining that at the opening rehearsal he knew only where the actors were onstage when the curtain rose. That is, he knew the setting and had chosen a position for the actors at the opening moment, after which, he and the actors worked out the blocking during the rehearsal process. As far as this author has been able to determine, most professional directors work that way. On the other hand, most textbooks about directing recommend preblocking the play outside of rehearsals. There seems to be a clash between actual professional methods and the methods being taught to students.

Examples from professional directors abound. Of his early career, Arvin Brown, artistic director of the Long Wharf Theatre, says, "I made some big mistakes initially. An example was walking into my first rehearsal with the blocking carefully planned out with my little stick figures from the night before" (Bartow, 1988, p. 25). He soon threw it all out and started with the actors from scratch. According to Gordon Davison, artistic director of the Mark Taper

Forum, "It is very important to create an atmosphere for actors that is conducive to *their* doing a great deal of the work" (Bartow, p. 77). "I used to block everything," says Zelda Fichandler of The Arena Stage. "I would map out the physical form in very great detail and then sort of parcel it out to the actors. Then, as I got more courage, I stopped writing the blocking on my scripts, and now I may have a vague notion of the physical design of a scene when I go into rehearsals" (Bartow, p. 115). "I don't 'block' in advance," explains Marshall Mason of the Circle Repertory (Bartow, p. 200). "We sit and run the lines until everybody feels comfortable. Then we explore the movement" (Bartow, p. 203). Harold Prince works with a model of the set, visualizing the possibilities: "I don't move little tin soldiers around on the model, but by the time I actually go into rehearsals, the space I'm going to work on has been ingested" (Bartow, p. 249). He describes his basic method as, "Just allowing people to create for me and then editing them" (Bartow, p. 253). From Tyrone Guthrie to Peter Brook, the vast majority of professionals work out the blocking in the course of rehearsals.

Arguments for Preblocking

The entire issue of preblocking deserves elucidation. At this writing, the most recently published text advises directors to preblock their plays for the following reasons:

1. to test the effectiveness of the arrangement of furniture and scenery

2. to avoid dealing with actors' egos

3. to avoid dealing with "whether the actor 'feels' like moving"

4. to save the actors' time

5. to help the technicians by allowing them to see early run-throughs

6. to avoid embarrassment.

"There is a notion that the director who preblocks deprives the actors of some of their chance to work collaboratively with him. I think all the actors are deprived of is their chance to see the director floundering" (Vaughan, 1993, p. 128). This justification clearly condemns itself by saying that one should preblock to avoid dealing with actors, their egos, feelings, and input, and, perhaps more important, to avoid showing moments of personal weakness or indecision. The director conjured up by this vision is an autocrat who knows all, who needs no input from co-workers because he is always certain of the correct choices.

This text contends not only that most professional directors do not preblock, but also that most experienced actors will be dissatisfied and, perhaps, even refuse to be directed in this fashion. According to actor Kevin Kline, "The rehearsal process to me is a process of exploration and discovery. If it has already been

In the Director's Chair

Vsevolod Meyerhold (1874–1940)

Vsevolod Meyerhold was an actor at the Moscow Art Theatre from its inception in 1898 until 1902. His revolt against Naturalism early in the twentieth century led Stanislavsky to put him in charge of the newly organized Studio in 1905, which was to be an experimental laboratory in the style of the Symbolists. Meyerhold wanted to produce a kind of abstract theatre in which the actor was reduced to one more plastic element, equal to but not greater than other elements such as scenery and lighting. The Studio lasted less than a year, but he was able to try out his ideas at the theatre of Vera Komissarzhevskaya from 1906 to 1908. At his own studio from 1913 to 1917, he adopted methods of improvisation and the Commedia dell'Arte. After the Russian Revolution, the idea of a revolutionary art form seemed appropriate. Meyerhold developed a scenic style called Constructivism in which the stage was an abstract scaffold of platforms, ramps, and stairs, simply an object for the use of the actors. He also developed a distinct acting style called *biomechanics,* in which the actors performed in an abstract, symbolic fashion—showing joy, for example, by doing a back-flip or some other overt gymnastic activity. However, Meyerhold's approach to the production and actors was one of improvisation rather than the careful and total preplanning characteristic of Max Reinhardt (see page 136). To find the thought of the playwright and turn that thought into a theatrical form was Meyerhold's goal. He and his actors would do lengthy improvisations that wildly elaborated a simple moment in the original script. Yet Meyerhold was the sole creative artist in his theatre; he used his actors as a sculptor molds his clay. Throughout his career, Meyerhold was constantly experimenting and inventing, never settling for one style. He has been called the Picasso of the theatre. In the early 1930s, Meyerhold fell from grace with his Soviet masters; and in 1938, he simply disappeared. His death was announced by the Soviet government in the 1960s, although it is thought that he died much earlier.

discovered and is being explained to you in rehearsal, I get enraged" (Cole, 1992, p. 172).

Blocking as a Process of Exploration

In her book, *Directors in Rehearsal,* Susan Letzler Cole observed the directing methods of a dozen professional directors. She discovered none who preblocked. The key term from her observation seems to be exploration; the purpose of rehearsals is to explore. The major difference among these directors appears to be based upon who is doing the exploring and for what purpose. Directors of highly abstract works, notably Richard Foreman and Robert Wilson, seemed to explore the movement by themselves and for themselves, without significant input from their performers. Actors were moved around by the director, often without any sense of reason or character motivation. When the plays are more lifelike—works by Shakespeare and Chekhov, for example—the directors appear more likely to work in rehearsal with their actors, exploring the movements, meanings, and motivations together. They attempt to "illustrate" the text, using blocking which "functions as a kind of objective correlative for a character's 'inner life' or for the buried situation in a scene" (Cole, 1992, p. 18). While not denying the value of more abstract works such as those produced by Wilson and Foreman, this author is promoting directing methods of the latter type, methods that privilege psychological realism and emphasize the free play of feeling and impulse during rehearsals.

Is there a logical contradiction created when we say that the director should develop a concept, a production plan ahead of time, "seeing the whole" by means of intense analysis and synthesis, and yet not be expected to preblock the movement of the actors (unless dealing with large groups of players or formal dance choreography)? Is it possible for one to see the whole without picturing actors in action? Of course not. Clearly, the director is likely to visualize some of the blocking in his or her mind while planning the production. And taking down a note about a wonderful idea is perfectly acceptable behavior. This author simply discourages directors from forcing themselves to visualize and write down blocking, in detail, to be read aloud to the actors at a later date during rehearsals.

Preblocking has always been a useful training tool in an academic setting. If working with the actors is impossible for one reason or another, a student director can preblock on paper so that the master teacher can view and criticize the work. The process is difficult; not only must the paperwork be visually clear, but both parties must have reached agreement concerning the subtext in order for the motivations for the movement be understood. Problems arise, however, when this academic tool is substituted for the real process of directing: creative exploration by director and actors during rehearsals.

Actor Participation

High school directors might argue that their student actors must be preblocked; however, it is the level of experience, rather than age, which tends to control the amount of creativity that the actor can offer. Creativity requires self-confidence. When actors are new to the stage, they cannot know whether an action is right or wrong; therefore, they will be afraid to try things on their own. An actor who has been onstage a few times and had the experience of doing it right will be able to sense the "rightness" of a movement. If the director sets up the proper creative atmosphere, that actor will feel confident to experiment at rehearsals.

On the other hand, a beginning actor may need a great deal of help from the director. Very early in this author's acting career, he was cast in the tiny comic role of Le Beau in Shakespeare's *As You Like It,* performed in Los Angeles. The director, who is now a successful professional in television, desperately tried to be creative with his young actor. Finally, he came over and said, "Okay, on this line, take three steps to here. Then turn, and on this line take four steps to here," and he demonstrated the movements as he described them. This direction was very mechanical, but it was exactly what the actor needed at his level of experience. He was totally new to the stage and, fearful of embarrassing himself, he was not about to try anything on his own. However, once given this basic framework of movement, the actor felt secure and was able to elaborate on it with ease.

The director should try to work openly with actors, allowing them to be as creative as possible. But the director must also adjust to the needs of the actor, often becoming a teacher of acting for inexperienced performers. For example, a 9-year-old girl played her first major role in a production of *Wait Until Dark.* Not having been in a substantial role before, she did not know the basics, such as standing onstage in an open position rather than with her back to the audience. In this case, the leading lady taught these basic rules to her as rehearsals went along, but the director must be prepared to take on such elementary actor training when the need arises.

When Preblocking Is Necessary

We are talking about creative staging during rehearsal as opposed to preblocking done solely by the director before rehearsal. Preblocking clearly prohibits the creative input of the actor, and preblocked scenes tend to have too little movement in them. Nevertheless, all directors should preblock in certain situations. When working with a small group of actors, it is easier to keep them constantly in focus. When a director has large numbers of actors onstage, it becomes necessary to preplan the stage positions and movement. Clearly, crowd scenes and musical dance numbers require preblocking;

however, many crowd scenes actually consist of a scene between two or three characters being watched by the remainder of the crowd. In such a case, the director might preplan the positions of the watchers, but leave the staging of the characters being watched for the rehearsal.

The Actor as Creative Artist

Even the most logical and well-organized theatre artists often operate from moment-to-moment intuition—that unspoken feeling for, and understanding of, the artwork. Sensing a problem but unable to pinpoint it, the director may simply ask the actor to try something different. Those motion picture directors who don't know acting well often require the actors to do it all on their own. The actor produces something and then the director alters or corrects it in slight ways. Or the director finds the whole concept wrong, expecting the actor to come up with something completely different, and the process begins again. The example Buzz Kulik uses to illustrate this process is: "William Wyler, who could never articulate what it was he wanted from an actor, but his genius was that when he saw what it was like . . . he recognized it" (Sherman, 1988, p. 163). For a more extreme example, witness the story of two young actors working on a film for American International. Asked to do a scene as dentist and patient, they were given neither script nor blocking; they simply went in and improvised. The actor must be prepared to adjust to any position from detailed preblocking to completely creative improvisation.

Such improvisational creativity is basic to the actor's trade, not only in extreme situations but also in working out the details of any role. Even after the actor knows the lines, the blocking, and what the director wants, the actor often must fill in for the playwright. If the scene continues for a few beats without going anywhere, the actor must invent places to go. John Dennis advises the actor not to tread water or repeat. "Even if the writer had given you no edge to swim to, do an Esther Williams out there—find new things to do" (1982). In this sense, one can visualize the director not as the leader of the actors, but rather as the person standing behind them, chasing, encouraging, prodding, pushing them along as they create the characters. Such a director realizes that the actor must create, using the guidance of the director. But the actor must also adjust to directors who create, who are simply using the actor.

As directors, we never have complete control of the events taking place onstage. We can't play the roles for the actors; they have to act for themselves, because we will be in the audience during the performance. The same is true of rehearsals. All the way through, the actors have to accomplish the task. The director can suggest, hint, prod them along, point the way, but ultimately, the actors must create the characters.

The Actor's Understanding of the Role

Let us continue with our study of the actor's job, from the actor's point of view. Our original premise was that the actor's job is to find what the director wants and what the playwright intends. Script analysis is too complex a process to discuss here in detail, but some ideas may be helpful. The actor traditionally concentrates upon the patterns of desire/obstacle/resolution: what the character wants, what stands in the way of these desires, and what he or she does to solve the problem, moment to moment, in the script.

Roger Gross, in a paper presented at a meeting of the American Theatre Association, introduces a schematic concept in which the actor determines the parameters of the role—those things that must be contained in the character—and the tolerances of the role—those things that cannot be part of the character. The range of latitude between the parameters and tolerances, then, is where the actor's artistic choices must fall. In order to arrive at the most apt understanding of the character, Gross says, "Our job is to persist in conceiving rationales until we find one that makes all of the character's choices inevitable: this is the actor's fundamental task" (1981, p. 7).

Parameters and tolerances may or may not be useful as a practical guide for actors, but the concept serves to remind us that no particular choice of reaction, movement, or pattern of line delivery is necessarily the correct one. Actors must find ways of trying different possibilities, either during rehearsal or on their own. They should deliberately experiment with alternative patterns of line delivery, even if they decide to return, ultimately, to their original choice as being best. If the actors fail to investigate alternate possibilities when rehearsal time permits, they limit their choices to their first reaction, even after they have gained a more thorough and sophisticated grasp of both the script and their character.

Similar Principles for the Director

The director should also be reminded that no particular choice of movement or pattern of line delivery is necessarily the correct one. There is no single, perfect way to play a role or to block a scene; there are a number of possibilities. There are also a number of clearly wrong choices. Each of us could block the same scene and come up with fairly different blocking and all of our scenes could be right in the sense that they seemed appropriate and worked well on the stage. Some years ago, a young director and his master teacher were watching a run-through of the director's blocking. The young man asked "Is that right?" and his teacher responded in the affirmative. He meant that everything the actors were doing up there on the stage was within the range of choices that could be described as "right." Directing is an art. In an art, there are seldom any absolutely right answers. If there were, computers could stage plays, compose music, and paint graphic artworks better than human beings could. As artists, both the actors and the director should remain open to new discoveries, because they will learn more about the play and the characters during the rehearsal period than they knew when rehearsals begin.

Where Perspectives Diverge

Finally, actors should recognize a clear difference between their approach and the director's approach to analysis of the script. The director views the characters as a device used by the author—along with other devices—to accomplish the goals of the dramatic structure. The director is looking at the character's function in the overall pattern of the script. On the other hand, the actor views the character as a living human being. An actor must love his or her character. The actor can never think of the character as being crazy or a villain; that is the director's and audience's point of view, never the actor's. Often the actor will receive instructions from the director that show little recognition of the actor's viewpoint. The director will ask for changes based upon simple practicality or upon the character's function in the script, leaving the actor to translate these instructions into actions that are rational and logical for his or her view of the character as a consistent human personality.

Every actor has had difficulty at one time or another trying to deal with a direction that seems inconsistent with his or her vision of what the character would or would not do. Discussion of the problem with the director may help, but ultimately, the actor must find a way to accommodate the character to the director's wishes because that is the actor's job. Jack Nicholson has said of the actor's job, "I feel that the actor, if he's in conflict with the material, just simply brings that argument to the director, espouses it for as long as it's creative, and then after he's done that, he does what the director decides that they should do" (Sherman, 1988, pp. 191–92). A common joke in the theatre tells of an actor constantly interrupting the rehearsal in order to ask the director, "What's my motivation?" However, this joke contains the implication of a serious communication problem that may arise in the actor-director relationship. At that moment, the actor is saying to the director, "I don't understand why the character would do what you are asking me to do here. I need to understand that." And the director must help the actor to gain that understanding; that is the director's job.

Basic Acting Style

According to Roger Gross, the basic challenge in acting is to create appropriate expressive behavior on the stage or screen. Theorists have argued for many years about the means of achieving believable human behavior on the stage, particularly the issues of whether the actor must truly feel the emotions of the character in order to create the correct illusion for the audience. How far do actors remove themselves from being the actor/craftsman to actually becoming the character? In American theatre, although actor training may vary, the answer to this question is almost universally influenced by our interpretations of the Stanislavsky method of acting. Gross describes the choices as being imitative or organic. The imitative actor copies cliché manners of expression, either subtly or in an enlarged manner for symbolic effect. The organic actor attempts to think the thoughts of the character, moment to moment, living a fantasy life, on the assumption that all resulting reactions will be both natural and appropriate. Gross concludes that "We are not capable of creating the full illusion of human behavior on stage purely by imitative means" (1981, pp. 3–4).

Hal Klapman, who worked at the old Actors Lab in Los Angeles, argued that thinking the actor's thoughts (what the cue and next line are, and the like) is what the actor does naturally. Therefore, actors must force themselves to think the character's thoughts as much as possible, knowing that they will never completely escape from their natural concerns as actor/craftsman. For most actors, pushing themselves as far as they can toward the organic approach will result in a balance between actors' and characters' thoughts at best. Certainly, the majority of the acting workshops that this author has attended in recent years focuses the actors' concentration on specific, concrete details of the imaginary place on the stage, calling on them to play all of the reactions to specific senses of the moment and to avoid playing generalized emotional states. In his advice to actors, John Dennis says that actors must play what they want to do rather than how they feel or the mental, inner circumstances of the particular moment or situation. And, most important, the actor should not try to symbolize or "indicate" information for the sake of the audience; they will figure it out without his help (1982). In life, we concentrate on what we want to do at any moment, and we continually react with all of our senses to the objects, people, and events around us. Adapting these reactions to the imaginary setting and life of the play, according to the organic theorists, will produce appropriate, lifelike behavior on the stage.

Too often, acting is treated like a mystical experience—an activity that requires some ineffable talent and inborn genius. Actually, the quality usually described in such mystical terms boils down to an ability to hurl oneself totally (physically and mentally) into the game or role without reserve, embarrassment, stage fright, or other hang-ups which cause tension and holding back. This ability doesn't necessarily indicate a lack of control, but it is most spectacular when it leans in that direction. Barbra Streisand described it as a state of being unfragmented, clear, intuitive, and simple, the complete ability to be sensitive to, and react to, events and other actors on the stage (1979). Truly, it is a more open and sensitive state than we usually achieve in ordinary life.

When accepting her Academy Award as best actress for her role in *Sophie's Choice,* Meryl Streep made a comment which illustrates this concept. Her exact words are difficult to recall, but she said something to the effect that she had created the role from what she saw in her fellow actors' eyes. If her performance was successful, she credited much of that success to the brilliant performances of her two costars who gave her so much to which she could react. What a fine description of acting this is. Being open and sensitive, the performer feeds on the signals coming from other actors. The ability to reach this state of sensitivity, combined with some experience in the craft of acting, will carry the actor far.

Basic Acting Technique

Drawing from his own experience, this author has concluded that the basics of the craft of acting are:

1. the discovery and use of one's own best orotund voice quality (that quality produced when actors make maximum, proper use of their natural resonance cavities and bone structure);

2. the ability to switch into "stage English" (Southern British, standard speech of the BBC);

3. freedom from tension so that one can move and gesture gracefully and naturally; and

4. knowledge of when to move (catching attention) and how to blend into the stage picture (giving focus of attention to another), while remaining a reacting, living person rather than a frozen statue.

Obviously, this list of technical abilities is simple and minimal; however, these are the abilities which the director will find most useful. Acting is a matter of integrating the mind with the body; therefore, the actor's technical abilities should be derived from an organic basis, in the mental and emotional subtext of the events of the play.

Perhaps the usefulness of **stage English** needs elaboration. For one thing, it is a good way of learning to use the voice in ways different from the actor's ordinary patterns. It is particularly useful in allowing the actor to gain the universal sound considered more acceptable in classic roles and mature, sophisticated characters. Roger Gross describes actors' styles as being universal or time-and-place oriented (1981, p. 8). Frank Sinatra, for example, has a colloquial and particularly modern style of delivery which might not be appropriate in a Shakespearean play. On the other hand, Laurence Olivier and Charlton Heston perform in a style more acceptable to roles that are both contemporary and classic.

The ability to use stage English is one key to this quality of universality so valuable to the actor. The director should be able to train his or her cast in British dialect during rehearsals when necessary because, of all dialects, this is the one that will be needed most often. Typically, stage English is used in productions of most classic plays. Even in a contemporary play, a young actor can gain considerable maturity for his character by adding a touch of British dialect.

Thus, the basics of craft are fairly easily attained skills in voice quality, stage English, and movement. And we can conclude from our earlier discussion that an actor needs excitement and energy, believability in both line reading and movement, and inventiveness in terms of adding details, discovering new actions, and generally elaborating on the role.

Summing up the Actor's Job

What job is required of the actor in order to fulfill his or her role in a production? First, the actor must understand what the director wants, adjust to his or her working methods, and—being aware of the different point of view from which directors and actors analyze the script—seek out an understanding of the character that makes all of the character's actions and choices sensible and consistent. Second, the actor must be ready to create, to improvise when appropriate and necessary, be willing to experiment with various forms of line delivery and action, and be prepared to fill in for either playwright or director when no help is forthcoming from these sources to keep the work alive and interesting. Third, the actor must be trained in moment-to-moment concentration on the character's thoughts and desires, finding the total openness and sensitivity necessary to sense and react to all of the stimuli in the character's life. Fourth, the actor must learn through experience the rules of the game in terms of stage techniques, human behavior, and social conventions. That is the actor's job.

A Positive Working Atmosphere

Because the director must deal with actors, it is appropriate for the director to understand the job of the actor and its challenges. The director attempts to create a pleasant working relationship among the actors. Occasionally, actors have personality clashes, such as two people in the cast who hate one another, yelling and calling each other names. As a cure, the director might try the well-known "you are all professionals" speech. Whatever personal feelings exist among people in the cast, these feelings should be taken care of outside the rehearsal. In rehearsal, the actors are a group of professionals working together; even God and the devil ought to be able to get along while rehearsing a play. Although the director is using the speech as a device to maintain good relations, the speech is one of the great truths of the theatre. It is difficult for young performers to see themselves as working artists first, who leave their personal needs, ambitions, and drives in a sort of limbo while working on their art. Actors should regularly remind themselves that they are artists. They must learn to give complete concentration to "the work"—the craft—leaving personal problems outside the rehearsal.

In the professional theatre, people often call one another "darling," hugging and kissing each other although they are mere acquaintances. These people are deliberately creating a positive working atmosphere; thus, working together is fun. If performers have bad feelings about a co-worker, it is best to keep these feelings to themselves. To the outside world, a performer seldom says anything bad or critical about other performers or their work. At some point, they may have to work together, and bad feelings do not lead to good work. The famous cinematographer, William Fraker, was asked about his criteria for choosing a film project. Quite often, if he knew the people involved and knew he would enjoy working with them, he'd accept the job. To hear a major professional say that he would choose a project because he would have fun in the work demonstrates the value that artists put on a positive working atmosphere.

Summary

In this chapter, we have surveyed the job of the actor and the implications of that job for the relationship between the director and the actor during the rehearsal period. By way of summary, let us look at the comments of actress Jessica Lange concerning directors' approaches, made in an interview at the American Film Institute. The only director she had met who gave meticulously detailed directions—even to the point of giving line readings to his actors—was choreographer Bob Fosse. Lange found it very difficult to work this way. Of another director, she said: "Sometimes he'd talk to me, but he'd talk in such ways that I couldn't even understand. It was like, What the hell do you want? Just tell me." When asked about her best experience with a director, Lange spoke of her film *Music Box:*

> Working with Costa-Gavras was probably the best experience I've ever had as an actress working with a director because of his amazing sensitivity and kindness and intelligence. Costa creates a situation that's very productive. For the actor he makes—at least for me he did—an environment that was very supportive and very nurturing, which allowed me to really try and experiment. . . . Words can have such an impact; they can either move you positively or they can shut you down, and Costa was just amazingly intuitive and intelligent as to when to stay out of the way and when one or two words needed to be said. (1990, pp. 16–17)

As we have seen in this chapter, actors must often adjust to widely different directorial approaches. In truth, actors run the distance parallel with the director but ultimately alone. They communicate with themselves and with the art. The effort used to conquer the artwork is what communicates. In order to get the best work from the actor, the director should try to develop a climate of trust, cooperation, and creativity.

CHAPTER 12

PRINCIPLES OF ARRANGEMENT

In order to arrange actors on a stage, the director must develop a sense of the artistic principles of composition. Whereas many of these concepts also relate to the placement of furniture and scenery, the director is particularly interested in arrangements of actors. The principles of arrangement, balance, and focus on the stage are the same in the graphic arts, as if the director took a photograph of any moment during the play in order to analyze the way in which the objects in that picture were organized. Because of this similarity between stage and graphic arts, we shall study a series of photographs and famous paintings and attempt to illustrate those principles of arrangement.

Central Position

Look at Figure 12.1. Is something wrong with the picture? If it is intended to be a picture of the house, then the photographer has failed to take a successful picture. We expect the house to be in the center of the picture. In fact, we expect the important information in any picture to be in the center. Here, we see nothing of obvious importance in the center; thus, we wonder what the picture is supposed to be about, and perhaps we assume that the photographer made a mistake. When textbooks describe the power of different locations onstage—for example, center is more powerful than the corners and downstage is more powerful than upstage—it is because we expect to find the most important information in those locations. Therefore, when the director wants to focus the audience attention on an actor or event, locating that event at the center of the picture will help because that is where everyone expects the important information to be.

Figure 12.1 A View of the Swiss Alps

Symmetrical and Asymmetrical Balance

Figure 12.2 is another view of the Swiss Alps taken near Saint Moritz. Although the river winds up through the center with mountains on either side, the picture seems to be centered, and, in some way, properly arranged. What does this idea of "properly arranged" mean? There is a **balance** of weights on either side of the center that has a feeling of orderly arrangement. Such an illusion of balance is created on the principle of an old-fashioned seesaw or teeter-totter, running left to right with the fulcrum or turning point at the center of the picture. The reader

Figure 12.2 The Swiss Alps near St. Moritz

will recall how a teeter-totter works: When two people of equal weight sit on each end, they balance one another with no trouble; this is called symmetrical balance. However, when two people of unequal weight try to teeter-totter, they must make an adjustment to compensate and gain balance. If the lighter person moves out as far as possible to the end, and the heavier person moves a little more toward the center, often they can balance one another; this is called asymmetrical balance. Thus, the actual weight of a person depends not only upon his or her heaviness, but also upon the distance from the center. An object farther from the center is heavier on the teeter-totter and seems heavier in the picture. When two unlike objects balance one another because they are at different distances from the center, that is called asymmetrical balance.

Focus of Attention

Let us look at Figure 12.3 with two ideas in mind: balance and **focus,** or control, of attention. Here we have Mother Mary and baby Jesus surrounded by people and angels in a painting by Giotto De Bondone, located at the Uffizi Gallery in Florence, Italy. The two angels at the bottom and the people at left and right balance each other symmetrically. Looking carefully at the picture, one can see that Mary and Jesus are intended to balance one another as well. Baby Jesus seems much smaller and less heavy than Mary. Mother Mary is a bit off to the right of center; the baby is quite a bit farther to the left. Therefore, the weight of her upper body and that of the baby are intended to be in asymmetrical balance.

When arranging people, the painter and stage director wish to control the attention of the audience, focusing it on whatever that artist thinks is important. The question is: "What does one look at first in this picture of Mary and Jesus?" One looks at Mary's face. What draws our attention? She is centered, she is tallest or highest in the picture, she is isolated by frames around her, by both the halo around her head and the high back of the chair behind her. The artist has used a number of devices to draw our attention to her. He also controls where we look next: at the baby. The frame of the chair and the black gown stop us from looking in other directions. Our eye is drawn down the white front of Mary's dress, while her hand seems to point to the baby. We can conclude that centrality, height, and isolation from other elements in the picture are useful devices for the control of attention. This main focus of attention is often called the **dominant contrast.** The first focus of attention is called the dominant in any still picture, even in the single frame of a movie.

Figure 12.3 Giotto Di Bondone, *Madonna Ognissanti* (1300–1310)

Courtesy of the Uffizi Gallery, Florence.

Following the Actor's Line of Sight

Figure 12.4 is a portrait of Leone X by Raffaello Sanzio. Clearly, the focus of attention is the brightness of the central figure's face against the dark back-

Figure 12.4 Raffaello Sanzio, *Leone X con i Cardinali* (1518)

Courtesy of the Uffizi Gallery, Florence.

ground. If the portrait is read from left to right (a typical way of reading in Western society), one would first see the man on the left and follow his glance to the central figure. Onstage, the director will want all of the actors to watch the center of focus at any one moment. Thus, if the audience looks at one of the other actors, they will follow that actor's eyes to the important center of focus. In terms of balance, this portrait is simple and symmetrical.

Body Position and Height

Figure 12.5, another Madonna and child, is by Andrea del Sarto. The balance is generally symmetrical, two little angels below, two figures left and right of approximately the same size. In theatrical terms, the figure at the right is turned three-quarters back while the figure at the left is in one-quarter turn, gaining more attention and emphasis. The artist must think that the figure in white draws too much attention and so de-emphasizes him by use of body position. So close

Figure 12.5 Andrea del Sarto, *Madonna delle Arpie* (1517)

Courtesy of the Uffizi Gallery, Florence.

together, Mary and Jesus dominate as a single unit, not only because they are centered, but also because they command the height. Onstage, the director can use height to gain emphasis by having the focal person standing while everyone else is sitting or by raising the focal person on a platform or stairway.

Breaking the Line-up

Figure 12.6 is the famous *Last Supper* by Leonardo da Vinci. The original is a fresco, painted in the still wet plaster of a wall in Milan, Italy—a wall that is deteriorating rapidly. The focus of attention is on Jesus because he is centered, isolated from everyone else, and framed by the window in the background. The balance is symmetrical with six men on either side. Rather than a simple line-up of people, the artist has broken the men into little conversational groups with three persons in each. This is also an excellent principle for breaking up large groups on the stage in order to avoid the look of a chorus line.

Figure 12.6 Leonardo da Vinci, *The Last Supper*

Circular Arrangement

Figure 12.7, of the Sacred Family, is by Michelangelo, who is better known to most of us for his sculpture. In previous paintings, the center of attention held the height in a triangular arrangement; here the triangle is turned upside down. The point of focus is Mary's face, brightly lit, centered and framed by the other figures. Our gaze is then drawn to the baby, because Mary's arm points the way and that is where she is looking. We probably look at Joseph last, working our way around that group of faces. In terms of balance, Mary is centered, but the baby must be balanced by Joseph. Joseph's head, seeming heavier and more massive, is a bit right of center, whereas the baby is considerably farther off left, creating an asymmetrical balance.

Figure 12.7 Michelangelo Buonarroti, *Sacra Famiglia* (1503–1512)

Courtesy of the Uffizi Gallery, Florence.

Horizontal Arrangement

Figure 12.8, by Leonardo da Vinci, shows the angel coming to Mary with the news that she is pregnant. The horizontal arrangement of the painting is like that of a stage. Nothing of importance is located in the center. The dominant focus is probably Mary's face, framed against the dark wall. If one reads the picture from left to right, one will see the angel first, but will follow in the direction he is pointing and looking, finishing on the face of Mary. In terms of balance, Mary is surrounded by a massive wall and a very heavy-looking desk. While the angel is bulky, he does not seem heavy enough to balance all of that weight around Mary. Therefore, the artist has added a group of trees behind the angel to achieve balance.

Figure 12.8 Leonardo da Vinci, *Annunciazione* (1472–1475)

Courtesy of the Uffizi Gallery, Florence.

Symbolic Value of Line Patterns

Each of the paintings mentioned previously are located at the Uffizi Gallery in Florence; the final examples come from the Louvre in Paris. Figure 12.9, also by Leonardo da Vinci, shows Saint Anne, Mary, and Jesus. Rather than being arranged in vertical and horizontal patterns—as were our previous pictures—this painting is organized on a diagonal, running through the faces of the three figures. The arrangement of a graphic artwork is often described by means of the main lines of the picture, created by the objects. Visualize a line as if it was a real object such as a telephone pole. If the line is vertical, it is poised with energy, but it could fall over. It has a kind of balanced tension. If the line is horizontal, it is at rest, as if it has already fallen down. If the line is diagonal, it seems as if it is in the process of falling at that very moment. Thus, a diagonal line has a feeling of

Figure 12.9 Leonardo da Vinci's Painting of St. Anne, Mary, and Jesus

From the Louvre, Paris.

movement about it, even though nothing is really moving. Figure 12.9 is arranged in diagonals. If this picture were to come to life, the woman could not hold her position; she would fall off of the lap. One can almost feel the sense of movement implied by this diagonal arrangement. First focus is probably on the central woman's face, then moves to the baby and lamb at which she is looking, and finally back up the diagonal to the woman above.

Figure 12.10 also has a diagonal pattern of organization. This is an action-packed painting called *The Death of Sardanapalus* by Delacroix, which deals with a historical event in which a sultan calmly watched the slaughter of his own harem. Although there is action everywhere in the picture, our attention is drawn to a diagonal from upper left to lower right which is created by the lighting. The artist enhances the feeling of action by the use of a diagonal arrangement. We may look first at the woman's body at the feet of the sultan because she is centered and brightly lit. Our gaze will then move to the sultan or to the woman being murdered at the foot of the bed. We look up and down that lighted diagonal before we ever notice other action, such as the man struggling with the horse in the lower-left corner.

Figure 12.10 Eugène Delacroix, *The Death of Sardanapalus*

From the Louvre, Paris.

Summary of Basic Concepts

All of these pictures illustrate concepts of arrangement which are relevant to the theatre. The idea of balance and orderly stability is a major force in the design of scenery and the staging of larger groups of people. In a scene with only two characters, balance is not important or meaningful. That is, two characters face-to-face either stage right or left of center obviously will not balance the stage. The director would be required to have those actors play only in the center to create overall stage balance. Such positioning would clearly be too restrictive. Audiences tend to focus their attention on the area of the stage being used by the actors, generally ignoring the remainder of the setting and stage for that period of time; thus, the lack of overall stage balance will not seem disconcerting.

The concept of controlling and focusing the audience attention is relevant at all times. Of course, this focus can be achieved with lighting, as in Figure 12.9, but lighting is difficult to alter, as is an attention-getting, brightly colored costume. The director is interested not only in the means to focus audience attention, but also in devices that will switch that attention from one actor to another at a moment's notice. What are some of these devices? Body position—the actor facing forward in a group will achieve greater emphasis. Isolation—the actor separated from the group in some way—physically separated in space, standing while others sit, or sitting while others stand—will achieve greater emphasis. Stage location—the actor more center or more downstage will gain the most attention. Height—the actor up on a platform or stairway will gain more emphasis. Visual focus—the actor toward whom all the other actors are looking will become the center of focus. Action—the actor who is moving onstage will gain attention.

Philosophy of Staging Arrangements

Now that we have surveyed a group of basic concepts which are used in the arrangement of actors on the stage, let us study some of the reasons commonly given for the use of these ideas—the justification for arranging in this manner rather than in some other, more haphazard fashion. In trying to discover the philosophy behind staging arrangements, we shall look at what traditional textbooks concerning directing, choreography, and the other arts have had to say on the subject.

In his book concerning directing for the stage, Charles Lees gives three goals or purposes for the design of stage pictures: (1) to control audience attention and focus it on the important lines and actions, (2) to point up conflict, and (3) to make the play a thing of beauty through stage pictures (1951, p. 83). The aesthetic principles or the philosophical bases that seem to underlie and justify these stage pictures are usually summed up in words such as unity, balance, grace, and rhythm.

Unity

Unity is often defined as understandable organization and arrangement, designs, and patterns. In his book *The Art of Play Production,* John Doleman says of unity, "Singleness of effect is, if not essential, at least conducive to understanding, to interest and to aesthetic pleasure. . . . Interest depends upon attention, and lack of unity represents diffusion of attention" (1946, p. 55). Unity, then, is a quality that catches and focuses the attention of the audience on one particular person or one particular point in any scene. We have pointed out that the audience will follow the glance of the actor, so that if all of the other performers are looking at one person, no matter where the audience looks first, their glance will be directed to that particular person. Here is a simple and obvious stage technique for control of attention and, consequently, for unity. All of the devices listed earlier which are used by the director to control and focus audience attention at any moment are devices that aesthetically unify the stage picture. And unity itself is the underlying artistic justification for Lees' first goal for the design of stage pictures. What about the audience interest? Perhaps we can postulate that interest and voluntary, or natural, attention are so closely allied that the control of one is equal to the control of both. If directors can control audience attention, they are most likely controlling interest as well.

Yet the concept of unity is not as simple as we have made it seem. Unity, which is too simple, brings monotony, and, as Doris Humphrey illustrates in her book, *The Art of Making Dances,* monotony is fatal to any artistic venture; one should look for contrasts (1959). Doleman agrees when he says, "Sustained interest lies rather in the discovery of singleness in multiplicity, of unity in variety" (1946, p. 56). Thus we see the necessity of focusing the audience attention, but in a variety of ways so that similarity will not bring monotony and ultimate loss of attention.

Balance

Lees' third goal for design of the stage picture—to make the play a thing of beauty—is the most difficult to understand. Beauty may be added to a stage picture through color, costume, pageantry, and the like, but we are talking about the actual positioning of the characters alone. Balance seems to be the key word in this concept, and Doleman briefly defines it as the "maintenance of stability through equalization of contending forces" (1946, p. 61). We have discussed the common rules for stage balance based upon the fulcrum and lever principle of physics. Two figures or groups of generally equal weight placed at an equal distance from the center of the stage opposite one another are in balance; a figure half the weight of another will create a balance by being twice as far from the center as the heavier figure or group. The former situation is called symmetrical balance; the latter, asymmetrical. Balance seems to give stability and order (a form of unity) to a composition which is inherently relaxing and pleasing to the audience. Unity seems to be the primary aesthetic goal, and it was defined as focus upon or emphasis of a single point in the stage picture; now we see that an aesthetic quality of organization and balance is also a part of unity. Again, these qualities are alike in that too much of a particular focus or type of balance becomes monotonous, too restful, and ultimately not interesting.

Grace

Whereas unity and balance are terms primarily related to the stage picture, **grace,** as an aesthetic term, is most relevant to movement and scenic design. It is usually defined as the quality of seeming effortless and natural, as opposed to being obviously patterned. An irregular curve, for example, is supposedly more graceful than a straight line or a perfect geometric pattern. It has often been stated that patterns that are subtle, rather than those that blatantly draw attention to themselves, are the most pleasing to an audience. This whole idea of seeming irregularity and subtleness may seem to contradict the former concepts of unity and balance, but this is only an apparent conflict; the irregularity and "naturalness" associated with the concept of grace, are a far cry from disorder and complete lack of pattern. Thus, subtlety and seeming ease of organization and pattern would be termed graceful—a characteristic of the quality of beauty in the stage picture.

Rhythm

Another major artistic goal in the design of stage pictures is **rhythm.** Rhythm is created by the regular recurrence of any event, pattern, sound, and so forth, in time intervals. Alexander Dean carried this idea one step further in *Fundamentals of Play Directing,* in his concept of sequence in the stage tableau—the "rhythm of distances between figures or groups of figures on stage" (1980, p. 179). Repetition in spacing and grouping, either equal or proportional, adds a quality of rhythm to the stage picture. Doleman defines the psychological basis of rhythm as follows:

When we contemplate an object of beauty we experience imitatively the motor responses suggested by it. If those responses are rhythmic, they tend to fit in with the natural experience of the body {heartbeat, breathing, and electrical brain waves are rhythmical}, and it is not difficult to see that they are more likely to be pleasing than if they fail to fit in. (1980, p. 58)

Rhythm, along with balance and grace, is another characteristic of the quality of beauty in the stage picture. Although rhythm basically involves motion—a pattern in time rather than space—we continue to find these concepts applied only to the visual arrangement of still pictures in most texts.

Symbolic Blocking

As mentioned earlier in this chapter, Lees gave three goals for the design of the stage picture: To focus attention, to create beauty, and to point up conflict. Illustration of the emotional relationships of the characters by means of their physical relationship in the stage picture is probably the most common reasoning behind most **tableau** designs. The concept is usually called **symbolic blocking, or picturization.** The rationale behind this concept is based upon a simple, general psychological fact, illustrated here by Dean: "Instinct keeps us away from those whom we dislike, suspect, oppose; near to those whom we trust, endorse, agree with, love" (1980, p. 204). By carrying this idea further, we may see humbleness, weakness, or poverty contrasted with haughtiness, power, or wealth by the use of lower and higher stage levels respectively. It is this concept of symbolic blocking, even more than the need for emphasis, that leads director-scholars like Dean to study the relative strength of different positions on the stage and different movements across it.

These approaches to the blocking of a play typically concentrate on still pictures or tableaux rather than on the movement of the actors. In a previous chapter, we discussed methods of blocking the action of a play, including the concept of preblocking. One of the approaches to directing implied by the concept of preblocking involves carefully arranged still pictures, the sort of approach discussed in this chapter. The director plans a well-organized still picture, just like a photograph or painting, for a particular moment in the play. Then, another still picture is planned for another key moment following in the script. As a result, the director ends up with a whole series of still pictures. All that remains is finding a way for the actors to move from one still picture to the following still picture. Although this method is described in textbooks, this author has never met a director who uses it.

Briefly, then, these are the basic philosophical goals recognized for the stage tableau by major writers in the theatrical field: unity, balance, grace, and rhythm.

In the Director's Chair

David Wark Griffith (1875–1948)

A minor actor and playwright, D. W. Griffith sold several stories and did some acting for the Biograph movie company in 1908. He soon had a chance to direct, and, during the following five years, he directed hundreds of short pictures for Biograph. He formed his own company in 1913 and went on to produce his epic, full-length masterpiece *Birth of a Nation* in 1915. He was responsible for introducing such famous film stars as Mary Pickford, Lillian Gish, and Lionel Barrymore. He was a cofounder (with Mary Pickford, Douglas Fairbanks, and Charlie Chaplin) of United Artists in 1919 and a director of note throughout the silent film era. Together with his famous cameraman, G. W. "Billy" Bitzer, Griffith revolutionized the art of motion pictures. Up to this time, cameras simply stayed back in a long shot to watch the action from eye level. Griffith is responsible for either the invention or the development of the close-up, high and low camera angles, extreme long shots, night shots, and the moving camera. In effect, he is the founder of the Hollywood technique called *classical editing*.

Obviously, these goals involve innumerable rules of thumb and practical suggestions. Few of the books written about play direction and production even go so far as to state such underlying principles.

Symbolic Value of Line and Mass Patterns

Obviously, these principles for the design of the stage picture are parallel to, and probably derived from, the study of graphic artworks. Such works are studied in terms of both their subject matter (picturization) and their formal structure (unity, rhythm, balance, grace). A common suggestion is that one should turn a painting or print upside down to view its use of line, mass, color, and so forth, without being prejudiced by the quality of the subject matter. In *How to See Motion Pictures,* R. M. Pearson, who would derive for the graphic arts a series of laws or mathematical rules of form much like the laws of music, says of the artistic use of line: "All of these line arrangements have for their conscious or unconscious purpose the control or entertainment of the eye" (1934, p. 92). By entertainment, he means that these line arrangements appeal directly to our sense of order and controlled relationships. He goes on to delineate the basic values symbolized by the use of line in the following summary:

> The vertical straight position spells poise or a balance of forces which can break into action at any moment. The diagonal line is action. The horizontal line has acted and is at rest. Curved lines can also be thought of as symbolizing action—the small quick curve with its rapid change of direction symbolizing unrest, the staccato; the slow curve, the dignity of flowing movement. (1934, pp. 72–73)

In relation to the human figure in a stage picture, Dean gives a similar list of symbolic meanings summed up as follows (1934, p. 197):

1. Horizontal lines: restful, oppressive, calm, distant, languid, reposeful. They express stability, heaviness, monotony, restfulness, and so forth.

2. Vertical lines: height, grandeur, dignity, regal or forceful impressiveness, frigidity, spiritual, ethereal, soaring, and aspiring.

3. Diagonal lines: (seldom used) express a sense of movement or an unreal, artificial, vital, arresting, bizarre, or quaint quality.

Clearly, there seems to be agreement upon the symbolic value of a single line. Dean discusses mass in terms of weight and balance of stage groupings within the following forms: symmetrical or irregular, shallow or deep, compact or diffused. Thus, a particular relationship of masses might be described as symmetrical, compact, and shallow. Take note of the static and stable quality implied in the majority of the words used: oppressive, distant, grandeur, dignity, impressiveness, artificial, arresting.

Implied Conflict

A different approach can be seen in the discussions of some of the other arts. The Russian film director, Sergei Eisenstein, when talking about the single motion picture frame, analyzes the picture wholly in terms of conflict. Lines and planes that meet and cross one another show graphic conflict, seemingly in relation to the angle of their intersection. Volumes (masses) and spaces of different sizes create conflicts of volume and space when juxtaposed. This is an active rather than a stable approach; although, perhaps, the same general principles are valid in both cases. Eisenstein seems to be interested in the creation of tension and movement through the implied conflicts within a still tableau (1957).

Doris Humphrey also gives voice to the ideas of symmetry, balance, and stability, but she gives greater emphasis to asymmetry, contrast, unevenness, and stimulation. "Art is for stimulation, excitement, adventure" (1959, p. 50). Like Eisenstein, Humphrey seems more interested in the relationship between one line or body and another in terms of the vitality and movement that the relationship can create. Any arrangement can be successional or oppositional: the latter having lines in opposition or conflict with one another, the former being a lack of that conflicting relationship. Humphrey notes, "Opposed lines always suggest force; energy moving in two directions dramatizes and emphasizes the very idea of energy and vitality. . . . It {oppositional design} is indispensable for any idea of conflict, either emotional and subjective or with some outside person or force" (1959, pp. 57–58). This emphasis on movement or activity in the fixed tableau seems to be a growing characteristic in the aesthetics of modern art that has yet to become part of the accepted theory of directing the play. Twentieth-century art tends to emphasize the dynamic sense of movement rather than static picturization. "Every drawing," writes Laslo Maholy-Nagy in *Vision in Motion,* "can be understood as a motion study since it is a path of motion recorded by graphic means" (1947, p. 36).

Formalism and Realism

Perhaps another concept—that of open and closed forms—will serve to sum up our vision of stage compositions. **Closed forms** are emphasized by formalists and are characterized by precise placement of objects, balance, order, symbolic expression of ideas, and formal beauty. Closed forms present a perfectly organized, complete, meaningful world—a perfect portrait. Open forms, on the other hand, tend to sacrifice formal beauty for realism and naturalness. **Open forms** present more informal designs and patterns, a seemingly random organization of objects, as if these objects were only portions of a continuous reality stretching offstage, out of and beyond the frame. Often chosen by realists, open forms—like the snapshot as opposed to the formal portrait—prefer the visual ambiguity of reality to the meaningful symbolism of art.

The creation of a successful artistic product is the goal of every artist. The means used to produce that artwork may vary enormously; however, all means are valid as long as they produce a worthwhile result. A theatrical director who emphasizes preblocking and picturization will create a dramatic production that is composed of closed forms. The emphasis of this textbook on movement over picturization implies a clearly realistic motive on the part of the author, a preference for open forms, punctuated only occasionally by closed visions of beauty or symbolic import. Yet even this preference will be modified by the specific script and production at hand, because the director's analysis of each new script should lead to a production that has its own appropriate stylistic and technical characteristics.

Summary

In this complex chapter, we have studied the principles of artistic arrangement and the underlying justifications for their use. The ability to control and make use of these tools of arrangement is vital to the director. We have pointed out that their descriptions in traditional textbooks about theatrical directing tend to focus exclusively on frozen, still pictures, with very little discussion of the dynamics of movement and conflict. This author notes his own tendency to privilege realism over formalism, action and conflict over the carefully arranged tableau. However, these tendencies are often overridden by the demands of a particular script, because the choice of style may well be controlled by the script's own unique commanding form.

CHAPTER 13

STAGING CROWD SCENES

Crowd scenes—moments in the play when large numbers of performers are onstage—are seldom found in the majority of contemporary plays. However, the director must deal with crowds in many musicals such as *South Pacific* and *Carousel,* as well as in dramas such as *Inherit the Wind.* Earlier in the text, we discussed the principles of organization in the arrangement of a still picture or tableau, concepts of line, balance, and focus of attention. Essentially, concepts of balance are meaningless when dealing with just two actors onstage. When arranging a crowd on the stage, these values become much more important.

Organizing the Crowd

The standard method of staging crowds was developed by George II, the Duke of Saxe-Meiningen, in Germany, in the latter half of the nineteenth century—the period when realism was introduced to the theatre. The Duke became famous for his realistic staging of crowds; when his little company toured the major cities of Europe, audiences were amazed by the powerful, lifelike illusion he created. The typical crowd scene of the period received little direction. The stage manager went into the streets, hired a group of itinerants, put them in costumes, and told them to line up on the stage. That was it. There they stood, like statues, in some fixed position. In fact, it was common to hire a few crowd members and have the remainder of the crowd painted on the backdrop. The Duke wanted the crowds in his productions to be believable, lifelike, realistic. The system that he devised in order to achieve this goal is fairly simply; in order to avoid the look of a chorus line, he divided his crowd into small units of four or five actors. Then he arranged those units into a perfect tableau—a beautiful, still picture that illustrated the key elements of the particular play in terms of mood, intensity, and focus of attention. He called this tableau **home position.** Each of the units had a leader, a more experienced actor to control the group and advise the inexperienced members. Finally, each actor in the crowd was given a specific character and specific reason for his or her presence in the crowd. For example, one player might be told that he was the local baker who thought well of the king. Then, when the king arrived in his town, the baker came out to admire and cheer the king. The baker attended the event with a small group of close friends, a group that constituted his unit in the larger crowd. Each actor, then, was playing a specific character with a concrete goal rather than simply playing a crowd member.

The Duke believed that a member of the crowd was just as important to the success of his production as was the leading actor. An actor who had a large role in an earlier production was required to head a crowd unit in the next play. When a leading actress refused to play a lowly crowd member, she was fired. As far as the Duke was concerned, all of the roles in a play were of equal value.

Moving the Crowd

A crowd member had a specific purpose and character to play; he or she was part of a unit with a more experienced leader, and that unit was located onstage in a place called home position. The movement of the crowd was developed from this basic situation. At some point of high emotion, the entire crowd might go into action, but when that purpose was complete, the crowd would return to home position. In other words, home position was the place to go when no other action seemed appropriate. In order to vary the home position and add life to this nearly still picture, a character or two might change units, leaving one small group to join another. Finally, if the crowd scene lasted a long time, the Duke might develop a second home position, a second "beautiful tableau" to which the actors could retreat. Thus, the crowd would begin in home position, then, after some flurry of activity motivated by the events in the story, the crowd would settle down in the second home position. Another active movement would be followed by a return to the first home position, and so on.

Blocking the Crowd

Earlier in this book, directors were discouraged from preblocking the action of their scenes. However, it is obvious that the system for dealing with crowd scenes must be preblocked in detail. Some directors do their planning on sketches of the set; some use models with common pins or toy soldiers to represent the actors. Whatever the working method, crowd scenes must be preplanned because the director will not be able to watch the action of the crowd during the scene. The attention of both the director and the audience will be focused on the leading actors. By careful use of this system for staging crowds, the director will avoid the typical problems associated with crowds, such as loss of focus in the scene because many people are wandering around aimlessly, or the unnatural look of a chorus line, with all of the crowd members standing in neatly geometric lines—much like a group of soldiers standing at attention.

No one had described a better system for handling crowds in a realistic manner than the Duke of Saxe-Meiningen. His most famous production was *The Weavers,* by Gerhart Hauptmann, a superb play about the revolt of a group of peasants against the manufacturers who were starving and oppressing them. In the play's climactic scene, the poverty-stricken weavers break into the wealthy manufacturer's mansion and tear the house to shreds, destroying the pictures, the furniture, the very walls of the set. In order to create the illusion that the crowd was of enormous size, the director brought his actors into the room for their destructive activity, had them pass through an archway, circle around the back-stage, quickly change bits of costume such as hats and scarves, and reenter the set for more destructive activity. Thus, thirty crowd members were able to give the illusion of two or three hundred people. Throughout Europe, audiences rose to their feet and cheered this magnificent scene.

Staging: An Example

In this author's experience, a production of *Marat-Sade* provides the best example of the staging of crowd scenes. The full title of the play is *The Persecution and Assassination of Jean Paul Marat as Performed by the Inmates of the Asylum of Charenton under the Direction of the Marquis de Sade.*

Marat was a leader of the French Revolution, while de Sade was a famous libertine whose legacy became a common word: "sadism." The story takes place in an asylum at the height of Napoleon's dictatorship. There, the inmates produce a play-within-a-play about the events in the French Revolution, 15 years earlier. Ideas in the play seem to comment on the time of the Revolution, the time of Napoleon, and the time of the present-day audience as well. The play is structured as a series of alternating scenes—arguments between Marat and de Sade, reenactments of historical events and song numbers—all introduced by a narrator and continually interrupted by the fact that the inmates are too crazy to stay in character. For example, Charlotte Corday appears with a knife in her hand, ready to murder Marat numerous times during the play. Each time, de Sade stops the action in order to move on to some other historical event. Finally, he allows her to finish the deed, which is the climax of the play. In the finale, the inmates go berserk, murdering their keepers in their own little revolution for freedom. The play is typically German, structured in the fashion of expressionism and the works of Bertolt Brecht.

Thirty-three characters were in the cast, and all of them remained onstage for the entire length of the performance. There were eighteen inmates, a troupe of four singers, three musicians, the director of the asylum and his family, and five nuns whose job was to control the patients. The set was a giant platform, tilted toward the audience. Marat sat in a tub at right center, de Sade in a chair at left center. Down left, the director of the asylum and his family watched the performances; down right, the musicians played. At the back of the set were platforms, raised up on scaffolding with small curtains that could be drawn to hide the players. The director's job was not only to stage the scenes that involved all of these characters, but also to decide what to do with them when the scene involved only two or three characters.

In order to preblock the position of the crowd, the director had to preplan the general location of most of the individual scenes. For example, knowing that a song number would take place down center, the location of the crowd could be preplanned. Knowing that a particular scene between Marat and de Sade would be staged around Marat's tub allowed the director to place the crowd in appropriate positions.

In the Director's Chair

Charles Chaplin (1889–1977)

A British music hall performer and vaudeville comedian, Charles Chaplin came to the United States and entered the blossoming movie business in 1910. As a writer-director of silent films, Chaplin is universally acknowledged a genius. After beginning with Max Sennett at Keystone Films in 1913, Chaplin moved from one company to another until he formed his own in 1917 and became a cofounder of United Artists in 1919. Chaplin built his career on a particular character, "the tramp," which he developed in 1914. Writing, directing, producing, and acting in his own films, Chaplin produced a series of masterpieces, including *The Tramp* (1915), *The Kid* (1921), *The Gold Rush* (1925), and *City Lights* (1931).

The director made a sketch of the set on a ditto master and ran off copies (see Figure 13.1). On the first copy, he planned a home position for all of the characters: the narrator down center, Marat and his nurse on a small platform at right center, de Sade on a matching platform at left center, the four singers up center, the nuns and Charlotte Corday on benches below the rear platforms, and the inmates arranged across the platforms in back. When the inmates returned to home position, their appearance could be varied by having them stand or crouch or sit down. Also, they could disappear by closing the curtains which hung from the scaffolding above their platforms.

Using twenty-five copies of this sketch of the set, the director planned each key placement of the crowd throughout the thirty-three scenes of the play. Each song number was preblocked in detail, as well. Finally, the director summarized the list of crowd positions and ran off copies of that list to be passed out to the actors at rehearsal. The following is that list (the numbers refer to scenes):

Figure 13.1

The director's sketch of Christopher M. Paul's setting for *Marat-Sade.* Using many copies of this sketch and placing the groups of actors in the set by drawing stick figures, the director preblocked the location and arrangement of the crowd from scene to scene.

Act I

Opening		Straight line with Military Regularity upstage
Begin	5	Cowering in upstage corners around 1st platform
	6	Group spreads out around stage on cry of "Freedom"
	7	Patients sit or lie where they happen to end up
End	11	At close of mime, everyone ends up seated in general place
	13	Patients kneel about Marat for his liturgy
	14	After priest speech, patients pushed up right, half sitting, half standing
	16	Patients surround Marat on chorus
	18	Run in circle around him, end up seated where they finish, upstage
	19	Crawl toward platforms one by one—later, stand

20 Watch de Sade whipped

21 Come down slowly and low on chorus, encircle Marat, rise on last few words; after chorus, patients to general position and curtains closed

23 As Marat speaks, patients come slowly forward, end up scattered about stage and standing

Begin 25 Crowd back to general position and standing

26 Marat's nightmare: final song around cart at center

Act II

27 Opening as legislature on platform; at close, retreat to general position and close curtains

28 Singers lay downstage

30 Open curtains on copulation round

31 Pour off platforms for "15 glorious years"; after song, crowd around Marat to watch murder

33 (Burn Flag)

Thus, for a particular scene involving Marat, de Sade, and one or two other actors, the director would decide ahead of time where that scene would be located in general, in order to choose specific positions for the crowd. The details of the blocking for Marat and de Sade were worked out between the director and his actors at rehearsal in the typical manner. The director is able to watch two or three actors at rehearsal, but the other thirty people must be preblocked. Although the singing group involved only four performers, blocking of the songs did not consist of realistic movement—that is, of characters moving toward or away from one another to illustrate their relationship. During the songs, the actors were playing games among themselves or with the audience, games which had to be planned ahead of time because they did not flow naturally from the dialogue. Each of the actors in the crowd had developed a unique character with a definite attitude and purpose. When a particular scene did not call for their participation, the director found an immediate neutral position for them—as in scene 7—or he sent them back to home position, as in scene 25. This example of *Marat-Sade* gave this author his greatest challenge in terms of blocking large numbers of actors onstage. While the director used many devices in dealing with crowd from one scene to the next, he based the entire play upon the principles first developed by the Duke of Saxe-Meiningen.

Summary

In this chapter, we have talked about the proper method of staging crowd scenes. A crowd member should have a specific purpose and character to play; he or she should be part of a unit with an experienced leader, and that unit should be located onstage in a home position. The home position should be an ideal tableau, a living picture which utilizes the same principles of artistic arrangement that appear in famous paintings—those ideas discussed in Chapter 12. In the next chapter, we shall elaborate upon another idea mentioned earlier in the book— that of directors being encouraged to develop an atmosphere at rehearsals that inspires experimentation and creativity in the performers. Such creativity will be the subject of Chapter 14.

CHAPTER 14

CREATIVITY IN REHEARSAL

Ultimately, actors will be alone on the stage. The director will remain in the background, encouraging the actors, building their confidence, helping them to create their characters. No matter how strongly the director desires to generate a fine performance from the actors, he or she cannot do the performing for them. The director's task is to do whatever it takes to guide the actors toward their best performance. That is the key to the relationship between actor and director. In this chapter, we shall discuss some of the approaches that the director can use to accomplish this goal.

Creativity and Rehearsal Atmosphere

Research indicates that creativity requires a certain kind of mind-set and a certain kind of atmosphere. In order for people to be creative, they need a climate in which they can experiment with different things, try different and unusual approaches without being criticized. In a classroom situation, many teachers say that they are open to questions, but if the students discover that raising their hands to ask questions invariably draws a response that seems like a put-down, a personal criticism, the students soon sense that this teacher has no interest in their contributions. Thus, the teacher has created an atmosphere that will discourage creativity.

Elementary school teachers soon learn that when one student draws a beautiful picture and another paints the strangest thing ever seen, both pictures must be treated as equally good work. The teacher cannot criticize that strange, creative painting as if it were some kind of test that the child failed—not if he or she ever wants that child to paint again. A creative climate makes the participants feel psychologically safe. The participants must feel respected and valued as human beings and free from negative external evaluation.

The director should develop a rehearsal atmosphere in which people will feel comfortable and, it is hoped, creative. We have talked about the process of blocking the play. The actors move at moments that seem appropriate. The director adds some actions, takes some back, suggests new alternatives. The actors and director create the blocking together. If the director provides an atmosphere in which the actors feel that their contribution is going to be ignored, they will just stand in one place, forcing the director to move them around all the time. Even if they are capable of doing it on their own, they will not make contributions when they sense that this is not what the director wants. In good staging, the director wants to encourage the actors to be as creative as possible. Certainly, the director should avoid doing anything that will discourage them.

Evaluating Contributions

Obviously, the director cannot accept every contribution made by the actors at rehearsal, but he or she must find ways to criticize that will not hurt the actors' feelings. This is a common problem for experts who are assigned to view and evaluate theatrical productions for contests such as The American College Theatre Festival. Such experts dislike the term, "critic," because it has negative connotations which imply that their job is to be "negatively critical." They prefer the terms "adjudicator" or "respondent" to describe their work. Adjudicators do not want to interfere with the creativity of the people they are judging. Rather than cause those people to be so discouraged that they will quit the theatre forever, the adjudicator wants to encourage the performers to improve their art. Suggestions for improvement must be given without creating a defensive situation, one in which feelings are hurt. If the performers are offended, they will stop listening, tune out, or simply refuse to accept any opinion from the adjudicator as worthwhile; thus, the adjudicator becomes completely ineffective. Because the director does not want to create an atmosphere in which the actors feel stifled and defensive, the director, like the adjudicator, must choose methods for evaluating the actors' contributions which encourage new and greater creative contributions.

Interpersonal Communication

The method by which the director achieves these goals when dealing with the actors is a matter of general attitude or approach, coupled with common sense. The director wants to be forthright and open, using the least manipulative tactics in dealing with the actors. In order to inspire actor-initiated work, the director can ask more questions, be open to actors' ideas, be cognizant of their feelings, and offer both praise and encouragement. Film director Ronald Neame recalls working with Alec Guinness and finding him more and more sulky and depressed. When asked about the problem, the actor responded that he had been at work on this picture for two weeks and had not heard a single word of praise. Actors, says Neame, "need praising. We need to be encouraged and patted on the back when we have done well" (Sherman, pp. 180–81). Because directors tend to concentrate on improving those aspects of production which are not going well, all too often they fail to compliment the positive achievements. Be reminded that praise is an important aspect of directing, simply because people will naturally assume that they are doing badly unless they are told otherwise.

Negative Contributions

At the same time, the director must maintain control of the rehearsal situation and the overall production. Some contributions and some ways of contributing are unacceptable. Comments from outsiders and from the technical crew

In the Director's Chair

Alfred Hitchcock (1899–1980)

Alfred Hitchcock went to work for Famous Players-Lasky Company, the forerunner of Paramount, in his native London in 1920. In 1923, he moved to Gainsborough Pictures where he worked his way up to directing in two years. He directed in Great Britain, becoming known as a master of suspense, until 1939, when he emigrated to the United States. From *Suspicion* (1941) and *Spellbound* (1944) to *North by Northwest* (1959) and *Psycho* (1960), hardly a year went by without a new movie. He also hosted a television mystery program from 1955 to 1965. Hitchcock was known for his meticulous preparation before filming actually began. The director would create a complete storyboard consisting of a sketch of each shot that the camera would take, in sequence, for the entire film. His preproduction preparation was said to be so thorough that his crew knew exactly what to do without his instruction. He would sit, quietly smoking his cigar, until some problem arose that he was needed to solve. Much admired by the French New Wave filmmakers, Hitchcock was lionized and knighted toward the end of his career.

made directly to the actors should be avoided. Feedback from outsiders should be given to the director in private, never in front of the cast. In this way, the director can pass on suggestions that he or she deems useful and simply ignore those that might be out of keeping with the interpretation of the script or detrimental to an actor's performance. Even comments from one of the actors concerning scenes in which that actor is not involved can be troublesome. On occasion, the director must discourage young "would-be directors" who wish to make excessive contributions to the creativity of their fellow actors.

Working Together

The director wants to develop a cohesive group of people, working together to create the production. Petty squabbles, jealousy, rivalry, and the like all interfere with this goal. Therefore, the director is well advised to lecture the cast at an early rehearsal about professionalism and what it means to be an artist in the theatre. When an actor arrives at rehearsal, he or she must leave personal problems and animosities outside, devoting all of his or her energy to the creative work with other actors—to the creation of the final work of art. Once they know what is expected of them, most actors are able to demonstrate true professionalism.

The director is trying to create a milieu that encourages creativity at rehearsals. When actors goof-off backstage and have a good time, some directors become frustrated. But in rehearsals, unless such activity becomes disturbing, the atmosphere should allow the performers to have fun. If theatre isn't fun, why should they do it? Unless they are professionals, they are not being paid. And even if they do theatre for a living, they should enjoy their work. "I hate this job, but it's a living." How many people live their lives like that? The director should not be upset when people have fun at rehearsals. A typical situation is one in which everyone gets the giggles because someone has bobbled their line in some silly way. When the entire cast falls apart, unable to stop laughing, this is a great moment. Woe to the director who gets angry at the cast; this director is making a big mistake. This time of laughter will be well spent in the sense of having a rehearsal climate that is not repressive, but encourages creativity and enjoyment.

The transformational leadership theory proposed by James McGregor Burns (1978) seems most relevant to the relationship between director and actors. Many leadership theories presume that the leader must control everything, but the transformational leader recognizes that giving up power to other participants empowers them to think and motivates them to excel. Hackman and Johnson (1991) identify five key personality characteristics of such a leader: (1) creativity, (2) a posture of open participation with the followers, (3) the creation of a shared vision with the followers, (4) empowering the followers, and (5) possession of a passionate commitment to both the followers and their task. The theatrical director brings creativity, vision, and passion to the task of empowering the actors to explore, discover, and develop the work of art. Clearly, the director who operates as a transformational leader will generate greater creative activity in the actors.

Creative people need the freedom to work, to experience, to know the world around them. Creative people need individual independence without rigid boundaries. Creative people must enjoy novelty and change and free themselves from social pressures to conform. The atmosphere of psychological safety provided by the director must be complemented by the actor's own self-confidence, openness to experience, and willingness to experiment and to try new ideas.

Beginning the Rehearsals

Many directors begin every rehearsal with a series of warm-up exercises. After a hard day, actors often stagger into rehearsal half-asleep; thus the first 15 or 20 minutes of their rehearsal is dull and listless. Group exercises develop camaraderie and get the actors' blood and adrenaline flowing. Exercises and games can also be used to set the proper mood for the rehearsal. When doing a production of *Taming of the Shrew* in the style of Commedia Dell'Arte (rather like the Three Stooges doing Shakespeare), a director had her actors play tag for 10 or 15 minutes at the opening of each rehearsal, tag in all of its variations, such as freeze-tag and explosion-tag. According to the actors, this imaginative tactic was successful as well as enjoyable. Many years ago in an acting class at UCLA this author had begun to perform the Katherine-Petruccio fight scene from *Taming of the Shrew* when the teacher interrupted the scene. He asked the actor to go outside and run around the building—a very large building. After the actor returned to the class, the teacher told us to begin the scene again. After the performance, he asked the class to comment, and all agreed that the scene was enormously improved the second time around. It was a lesson well learned: Energy, vitality, and the release of tensions that interfere with acting can be achieved with physical exercise.

Ending the Rehearsals

The director's job on opening night is to maintain the creative atmosphere developed during rehearsals, to set a mood that will build the actor's confidence, much like the mood set by a coach in the locker room before the big game. Whatever the director does should help relieve the tension—the opening night jitters—created by the fact that there will be an audience for the first time. All through the rehearsal period, the director's job was to be the eyes of the audience. The actors have to feel that they are not going to look stupid onstage. The director has watched to make sure that would not happen to the actors and assures them, by being their audience, that nothing is going wrong, everything is going well. If the actors have complete confidence in this relationship—trusting the director not to let them make fools of themselves, trusting that they will do well onstage—they will then be able to perform with confidence and creativity. The director's job on opening night is to reinforce this relationship of trust and confidence.

Summary

Actor creativity can be encouraged by the proper atmosphere, a rehearsal climate that fosters experimentation without judgmental criticism. Interpersonal communication between director and actors should be such that it nurtures rather than discourages further creative contributions. Transformational rather than dictatorial leadership from the director is likely to generate greater creative activity. And, finally, the creative relationship developed between director and actors should carry through rehearsals and on into the performance.

CHAPTER 15

BLOCKING REHEARSALS

Let us return to our production of *Play It Again, Sam,* tracing the rehearsals from readings and **table talk** on into the blocking. After the first read-through, the actors were asked to write autobiographies of their characters which were discussed the following evening. During the second read-through, the director put the emphasis on locating the comedy in the script, pointing out which lines or sequences were funny and exactly how they worked. The actor's job is to be aware of the comedy and play it well, remaining, at the same time, a believable human being. In comedy, becoming mechanical, or acting like stand-up comedians playing for laughs, is a major pitfall. Theatre tradition has it that comedy is more difficult to play than tragedy, probably because the actor must blend and balance comic technique with believability of character. At this point in rehearsal, the director warned the actors about this problem.

Blocking took more time than usual. Typically, this author blocks approximately fifteen pages of a Samuel French or Dramatists Play Service script at a 3-hour rehearsal; however, with this play, we were able to block only ten pages at a time. The reason seemed to be that the comedy required us to work out more of the details. Usually, one blocks the major movements, leaving the tiny, intricate details for later rehearsals. But with *Sam,* what was funny about the scene often depended upon how the actor played those details. Thus, we found ourselves working on such things as a simple gesture or glance early in the blocking. Once the blocking was finished, a major proportion of the director's job had been accomplished. Creative decisions had been made that would make or break the show.

Playing by the Rules

The director might be wise to establish ground rules for his or her relationship with the cast at the opening rehearsal, explaining working methods and the overall pattern of rehearsals. Although the director is interested in and willing to discuss their suggestions, the actors should realize that when a disagreement appears, the ultimate decision must lie with the director, because that is the proper line of authority between director and actors. Directors tend to assume that their casts know about these matters; this assumption may be a mistake. Along with the discussion of the interpretation of the script, the director could describe the rehearsal process that they will go through together, the lines of authority, and the type of relationship that he or she wants to establish with the actors. Spending some time on these matters at an early rehearsal may save the director time and trouble in the long run.

In order to demonstrate the process involved in blocking a scene using the creative contributions of both director and actors, we have previously analyzed and staged a scene from *The Rainmaker* in Chapters 2 and 3. This chapter will present a second example of the process of blocking a scene creatively with the actors during rehearsal. It is presented as one example of the blocking process rather than as an ideal model to be followed and imitated in detail. This event is the record of an actual staging that took place in a directing class, with student-directors performing the roles. At this time, the reader may wish to review material presented in the early portion of Chapter 2, which dealt with the general principles of stage movements. The scene is that which closes the first act in the play *Blue Denim* by James Leo Herlihy and William Noble.

Background and Analysis

Blue Denim deals with two high school students who fall in love, a situation which leads the young girl through a pregnancy and an abortion, in the era before abortion had become legal. Our scene, at the end of the first act, is the initial incident of the play, the moment in which Arthur and Janet realize that they love one another. The scene takes place in the basement of Arthur's home, a room set up as Arthur's clubhouse where he and his friends can hide out, playing cards and occasionally smoking and drinking beer behind their parents' backs. In fact, that is exactly what Arthur and his comic, braggart friend, Ernie, were doing just prior to our scene. Their fun was interrupted by the arrival of Janet. Janet does not like Ernie, probably because she thinks he is a bad influence on Arthur. She and Ernie clash, and Ernie angrily leaves the basement.

Beat 1 Janet explains why she does not like Ernie. Arthur resents her interference.

Beat 2 Janet unsuccessfully tries to make up.

Beat 3 Arthur asks Janet about her relationship with her father.

Beat 4 Embarrassed by the subject, she finds music on the radio.

Beat 5 Janet makes Arthur dance with her.

Beat 6 Arthur breaks it off, making Janet angry.

Beat 7 Janet leads Arthur into confiding in her.

Beat 8 Janet asserts that she is in love with him. Arthur does not believe her.

Beat 9 Resentfully, she explains her feelings, as he questions her.

Beat 10 She is embarrassed. He tries to comfort her. They end up kissing. (Climax)

Beat 11 Arthur asks about her relationships with other boys.

Beat 12 When she asks him about other girls, he makes up a macho story that angers her.

Beat 13 They kiss and make up.

Beat 14 She asks him to teach her how to make love, forcing him to reveal that he has no knowledge or experience in lovemaking. She embraces him.

The scene climaxes with the idea of making love and concludes with Arthur's revelation that he was bluffing when he bragged that he had experience in these matters. Like Romeo and Juliet, Arthur and Janet are very young, naive, and vulnerable.

Blocking the Scene

In order to stage this scene from *Blue Denim,* the setting of Arthur's basement club room must be planned. Three folding chairs were set up stage right of center to represent an old couch. Behind the couch was a music stand which represented the punching bag called for in the script. Up center, against the "wall" of the room, was a chair which represented a small table with the radio. Stage left of center, balancing the couch, was a card table with one corner pointed toward the audience and two chairs set above it. The reader will recall from *The Rainmaker* scene that "D" means downstage, "R" means stage right, "L," stage left, and "X" means cross. For the opening moment, the director placed Janet up center at the radio and Arthur in the stage right chair at the card table. However, when she spoke of his being "sore," the boy immediately rose from the chair and found himself directly downstage of the girl (see Figure 15.1). Therefore, the scene began with Arthur seated in the other chair, farther left.

JANET: You sore?

ARTHUR: Naw!

JANET: For breaking up the game, I mean.

ARTHUR: Well, okay then! Why? (<u>RISE</u>)

JANET: I just don't like to see you—the way you act when Ernie's around.

ARTHUR: And how's that?

JANET: Oh—pretending so!

ARTHUR: Who's pretending? Ernie and me happen to like a couple of beers and hand of poker. Why do you have to act like somebody's mother? (<u>CIRCLE DOWN BELOW TABLE</u>)

The director suggested that Arthur cross above the table, toward Janet. The scene began again, then stopped at this same point. The director said, "You want

Figure 15.1

to get by her. You don't really want to go to her." The actor agreed, but asserted that his first move was better. "All right, try it that way."

JANET: You sore?

ARTHUR: Naw!

JANET: For breaking up the game, I mean.

ARTHUR: Well, okay then! Why? (<u>RISE</u>)

JANET: I just don't like to see you—the way you act when Ernie's around.

ARTHUR: And how's that?

JANET: Oh—pretending so!

ARTHUR: Who's pretending? Ernie and me happen to like a couple of beers and hand of poker. Why do you have to act like somebody's mother? (<u>CIRCLE BELOW TABLE AND X BEHIND COUCH</u>)

JANET: I'm sorry. (As he does not answer) I'm sorry, Arthur.

ARTHUR: Why don't you call me Art, like everybody else? (<u>TURN TO FACE HER</u>)

JANET: All right. I'm sorry, Art.

ARTHUR: Forget it. (<u>SITS ON BACK OF COUCH</u>)

JANET: (Searching for a topic) Want to go down to the drugstore? (<u>X AWAY BEHIND TABLE</u>)

ARTHUR: For what?

JANET: I don't know—Coke, soda. . . .

ARTHUR: On top of beer!

JANET: Oh. (A rather strained pause, Janet hits the punching bag with her fist) Ow!

At this point, the director realized that Janet was nowhere near the punching bag. Rather than reblock, the bag was moved up left of the table where she could easily reach it from her present location.

ARTHUR: Janet. What'd you mean, when you said you wished your father was different? (As she does not answer) The way he's so funny about lipstick and stuff? And doesn't like you to date guys?

JANET: I wish I lived downtown with Norma! I'm going to, the minute I graduate!

ARTHUR: What the hell, lots of parents are old-fashioned and raise cain with their kids. 'Specially girls.

JANET: Yes, but my father doesn't raise cain. He says: "How can you hurt me this way? How can you?" And then he—cries.

For the opening of this new beat, the director suggested that Arthur fall into the couch from his position seated on the back of the couch (see Figure 15.2). "A kid of his age would do that—just flop down into the couch." Where would Janet go? That depends upon how she decides to play the sequence about her father. If she just throws it off, that's one type of movement. If she is really upset, taking it seriously, the movement will be different. The actress decided to play the sequence with strong emotion.

Figure 15.2

ARTHUR: Janet. What'd you mean, when you said you wished your
father was different? (As she does not answer) The way he's
so funny about lipstick and stuff? And doesn't like you to
date guys? (<u>FLOPS INTO COUCH</u>)

JANET: I wish I lived downtown with Norma! I'm going to, the minute I
graduate! (<u>X D BELOW TABLE</u>)

ARTHUR: What the hell, lots of parents are old-fashioned and raise cain
with their kids. 'Specially girls. (<u>SITS UP</u>)

JANET: Yes, but my father doesn't raise cain. He says: "How can you
hurt me this way? How can you?" And then he—cries. (<u>X
AWAY, DL</u>)

ARTHUR: Cries?

JANET: (Nodding) Real tears. (<u>TURNS TO HIM</u>)

ARTHUR: But your dad's a grown-up man, a college professor!

JANET: I know. And he makes me feel so sorry for him, I—(Looking around desperately) Does your radio still work?

ARTHUR: Of course. Why shouldn't it?

JANET: (Switching it on) Good. Let's find some real crazy music. (<u>X TO RADIO</u>)

ARTHUR: You won't find anything at that end. (<u>FOLLOWS HER</u>) (<u>DIALING FOR HER</u>) How's this? Not very crazy, though. (Dance music comes on)

JANET: It's fine—Arthur, dance with me.

ARTHUR: You know I can't.

A lengthy discussion took place at this point. Arthur's back was to the audience and he was blocking Janet when he crossed directly up through the center to reach the radio. The director suggested that he circle right, around the back of the couch, in order to approach Janet and the radio from the side. Although it was a small movement, the director encouraged Arthur to take a few steps away from Janet, down to the edge of the couch, on the line, "You know I can't!" The following dance sequence took considerable time to stage (see Figure 15.3).

JANET: It's fine—Arthur, dance with me.

ARTHUR: You know I can't. (<u>X DOWN TO COUCH</u>)

Janet: It's no big mystery. (Walking to him, taking charge) Now—just walk in time to the music! (After a moment) It'll never work if you keep on being so stand-offish. Here, like this! (Walks into his arms. As he draws back) No, goofy, closer! (She presses tightly against him. After a moment) You catching on?

ARTHUR: (Breathlessly) Yeah, I—think so. (Acutely conscious of her) We—we better stop pretty soon, huh?

JANET: You're doing fine. Everybody's self-conscious at first.

ARTHUR: (Painfully) No—I think we better—(He breaks from her, hurries to the radio and turns it off)

The lines imply that Janet forces Arthur to dance. She must come down, grab him, and drag him to an open space, probably down center. What kind of music is this? Arthur wouldn't start with rock music because he is not a dancer.

Figure 15.3

Therefore, the music must be appropriate for a slow dance—simply walking in time to the music. As they tried the sequence a number of times, the director encouraged them to take longer pauses for dancing between the lines of dialogue. The pattern that appeared had them dance for a while, then Janet would stop, give new instructions; followed by a continuation of the dance. Overall, these movements included one half-turn, swapping positions onstage, followed by some simple swaying to the music at the end. Given this framework, the dance scene would require the real music and the point at which the actors were no longer carrying scripts in order to achieve a polished look. When Arthur broke away from the dance, he moved down right, in front of the couch.

JANET: It's fine—Arthur, dance with me.

ARTHUR: You know I can't. (<u>XDR DOWN TO COUCH</u>)

Janet: It's no big mystery. (Walking to him, taking charge) (<u>DRAGS HIM D. CENTER</u>) Now—just walk in time to the music! (After a moment) (<u>DANCE</u>) It'll never work if you keep on being so stand-offish. (<u>PAUSE</u>) (<u>PULLS HIM CLOSER</u>) Here, like this! (<u>DANCE ONE HALF TURN—PAUSE</u>) No, goofy, closer! (She presses tightly against him. After a moment) (<u>SWAY TO THE MUSIC</u>) You catching on?

ARTHUR: (Breathlessly) Yeah, I—think so. (Acutely conscious of her) We—we better stop pretty soon, huh?

JANET: You're doing fine. Everybody's self-conscious at first.

ARTHUR: (Painfully) No—I think we better—(He breaks from her) (<u>XDR, IN FRONT OF COUCH</u>)

JANET: What's the matter?

ARTHUR: Nothing. I told you—I'm no good at that stuff. (<u>AROUND COUCH TO TURN OFF RADIO</u>)

JANET: You'll never learn if you won't try! (<u>X TO COUCH AND SIT.</u>)

Since Arthur did not turn off the radio where the script indicated the action, the director suggested a way to do that on the following line. However, that placed Arthur directly upstage of Janet. The director cleared up this awkward position by having Janet cross immediately to the couch and sit in frustration (see Figure 15.4).

At this point, the director decided to rerun the blocking that had been done, going back to the beginning of the scene. Arthur changed the moment that he flopped into the couch. The dance was terrible, but everyone realized that it would not come together properly until polishing rehearsals. Arriving at the unblocked new beat, the director changed Arthur's cross to the radio to the opening line of the new beat, after Janet had seated herself on the couch, thus avoiding the awkward moment in which she was upstaged.

ARTHUR: Too bad Ernie isn't here. He goes to dances all the time. (<u>XR AND AROUND BACK OF COUCH TO TURN OFF RADIO</u>) real ones, downtown.

JANET: I wanted to dance with you, not Ernie.

ARTHUR: I'd give anything if I could be like him.

JANET: Now why?

ARTHUR: He's really got a smooth tongue on him. I admire that. With me things get all twisted up. . . .

Figure 15.4

The director said, "What might he do there? Walk forward, go down and head back over to the table. He's a kid; he could sit on it. I don't know what is coming up next. Maybe it will work." This movement did work, but Arthur did not remain seated long. The actor felt that his character was too upset to stay comfortably seated on the table.

ARTHUR: Too bad Ernie isn't here. He goes to dances all the time. Real ones, downtown. (<u>X AROUND COUCH. TURN OFF RADIO</u>)

JANET: I wanted to dance with you, not Ernie.

ARTHUR: I'd give anything if I could be like him. (<u>TURN TO HER</u>)

JANET: Now why?

ARTHUR: He's really got a smooth tongue on him. I admire that. With me things get all twisted up. . . . (<u>XDL IN FRONT OF TABLE</u>)

JANET: Arthur, what sort of things?

ARTHUR: Things I wonder about—One thing, it bothers me a lot. (<u>SIT ON TABLE</u>) I tried to tell Mom about it once, but. . . .

JANET: But what?

ARTHUR: Aw, every time my mother looks at me I feel like she's (<u>RISE AND XDL</u>) seeing something small and pink and wrapped up in a blanket.

JANET: Try telling me, Art.

ARTHUR: See . . . I've got this feeling I ought to be somebody special! (<u>TURN TO HER</u>)

JANET: Who doesn't? I want to be a poet, and what's sillier than that? (<u>RISE</u>)

ARTHUR: Yeah, but you got what it takes. I'm just—ordinary.

JANET: Ordinary! You think I'd hang around with you if I didn't think you were going to be—special? (<u>X TO HIM</u>)

ARTHUR: You do?

JANET: Of course. That's why you and I can talk.

ARTHUR: I guess we do talk better than most people. All the kids at school—even Ernie . . . I mean. I figured it out. I don't really know anybody at all. Not even my own folks. Does that sound bats?

JANET: Not to me!

After Janet crossed to Arthur, they seemed to be stuck in the middle of the stage because there were no lines that would allow either of them to move away from the other. It was decided that she should remain seated on the couch, allowing him to come to her, so that they could have this conversation on the couch together.

JANET: Try telling me, Art.

ARTHUR: See . . . I've got this feeling I ought to be somebody special! (<u>TURN TO HER</u>)

JANET: Who doesn't? I want to be a poet, and what's sillier than that?

ARTHUR: Yeah, but you got what it takes. I'm just—ordinary. (<u>X UP TO HER</u>)

JANET: Ordinary! You think I'd hang around with you if I didn't think you were going to be—special?

ARTHUR: You do?

JANET: Of course. That's why you and I can talk.

ARTHUR: I guess we do talk better than most people. (<u>SIT BESIDE HER</u>) All the kids at school—even Ernie . . . I mean. I figured it out. I don't really know anybody at all. Not even my own folks. Does that sound bats?

JANET: Not to me!

ARTHUR: Huh?

JANET: It seems to me the only people who really know each other are—people in love.

ARTHUR: Maybe so.

JANET: Arthur, how d'you suppose it feels to be in love with someone?

ARTHUR: Don't ask me!

JANET: (Bravely) Because—because I think I'm in love. With you.

ARTHUR: You . . . ! (Sharply) Whadd'ya want to kid like that for? (<u>SUDDEN RISE</u>)

The actor was correct in creating distance between them at this point. However, the director suggested that Janet might find it difficult to confess her feelings face to face with Arthur. Therefore, a line was found that would allow her to move away earlier. After Arthur rose from the couch in shock, he also moved away from her. That did not look right. The director said, "I don't like them going away. Is it possible that he could go toward her? He gets up in shock but goes toward her when he decides that she is just kidding. Then, when she gets angry, she could cross in front of him and go over there. Walking past him in an even stronger rejection. Try that."

JANET: It seems to me the only people who really know each other (<u>RISE AND XR</u>) are—people in love.

ARTHUR: Maybe so.

JANET: Arthur, how d'you suppose it feels to be in love with someone? (<u>TURN TO HIM</u>)

ARTHUR: Don't ask me!

JANET: (Bravely) Because—because I think I'm in love. With you.

ARTHUR: You . . . ! (Sharply) Whadd'ya want to kid like that for? (<u>RISE</u>)

JANET: I'm not!

ARTHUR: You are. And I thought we were talking serious. (<u>X TO HER</u>)

JANET: Well, if that's your attitude, I'm sorry I told you! (<u>JANET X HIM TO CHAIR AT TABLE</u>)

ARTHUR: Janet! Weren't you kidding? (<u>HE MOVED A BIT TOWARD HER</u>) Lordie, Janet. . . .

JANET: Don't worry about it. At my age it's perfectly natural to have crushes on people. (<u>XL ABOVE TABLE</u>)

ARTHUR: Yeah, but—why me?

JANET: Frankly, I don't know. You're not the handsomest boy (<u>SIT IN L. CHAIR</u>) in the world.

The actress said, "I feel like I'm backing up. And I don't know why I come over here and stand by this chair if I wasn't going to sit down." Of course, she was correct. It was decided to have her sit in the far chair, in case the scene allowed the boy to come and sit beside her (see Figure 15.5). Thus, the last two moves were created in the above blocking. As it worked out, Arthur sat on the couch while Janet delivered her long speech. The actress moved naturally on this speech, creating an excellent piece of blocking on her own.

ARTHUR: Thanks!

JANET: You see, I'm very objective about you, Arthur. My mistake was I told you. Norma says never let a boy know you really like him.

ARTHUR: Norma doesn't know everything. (<u>SIT ON COUCH</u>)

JANET: She knows plenty!

ARTHUR: (Stunned) When did you find out? I mean, about me?

JANET: I can tell you the exact second. (<u>RISE</u>) It was this morning. Remember the English test? I saw you trying to decide whether

Figure 15.5

or not to copy from Billy Robinson's paper . . . (<u>XD</u>) Turning sideways, leaning back . . . and all you had to do was look over! But you didn't. (<u>X BELOW TABLE TO HIM</u>) I started to laugh. At least I thought I was—but I was starting to cry. (<u>X BEHIND COUCH TO HIS RIGHT SHOULDER</u>) Now, almost everything you do is funny . . . and at the same time . . . not funny . . . Well—say something!

ARTHUR: I don't know what to say!

JANET: I guess you don't (<u>XDR</u>)

In the next sequence, Janet kept her back to Arthur as he came toward her. When she did turn, they were nose to nose, just in time for the kiss. The director pointed out how well that seemed to work, and the sequence was rerun.

ARTHUR: Don't be mad.

JANET: I'm not mad.

ARTHUR: Yes you are. (<u>RISE</u>)

JANET: I really made a fool of myself, didn't I? (<u>TURNS FULL BACK TO HIM</u>)

ARTHUR: No. God no. If you feel like that, and if—(<u>X TO HER</u>)

JANET: Norma was right. (<u>TURNS—FINDS HERSELF FACE TO FACE WITH HIM</u>)

ARTHUR: No! (<u>KISS</u>) (He kisses her quickly, awkwardly. Then, laughing self-consciously) Our noses got in the way.

JANET: (Softly) Goofy. Like this. (She tilts her head slightly, kisses him on the lips). (<u>KISS</u>)

ARTHUR: (Joking breathlessly) You seem to know a lot about kissing.

JANET: (Also breathless and joking) Enough to keep my nose out of the way. (They stand holding each other at arm's length, each of the verge of hysteria.) Arthur . . . I bet you like me a lot more than you think you do! (<u>PUTS HEAD ON HIS SHOULDER OR CHEST</u>)

ARTHUR: Maybe—I do. I feel—funny. Do you? (<u>BREAKS CLOSE EMBRACE TO PREPARE FOR MOVE</u>)

JANET: Kind of.

The director reminded the actors that the kiss should be reasonably naive; involving little activity with the hands. The actress asked what was meant by naive. The director explained: "Being naive doesn't mean you don't know about it—it just means you haven't done it." In the following sequence, Arthur moved away to the left to ask his question (see Figure 15.6). Janet went to him to reassure him. Then she needed a movement during her explanation. She crossed right. Seeing that, the director suggested that she cross farther, past the couch. That would allow a later move up behind the couch without circling and turning her back on the audience.

ARTHUR: Janet. I want to ask you something personal. Only don't get sore. (<u>X AWAY L, NEAR TABLE</u>)

JANET: I won't.

ARTHUR: Well—a guy's bound to wonder!

JANET: (Pleased) You're jealous! (<u>SMALL X TOWARD HIM</u>)

ARTHUR: You're crazy!

Figure 15.6

JANET: Yes you are! Well, you don't have to worry, Arthur. (<u>COM-PLETE X TO HIM</u>)

ARTHUR: You've never?—Not that I'd blame you, understand, I'm broad-minded.

JANET: I've thought about it for a long time, though. (Flaring) And that's perfectly biologically normal, too! (<u>XDR</u>) Lots of countries' kids our age are already married and raising families.

ARTHUR: Sure they are.

JANET: (Quietly) With me, I always get to a certain point—(<u>X UP BEHIND COUCH</u>) listening to somebody's line and kissing, and petting—then I get scared or disgusted and . . . (A helpless gesture) Do you think I've got a sex blockade or something?

ARTHUR: Of course not! (Then, treading softly) You simply didn't love
those other guys. (<u>X TO EDGE OF COUCH</u>)

The following beat had hardly begun when the director interrupted. When
Janet asked Arthur about his experience with women, he remained still during his
answer. The director said, "Lie—lie—you know it is a lie. Probably go away; that
is an away move." The director wanted the actor to play the subtext.

JANET: Arthur. Have you slept with lots of girls?

ARTHUR: Oh, the—regular amount for a guy of fifteen, I guess. (<u>XL,
ABOVE TABLE, TO L OF CHAIR</u>)

JANET: Is it—was it like you thought it'd be?

ARTHUR: (After a moment's deliberation) More or less. (<u>TURN</u>)

JANET: When it happened, were you in love with those girls?

ARTHUR: Hell, no! (Explaining) A man doesn't have to be. (<u>X TO
RIGHT CHAIR</u>)

JANET: That's not fair! (Suddenly) Art, let's not talk about it any more!
(<u>X TOWARD HIM—THEN DR IN FRONT OF COUCH</u>)

ARTHUR: What's the matter?

JANET: I think if we talk about it, it's going to spoil something.

ARTHUR: Okay, Jan.

Quite a bit of experimentation took place here. For example, Arthur tried
sitting down on "A man doesn't have to," but decided against that as the scene
continued. A number of possibilities appeared for Janet's beat change during her
line, "That's not fair!" At first, the director suggested that she move toward
Arthur, then stop. Director: "No, I don't like that." Actress: "Me too." Another
possibility was tried. Actress: "That doesn't seem right, either." Director: "Okay,
yeah, 'That's not fair' doesn't get you anywhere. Try your first reaction right from
there and, then, take the move on the next line." The final result was a small
movement to the edge of the couch on the first part of the line, followed by a large
movement down right on the second part. It was immediately apparent in the
following sequence that Arthur and Janet had to be close together.

JANET: I wish I was eighteen right this minute and knew all about
everything! (<u>SIT ON COUCH</u>)

ARTHUR: If you were, you wouldn't like me any more. (<u>X TO HER AND SIT</u>)

JANET: I suppose. (Looking at him) That's so hard to believe, though . . . (They stare at each other for a long moment)

ARTHUR: You're so—(Unable to find a fine enough word) Why didn't I know before what you were like? (They kiss tenderly, then nuzzle, forehead to forehead) (<u>KISS</u>)

JANET: (After a moment, softly) Are your eyes closed?

ARTHUR: Yes.

JANET: I love you, Arthur!

ARTHUR: (Crooning) Janet, little Janet, Jan. . . .

JANET: Arthur . . . Teach me how to love you? . . . (He draws back and looks at her, slowly comprehending her meaning)

ARTHUR: Jan, you don't mean—(Janet reaches up, covers his eyes with her hand so that he can't see her face).

JANET: Yes, Arthur. (Then, to Arthur's mortification and surprise, he starts to cry, knuckles fiercely at his eyes) Why, dearest . . . What's the matter?

Actress: "That sounds really stupid, 'My dearest.' How old am I supposed to be? I'm sure I wouldn't use that word." The director agreed, and the word was cut. With her line, "Teach me how to love you," Janet begins a new beat and Arthur is trapped. He must get away, but in the end he has nowhere to go.

JANET: Arthur . . . Teach me how to love you? . . . (He draws back and looks at her, slowly comprehending her meaning)

ARTHUR: Jan, you don't mean—(<u>TURN STRAIGHT FORWARD</u>)

JANET: Yes, Arthur. (Then, to Arthur's mortification and surprise, he starts to cry, knuckles fiercely at his eyes) Why, . . . What's the matter?

ARTHUR: (Sharply) Nothing! Don't look at me (<u>RISE AND MOVE L</u>) (After a moment he draws a long, shuddering breath, wipes his eyes, and tries to smile at her) Now, why'd I do a crazy thing like that!

JANET: Is it my fault? (<u>RISE</u>)

ARTHUR: (Strongly) No!

JANET: Then what?. . . .

ARTHUR: (Whispering, panic-stricken, his face averted) Janet—I don't know about anything!

JANET: What do you mean? (<u>MOVE A BIT TOWARD HIM</u>).

ARTHUR: I made it all up. About other girls.

JANET: (Tenderly, her voice shaking slightly) Why, you—you big phony! (<u>X TO HIM AND EMBRACE</u>) (She breaks into a slight hysterical laugh. After a moment they are laughing together, briefly, softly, with panic underneath. Then Arthur's breath goes out of him in a long sigh. He kisses her, straining his body against hers) (<u>KISS</u>)

"Why, you big phony!" may be the line on the surface, but the subtext is "I love you." Arthur and Janet embrace, and the scene comes to an end.

At this point, the director called for a complete run-through of the scene. Having blocked the action in little pieces, one cannot know what it looks like until it has been run through at the proper pace. The actors had to be reminded of some of their movements, and a bit of polishing took place, but no substantial alterations were made in the blocking during the run-through. The director and cast had arrived at an appropriate staging of their scene from the play *Blue Demin*.

In this chapter, we have illustrated the process of blocking a scene creatively with the actors during rehearsal for the second time. If the scene was to be fully produced, a few more run-throughs would lead to the learning of lines and scripts being put aside. Two or three polishing rehearsals to correct pace, emotional intensity, and timing—particularly for moments such as the dance and the kisses—ought to produce an excellent performance.

Problems of Blocking

On the whole, this textbook encourages the director to think of the process of blocking more as a matter of movement than one of creating still pictures. As we have seen, tableau values have considerable dramatic power; nevertheless,

In the Director's Chair

Laurence Olivier (1907–1989)

Best known as a superb actor, Laurence Olivier followed in the tradition of British actor-managers, often producing, directing, and acting in his stage presentations and motion pictures. Although he played in every type of show, Olivier is most associated with his productions of the classics, particularly the works of Shakespeare. Beginning with his performance as Hamlet at the Old Vic in 1937, Olivier was associated with that company for many years as both actor and director. His film version of Shakespeare's plays—*Henry V* (1944), *Hamlet* (1948), *Richard III* (1956), and *Othello* (1966)—made him famous throughout the world. He was chosen to head the development of the National Theatre of Great Britain, a task he carried out from 1963 to 1973. He was made Lord Olivier by Queen Elizabeth II in 1970, and the largest of the theatres in the National's complex is named for him.

dynamic movement will tend to dominate. We have discussed the typical procedures for blocking movement in both this chapter and Chapter 2. However, at times, the director must deal with blocking that does not follow typical patterns. When staging a character who is insane, for example, the director may find that movement which clashes with the lines of dialogue—rather than being appropriate to those lines of dialogue—will help to establish the character's unstable mental state.

Another example appeared in a student-directed scene of the play *Whose Life Is It Anyway,* a story about a paralyzed man who demands the right to decide whether he will live or die. The protagonist, who has most of the lines in this scene, cannot move; he is fixed in his hospital bed. The only person who can move is the female doctor. Should the director break the rules by having her move during his lines? Because of her role as the doctor, she could not sit down and listen to him as if she were a friend. Standing there in a very prominent position with nothing to do, she looked awkward. Careful study of the action of the scene led to a solution. The protagonist constantly needles her, trying to get to her with his comments, while she attempts to appear very business-like, pretending not to be affected by his lines. Obviously, she needed some business, something to do. She could pretend to be busy, thereby trying to cover up her reaction to his jolting comments. We located many objects in the imaginary room: a table with medical supplies at one end of the room, a window with blinds at the other, machines above his bed that dealt with his life-support system. The doctor used these objects to keep busy during the patient's lines, trying not to be too distracting. The audience watched him needle her and watched her reactions, thus accomplishing the purpose of the scene. Here was a scene that required the director to break with the normal rules of blocking.

Another unusual situation occurred when blocking the second act of the play *Noises Off.* The scene takes place backstage during the performance of the play. The angry actors are fighting with one another in pantomime, interrupting the battles only to rush "onstage" and out of audience view in order to deliver the lines of the play they are performing—the play-within-the-play. Thus, the audience heard dialogue being delivered offstage while watching the action of the actors who spoke no lines, action that had nothing to do with the dialogue. Clearly, the director could not use the dialogue to motivate the choice of movement, following the normal procedures for blocking. Ultimately, the backstage battles had to be staged as a gigantic pantomime, as if there was no dialogue in the script. A director must be prepared to deal with such unusual situations on occasion, situations that require inventive use of the normal procedures and rules for blocking the play.

Style of Movement

This seems a good time to talk about the style of stage movement. We have described the staging of a dramatic work as a process of actors moving toward or away from one another, physically illustrating their current relationship, and these movements are best when they seem normal, natural, realistic, and recognizably lifelike in style. In the most simple sense, stage movement is either realistic or nonrealistic, the latter usually described as "stylized" in some fashion.

Perhaps such nonrealistic movement is better described as abstract, or dance-like, because the term, "style," is not necessarily separated from realism. For example, "theatrealism" is a recognized conventional style of theatre in which the audience and theatrical situation are frankly acknowledged by the performers onstage. The character of Richard III and Woody Allen's Allan Felix address us directly concerning their problems and plans, and the Narrator of *Our Town* organizes the time frame of his world and its afterlife like a master magician. However, these openly theatrical events in the play's structure are not usually the cause of nonrealistic or dance-like movement by the actors. In fact, the contrast between the abstractly arranged and narrated events in *Our Town* and the extremely naturalistic performances of the actors creates much of the play's charm.

Abstract or nonrealistic movement is most common in the musical theatre, for example, when the New York teenage gangs of *West Side Story* dance down the streets and fight a major street battle with stylized, slow-motion dance movements. These events are abstracted and summed up in patterns of movement which universalize their meaning in an artistic manner.

Such nonrealistic, dance-like movement is also to be found in the nonmusical theatre. It was an integral part of the work of avant-garde theatre groups such as The Performance Group and the Open Theatre. And it is commonly used by the major British theatrical troupes. For example, when the National Theatre brought their touring production of *Fuente Ovejuna* to The Lope de Vega Theatre in Seville in the summer of 1992, they had added chanting, song, dance, and stylized movement to Lope's classic tragicomedy. The story concerns an evil local tyrant who oppresses the people of a town called Fuente Ovejuna. After the tyrant has abducted and raped a local maiden, the townspeople rise up and murder him. In staging this scene, The National Theatre abstracted the movement in a powerful, ritualistic fashion. The setting consisted of a rough, long table and some benches—rather like a picnic table—in an empty space, representing a local tavern. The villain is standing on the table, ordering the others around, when he is attacked. The townspeople surround him threateningly but at a distance. They never touch him physically. Each townsperson, one at a time, strikes a powerful blow in the air, as if the villain were in front of him. Alone, up on the table, the villain reacts as if he had received the blow. Finally, he is writhing in pain as the entire group beats him, symbolically, from afar.

How does one describe such blocking and what is its effect? Clearly, the imaginative staging of this scene from *Fuente Ovejuna* is abstract and symbolic—exactly like dance movement. While it has a strange and fascinating beauty, it is also emotionally distanced, losing the intensity and shock contained in a more violent, realistic depiction of a murder. Obviously, The National Theatre Company was enhancing the classic drama in an attempt to make it more universal and meaningful to a contemporary audience.

The point of this discussion is that movement for the stage may be realistic and lifelike or it may be abstracted in some degree toward dance. Many scripts, particularly for musicals, require dance-like movement, and a number of contemporary theatrical companies make imaginative use of this style in their staging. Once a director has determined that some dance movement would be appropriate for a particular production, such movement is not difficult to conceive and achieve in practice.

Summary

In this chapter, we have described the early stages of rehearsal, exemplified the process of blocking, described some situations in which the normal patterns of blocking must be altered, and, finally, talked about different styles of movement. Once the action of the production is blocked, the patterns of movement fixed, then the actors must learn their lines and lay down their scripts before the director can begin the polishing rehearsals.

CHAPTER

POLISHING REHEARSALS

16

We have now discussed two of the three major artistic segments of the director's work: interpreting the script and blocking the movement. In this chapter, we will deal with the third and last section of rehearsals in which the director's artistry is paramount, the polishing rehearsals. Between the blocking rehearsals and the polishing, however, the actors must learn their lines, divest themselves of their scripts, and make their minds available to new areas of concentration beyond the pervasive thought: "What is my next line?" Let us return to our example from *Play It Again, Sam* to show the line-learning process.

Learning the Lines

For *Sam,* the actors spent a whole week getting the script out of their hands and memorizing their lines. All directing ceases at this point. Because the actors concentrate so heavily on the memorization of lines, there is no room for new information from the director. We went over one act each night three times, once sitting in the audience and twice onstage with the blocking. By the third time, the actors found themselves calling for fewer cues from the stage manager, discovering that they knew their lines better than they thought they did at the beginning of the evening. Learning lines is easy for some and difficult for others. If the director can find time to run through the scenes often with script in hand, most actors will be surprised to discover that they have learned the majority of their lines without tedious labor. But the lines must be learned. The actors will not be able to take direction again until they are rid of their scripts and have the lines under control. If line-learning lags behind, the director will lose a day or two in the week that should be devoted to polishing the production.

Polishing

In some ways, polishing is the most difficult of the director's tasks. At this point, the director must attempt to solve persistent problems that he or she has failed to bring under control during the first three weeks of rehearsal. If one performer is not doing well, is not up to the level of the other cast members, the director must find some method or device to pull that actor up. Unusual problems arise, and the director may need to be inventive in trying to solve a particular problem. The director may feel less secure, as well. The director has more control of the entire situation during the blocking, but the further one gets into rehearsal, the less control the director has, and the more the burden falls on the actors. Finally, when performance time arrives, the burden has shifted entirely to the actors, and the director has no control whatsoever.

In polishing, there are no set rules; a problem arises and the director must invent a way to attack it. For example, an actress in *Play It Again Sam* was delivering her lines in an unnatural manner, entirely different from normal conversation. She tended to put equal emphasis on every word in a sentence instead of emphasizing the important words and throwing the others away. At times, actors sound like this when reading scripts, but as they become more familiar with the script, this quality naturally disappears. In this case, the reading had remained mechanical into the polishing rehearsals. Giving the performer a line reading, saying the line properly so that she can imitate it, should be the last desperate resort, because imitated line readings usually make actors sound like robots. Finally, the director suggested to the actress that she was saying the words without thinking about their meaning. She reentered as the character and did the scene in an entirely different fashion, much more believably. Luckily, the director had hit upon the proper key.

Another actress in *Sam* played a very small role as one of the protagonist's date memories. As they are sitting together on the couch, she tells him that she has had an amazingly prolific sex life; yet, when he makes a pass at her, she jumps up and says indignantly, "What kind of a girl do you take me for!" Clearly, her scene is a single joke with a punch line. One night, the director suggested that she make her entrance more like Marilyn Monroe. She came sashaying in, suddenly adding a whole new dimension to her character.

The actress had previously delivered her indignant punch line while jumping up from the couch. It was not funny. The director suggested that she jump up, take a moment to regain her composure, and then deliver the punch line. One of the keys to comic timing is taking a pause just before the punch line. In this case, it worked like a charm. Polishing is a tricky business. Sometimes the director can find the right key, but often a problem will remain unsolved.

Setting the Emotional Key

Polishing involves certain standard goals as well as finding solutions for unique, individual problems. The director always works on the **emotional key,** pace, tempo, and timing of the production during the polishing period. The idea of "key" in the phrase *emotional key* is parallel to the concept of musical pitch: The greater the emotional tension of a scene, the higher the key; whereas a calm scene is described as low key. Any scene played at a higher emotional key than the story seems to justify will appear to be a case of overacting. Just how angry are the characters at any particular moment? The director and actors are seeking the appropriate level of intensity, and that decision is made on the basis of instinct— the level of emotion that seems or feels right. Intensity can be achieved by yelling, but the same amount of intensity can be achieved quietly, even by a whisper. The latter method has great power because the character seems to be holding in the tension, about to explode at any moment.

This author once worked with a very solid, articulate actress who could not do emotional scenes that required the character to be nearly in tears. And the director was unable to help the actress solve this problem in the polishing rehearsals. Perhaps a sheer mechanical approach might have helped. What happens to people when their emotional key is high? Their muscles, throat, and voices become tense and tight. Perhaps if the actress had tensed her body muscles, she could have discovered the proper feeling and a method to reproduce it. Usually, the director can count on his or her actors to reproduce believable emotions because most people are able to do that with ease. Many famous actresses can cry on cue. However, as a young actor, this author could not laugh aloud onstage when laughter was called for in the role. Many hours were spent learning to laugh aloud on cue, something that can be done with little effort by most actors.

The director should encourage the actors to overplay or overdo such devices as vocal volume and dialects early in the rehearsal period. The actors will have little trouble making these more subtle in later rehearsals, but to make things bigger in later rehearsals often proves very difficult. After spending the entire five weeks of rehearsal in a small classroom on a production of Shaw's *Arms and the Man,* the cast was unable to achieve strong enough vocal volume for the large theatre space in which they performed. Even with great encouragement, they could not always overcome the habit of speaking at a volume appropriate for that classroom rehearsal space. For the performer, actions, volume, and emotional key always seem greater than they are in reality. An actor will be asked to talk louder when, in his own head, he feels as if he is already shouting. Thus, actors have difficulty making their efforts bigger without feeling absurdly broad. The best the director can do is reassure them that their bigger efforts seem natural and appropriate.

In one particular way, projection and emotional key are alike; actors cannot develop or maintain an emotional key unless their partner plays to them in that same key, and actors cannot maintain a certain level of projection unless their partner plays to them at that same level. When the partner comes in at a lower key, both actors will end up working at the lowest common denominator. One character speaking much more loudly than the other in a conversation will seem unnatural, unless one of the characters is supposed to be deaf. If an actor comes onstage with a considerably lower volume level than the others, sooner or later everyone onstage will come down to the lower volume. When the director encourages actors to begin each scene with strong projection, that level will become self-maintaining. The actors will not have to worry about projection for the remainder of the scene. Emotional intensity usually grows, step by step, between two performers. Such emotional key is impossible to maintain for long if the other actor is undercutting it with a lower key. And high-key emotion usually goes hand-in-hand with a quickened pace. If the partner takes long pauses or fails to **pick up the cues,** the actor will have difficulty maintaining a high level of intensity. When an emotional scene is not working, the director may find that one of the actors is undercutting the emotion. That actor must play into and feed the other actor's emotional intensity. If the lines are not well learned, lack of cue pick-up can be a common problem, deflating the emotional key of the scene.

In the Director's Chair

Elia Kazan (b. 1909)

The work of Elia Kazan was founded in his development as a member of the Group Theatre company in the 1930s, both as an actor and as a director, although he did not win acclaim as a director until the year after the Group Theatre disbanded and he staged *The Skin of Our Teeth*, for which he won the New York Drama Critics Award in 1942. The Group Theatre was home to the dramatic theories of Stanislavsky (see page 123), particularly his system of "method" acting. Method acting is a style based in deep psychological realism, involving a high level of actor creativity and improvisation. Kazan applied these ideas to the works of the finest playwrights of the era—Arthur Miller (*Death of a Salesman*, 1949), Tennessee Williams (*A Streetcar Named Desire*, 1948, *Cat on a Hot Tin Roof*, 1955, *Sweet Bird of Youth*, 1959), Robert Anderson (*Tea and Sympathy*, 1953), and William Inge (*Dark at the Top of the Stairs*, 1957) Kazan was equally at home directing films such as *Gentleman's Agreement* (1947), the film version of *Streetcar* (1951), and *On the Waterfront* (1954), for which he won his second Academy Award. Kazan could not understand why any director would block a play with a copy of the script in hand because what was being staged from moment to moment was the subtext, the underlying meaning, character goals and desires, rather than simple words that one could see on the pages of the script.

Setting the Tempo

The tempo of a play is created as a type of illusion. A play that lasts two hours can seem slow and boring, or amazingly quick and interesting. Tempo relates to that feeling of pace rather than to the actual time consumed by a play or movie or any other event. The director can increase the tempo of the production in four ways, only the first of which shortens the actual time consumed by the play: (1) have the actors pick up their cues, (2) have the actors increase their volume and projection, (3) create more movement in the blocking, and (4) raise the emotional key of the play to a higher level.

Picking up cues means that the actors leave no space between their lines; one says a line and the other actor comes in immediately with the following line. If all of the actors are leaving a tiny space between their cue and their own line throughout the play, the production could be as much as half-an-hour longer than it should be. Getting the actors to tighten up their cue pick-up is an absolute necessity during the polishing rehearsals. Of course, the actor should continue to take **dramatic pauses,** pauses which are consciously chosen to fulfill some logical purpose. But dramatic pauses are meaningless when there are pauses everywhere for no special reason. Often, the best place for a dramatic pause is within an actor's speech rather than between the lines of two actors. Dramatic pauses do not hurt the pace; dead space that is of no significance can be extremely detrimental.

Raising the level of projection—making it easier for the audience to hear the show—will make the tempo seem quicker. This author can give no explanation for this illusion, but experience proves it to be true. The addition of more movement to the blocking will also increase the tempo. Chase scenes and fights always seem to go faster because of all the intense movement; therefore, more movement onstage creates the illusion of a quicker tempo.

Finally, raising the emotional key of the production will enhance the illusion that the play is moving along more rapidly. Of course, individual scenes of high emotion always seem to have a quick tempo, but here we are talking about raising the general emotional key of the whole production. For example, in most musicals the performers are bursting with energy onstage, almost as if they had been injected with some drug. At times, this hyped-up energy seems a bit fake, but it is also joyous, happy, and quick in tempo. Directors commonly ask for more energy from their actors, clearly attempting to raise the general emotional key of the show. This situation is discussed in a recent book by Edward Dmytryk and his wife, Jean Porter, called *On Screen Acting* (1984, pp. 109–10). Dmytryk dislikes the word "energy" because he feels it pushes the performers toward overacting and looks terrible on the screen. He prefers the word "vitality." Even in calm and quiet scenes, great actors like Jimmy Stewart always seem to have a strong, underlying intensity which Dmytryk calls vitality. The actors seem alive and exciting, even in the calmest moments, and that is what makes them interesting. So, just before the cameras rolled, the last thing Dmytryk would say to his actors was, "Vitality—Vitality!" When a director calls for more energy, he is trying to make the production more exciting—raising the underlying emotional key, and, as a result, increasing the tempo. For Dmytryk, vitality energizes the acting without sending it beyond the bounds of believability.

Increasing the tempo is a standard goal of directing during polishing rehearsals. Throughout the play, the director wants the actors to pick up the cues, increase the projection, and raise the emotional key.

Playing Comedy

Experts have always said that the key to comedy is to play it seriously. Rather than trying to be funny, the actors should play their characters believably and the humor will take care of itself. When an audience fails to laugh, actors often start pushing for those laughs, overplaying the funny lines and action. This is a mistake. If the play does not seem to be as funny on one night as it did on another, the answer is to play it more seriously and honestly. Play the funny scenes for believability—not for humor—and, chances are, it suddenly will become funny. As mentioned earlier in the book, the actor's job is to be aware of the comedy and to play it well, at the same time, remaining a believable human being. For *Play It Again, Sam,* polishing rehearsals were a time for working to achieve this balance of precision in the comic timing and believability in the characterization.

Polishing Techniques

A number of general devices are available which the director can use during the polishing period. Three of those techniques will be described here—two involving the subtext, and the third, physical contact among the actors, as well as a brief comment concerning improvisation. The subtext is what the character is thinking; having the actor speak those thoughts aloud is commonly called **subtexting.** Using one of the polishing rehearsals, the director asks the actors to speak their subtext aloud. This is a crazy rehearsal because everyone is talking at the same time. However, subtexts are done softly, so that the actual lines in the script will stand out and the actors can hear their cues. At first, the director will have to make some effort to get the actors to take all of this silly-sounding subtexting seriously. However, subtexting forces the actors to discover if they really know what their character is thinking; it teaches the actors how to think like the character and avoid such actor thoughts as, "What is my next line? I'll just freeze here and wait for my cue. Oh, there it is." This type of mental activity causes the actors to be in character only when saying their own lines. Subtexting forces the actors to listen and react to the other characters onstage, just as their character would in real life. This type of polishing rehearsal will result in a series of revelations for the actors;

lines that they have been delivering in a certain way every night for weeks will suddenly change, because thinking and reacting to what the other person just said causes them to respond differently. A subtexting rehearsal will enhance the level of believability of the entire play in just one evening.

Subtexting is a wonderfully successful technique, particularly for a serious play. For example, a subtexting rehearsal for a production of Eugene O'Neill's *Long Day's Journey into Night* revolutionized the performances of the entire cast. The performance of the young man playing Edmund became so alive that the actor continued to subtext under his breath all of the time, driving the other actors crazy. Even in performance, he was mumbling his thoughts while they were trying to say their lines. And he was right to do this, because subtexting made the performance real for him. Actors should subtext at every performance, but they should do it silently, of course, rather than aloud. The actors can find out if they know what the character is thinking by subtexting. In many cases, the actors will discover that they do not know, and that discovery alone will make the rehearsal worthwhile. Subtexting will put the actor completely in the play—truly reacting to the other characters and listening to what they say.

This author was introduced to another method of subtexting at a midwestern theatre conference by a team from the University of Nebraska. One director had staged a scene from *Bus Stop,* by William Inge, rehearsing the scene until the actors had learned their lines and were ready for polishing. At the workshop, a second director, who had not participated in the scene up to this point, took over. Rather than have everyone subtext simultaneously, this director asked the actors to subtext their reaction aloud before saying their next line. For example, an actress might say, "Darling, I love you." Her coactor would respond with a subtext of his thoughts, "She loves me? But I can't stand her. How on earth will I get out of this situation tactfully?" Then, after the subtext, the actor would deliver his real line, perhaps something like, "That's nice." She would respond with her own subtexting before she said her line from the script, and so on throughout the scene. In the workshop, the actors ran through the scene before the subtexting, a performance that was smooth and well-done. But when they ran through the scene again, after the subtexting, it was considerably altered and obviously improved. Lines were being delivered in different ways and subtle, new dramatic pauses had appeared. Again, the actors have revelations which bring them closer to the character's reality, and it changes the way they treat crucial moments in the performance.

A third device that the director can use as a polishing technique—involving physical contact of the actors—is called a **touching rehearsal.** Unlike subtexting, this type of rehearsal requires the actors to alter the blocking for one session. Unless the characters are a long distance apart, when one character speaks to another, the speaker should walk up to the listener and touch that person in an appropriate manner. Actors break out of the blocking in order to touch the person to whom they are speaking, and they must decide what kind of touch is appropriate, both to the particular dialogue and to the relationship between the two characters.

As with subtexting, a touching rehearsal will lead to major discoveries. Such rehearsals always lead to some alteration in the blocking in order to incorporate some of the actual physical contact. An actor will feel that he or she has to keep that new touch because everything changed the moment it happened, and the new reactions and line delivery were so much better, so much more "right." Discovering how one would touch another person defines the interpersonal relationship between them. Touching will also help actors achieve proper physical contact for their characters. As characters they may be husband and wife, but as actors they are strangers; thus, the actors avoid physical contact that would be perfectly natural for the characters.

Another technique that deserves discussion is **improvisation.** Many directors use improvisation during the course of rehearsals to enhance the actors' understanding of their characters. Playwrights such as Edward Albee speak of this kind of understanding when they say that they come to know their characters so well, that once they put those characters into a particular situation, the characters' reactions seem to develop naturally and automatically, with little conscious interference on the part of the writer.

The type of creative blocking advocated in this textbook should not be confused with improvisation; true improvisation requires the actors to invent both the movement and the dialogue in an impromptu manner. During rehearsals of a particular show, the director might ask the actors to play out a situation in their characters' lives that does not exist in the script. Such improvisation will help the actors to focus their understanding of their character and their character's interpersonal relationships. This technique might prove useful early in the blocking rehearsals as well as in the polishing. However, elaborate use of improvisation may require a longer rehearsal period for the production.

Typical polishing rehearsals last one week. What the director does in those rehearsals depends upon the type of play, how well the lines are learned, how well the characterizations are coming along, and so on. If the production is going well at this point, subtexting and touching rehearsals may be extremely useful techniques. However, work on the tempo, by means of cue pick-up, projection, and emotional key, is always done at this time.

Finally, the production will move to a series of run-throughs, technical, and dress rehearsals. Scenery and costumes are added at technical rehearsal—items to which the actors will have some difficulty adjusting. The director's attention will be distracted by the addition of all of the technology and sound and light cues, as well. Because dress rehearsals are supposed to be exactly like the performance, the director no longer interrupts the performance to make suggestions or corrections. Sitting in the audience, the director makes notes about the problems. After the rehearsal, the director and the actors sit together and discuss the problems in the director's notes and any issues that the actors might raise.

Summary

In this chapter, we have discussed the later part of the rehearsal process, from line-learning through performance. Our particular interest was in the last of the three major sections in which the director's artistry is paramount—the polishing rehearsals. Among the topics covered was the polishing of emotional key and tempo, as well as a group of rehearsal techniques that can enhance the realism and believability of the performances. Polishing is a difficult and creative time for the director, a time when a good show can become a great show—a truly polished work of art.

CHAPTER 17

PREPARING FOR PERFORMANCE

In this chapter, we will concentrate on the close of the rehearsal period, particularly on the special problems of technical rehearsal, dress rehearsals, and performance.

Technical Rehearsal

Once the actors have put their lines and blocking to memory, the director can polish the details of the production. If the show is on schedule, the actors should be ready for performance before the technical rehearsal takes place. During the rehearsal period, actors have been working without proper costumes, without the actual set, and without such technical details as lighting and sound. With the outline of the set taped on the stage floor and using stand-in furniture, the director and actors have pictured these details in their minds, imaginatively working with them for weeks. All of these details—costumes, lighting, sound cues, and the like—are added at the technical rehearsal, allowing the actors a short series of dress rehearsals to get used to the new realities before the performance. The director and designer should have a private technical rehearsal at which they work out as many of the lighting and sound cues as possible without the presence of the actors. The major technical rehearsal will be much more efficient when it is not held up by discussions between the director and designer which could easily have taken place at an earlier time.

Even at this late date, the director must be prepared to ask for changes in any of the new additions which seem out of step with her or his interpretation of the show. For example, technical rehearsal for a production of Shakespeare's *Richard II* went well except for the costume of the leading lady, playing Richard's wife. It was frumpy and unflattering; it looked as if it had come out of the local dumpster. Telling the costumer—who had worked on this costume for weeks—that the costume must be changed was not an easy task; nevertheless, it had to be done.

For our production of *Play It Again, Sam,* the protagonist's friend—who is supposed to be a cool, good-looking businessman—appeared at technical rehearsal wearing a suit that was too small for him, with "high-water" trousers. And, in the third act, the actor appeared wearing what seemed to be the same clothes he had worn at rehearsal—jeans, sneakers, and an old sweat shirt. He had just flown in from a business meeting in Cincinnati, arriving directly from the airport with luggage in hand. Whereas the costumer thought the character might be wearing casual clothes, the director's interpretation required a stylish business suit. This problem could have been avoided by means of better consultation between the costumer and the director. Still, the director must be prepared to request changes at technical rehearsal when necessary.

Dress Rehearsals

Technical rehearsal is for the technical crew, not for the actors. Running the light cues, sound cues, and set changes, the designer will back up and repeat these cues again and again until the crew gets them right. Then, on three or four dress rehearsal nights, the play will be done "in full dress," allowing both the actors and the technical crew to practice their respective jobs exactly as they will be done in a performance. Because the actors must play the entire performance without interruptions, the director makes notes during the dress rehearsal, discussing the problems with the cast at the end of the run-through.

Early dress rehearsals present the director with a new problem. Whereas the actors—who have been in rehearsal for weeks—are performing rather well, the technicians have had only one or two rehearsals. Because the directors' attention is given to the aspects of the show which are in the most trouble, they will find themselves concentrating on disastrous technical cues at this point. Therefore, directors will have to make a conscious effort not to be dominated by the technical problems to the extent that they are no longer helping and directing the actors.

Another problem for directors at this time is that they no longer may be able to discern if the projection and articulation of the actors will be adequate for the audience. The directors are now so familiar with the lines that they will understand the actors easily. The question is, would someone hearing the play for the first time find the actors loud and clear enough? Many directors bring a friend to a dress rehearsal to get some outside feedback about such matters. The director may discover that one of the actors is not easily understood, either because the words are slurred or because they are delivered too softly. The director, who may not have been aware of this problem, can usually correct this defect with a simple suggestion to the actor. Because the designer has begun to attend the rehearsals regularly, he or she will be able to offer similar feedback. The wise director will pay careful attention to suggestions concerning such general matters as tempo and projection.

When *Play It Again, Sam* reached dress rehearsals, certain particular problems caused concern for the director. For example, how well would the actors play the timing and the comedy? Audience response is the major missing link that is needed for polishing a play like *Sam*. When the audience laughs, that laugh is just like a new line of dialogue in the play. The actors must pause to allow the audience their line of dialogue and then pick up their cue with the next line from the written script. Because the actors cannot know where the lines from the audience will come in, they must be ready to take new pauses at a moment's notice. If the actors go right on, running over the laugh with their lines, the audience will think they have missed some of the play. Because they do not want to miss anything, the audience will stop laughing; bit by bit, the laughter will diminish until only the biggest jokes draw a response. Therefore, the actor's job is to make it clear to the audience that they will not miss anything, that the play will stop while they laugh. After all, the actor certainly does not want to discourage the audience from laughing. Some directors attempt to polish this aspect of their production by inviting a small audience to one or two of the dress rehearsals. Actually, one great laugher—a person who laughs often and heartily—is worth a whole audience. Either way, helping the actors to discover where the laughs are likely to appear will improve both their confidence and their performance.

Flaws in the Production

The director also worries about the audience reaction to some of the actors' performances. Often, a director is very proud of a performer because he or she knows how hard that actor has worked, how much that actor has gained during the course of rehearsals. However, the audience judges only the finished product. If a young actor playing an elderly character does not create the total illusion of age, he or she might receive some criticism. For example, in *Sam,* the young man who played Humphrey Bogart was doing a fine job; yet he neither looked nor sounded like Bogart. It was a long stretch for this actor to create an illusion of Bogart. Would the audience find him acceptable? No one can predict this response. In a production of *Black Comedy* some years back, the old British Colonel—the most "British" character of all—was being played by a man with a blatant Texas accent. The result was an impure, corny-sounding mixture that the director was sure would receive some criticism. No one ever mentioned it. The actor played a very funny character, and the audience loved him. Not a single negative comment was heard about his truly odd accent, either from members of the audience or from two newspaper reviews. Nevertheless, the director worries about the imperfections in the production. With a little luck, the audience might never notice them.

Finally, the technical problems in the dress rehearsals may keep the director on edge. In our production of *Play It Again, Sam*, all of the dream scenes had background music and a multitude of light cues, all of which were driving the crew in the light booth crazy. Halfway through one dress rehearsal, a sound tape broke. By the time the crew member had it fixed, he was four or five cues behind and never again played the right music for any scene in the show. At other times, as we cut to a dream scene, there would be a major

In the Director's Chair

Peter Brook (b. 1925)

As codirector of the Royal Shakespeare
Company after 1962, Brook became world
famous for his daring productions. Influenced
by the theories of Antonin Artaud and the
innovative work of experimental theatres such
as the Polish Laboratory Theatre and the Living
Theatre, Brook won worldwide acclaim with his
production of *Marat/Sade* by Peter Weiss in
1964. Brook has continued his daring work
with both classical and contemporary plays.
Since 1971, he has worked in France, where he
founded the International Centre of Theatre
Research.

pause while the actor waited for the lights to change and the music to come
in before making his entrance. Everyone in the audience will notice a missed
technical cue. Such an error will hurt the performance because it pulls the
audience out of their emotional involvement with the story. Therefore, technical cues must be absolutely perfect. At this point, the director began to
question his decision to add so much music to the production; however, by
opening night, the crew had miraculously managed to bring this multitude of
technical cues under control.

Final Dress Rehearsal and Performance

When the rehearsal period is ended, what does the director do at the last dress
rehearsal and the first performance? At this point, the director's major goal is
to let the actors know how fine they are, to make them feel good about what

they are doing, to help them to go onstage with confidence and excitement. At the final dress rehearsal of a production of *The Night Thoreau Spent in Jail,* the director said that he would discuss notes in the dressing room the following evening. But when he arrived the next night, he decided not to give any notes. This was the correct decision. Rehearsals are finished, and it is too late to make any major revisions in the production. Instead, this director showed up with bottles of nonalcoholic champagne and a set of wine glasses. Together, as a cast, they toasted one another, celebrating themselves and their production. What a wonderful mood to create for the opening night of a show.

Very few directorial changes are allowed once the show has gone to performance. Acceptable alterations are always of a general nature. The director can make suggestions about projection, energy, and emotional key during the run of the show, without causing havoc in the details that have been carefully rehearsed for weeks. If an actor cannot be heard by the audience, he can easily adjust his volume, but alterations in such areas as blocking or line readings may well be disastrous. Such corrections should have been made during polishing so that they will be habitual by the time of the performance.

On the night of any play which this author has directed, he spends time in the dressing rooms trying to keep the actors from becoming nervous— chatting about other things, telling jokes, kidding one another—anything to get them to lighten up. The actors don't realize that, having been through five weeks of rehearsal, they have done this play so often that they could not fail to do it well on opening night. Doing it right has become a habit by this time. If they are well-rehearsed, the likelihood of something going wrong is extremely remote. New tensions, a new audience may make them a bit edgy, but they could perform these roles in their sleep without making a mistake. Why shouldn't they be confident about it? Therefore, the director wants to maintain an atmosphere that allows the actors to feel loose, confident, and creative.

During the performance, the director's place is probably in the audience. The one place the director should not be is backstage. The production now belongs to the stage manager and the actors. Just as a parent ultimately must allow the children to leave the nest and face the world on their own, the director must let go of the show.

What point of comparison does a director use to judge the production of a show such as *Play It Again, Sam*? When we perform Shakespeare, we cannot compare our production to one done by Laurence Olivier, for example. We cannot hope to reach that level of style and quality. But for a play like *Sam,* we should be able to do it as well as any professional company would do, even as well as the Broadway production itself. With the possible exception of the Bogart look-alike, we have the level of talent in our young actors to produce most contemporary comedies with professional quality. That quality is what directors should expect of themselves and of their cast.

Special Problems

Second Nights

According to tradition, directors should warn their cast about a potential problem commonly called "second night let-down." Opening night is filled with electricity, excitement, and flowing adrenaline. After a successful opening, actors may breathe a sigh of relief, relax a little too much, and have a poor second performance, filled with easily avoided errors. This author has never seen this happen. On the contrary, the second performance is usually better than the opening night, because all of that early tension has been relieved by the successful opening which has given the actors self-confidence. However, the second-night audience may present a new problem. Opening night audiences tend to be filled with people who love the theatre, people who laugh and applaud, who are obviously having a good time. In contrast, the audience on the second night is often much more reserved, and their lack of reaction causes the actors to assume that this performance is not going well. The director should remind the actors that audiences differ and their reactions will vary. The second-night response is seldom as overt as that of an opening night. The actors must not start playing the show for laughs or changing the way they have done the show as a reaction to this lack of response from the audience. In all likelihood, this audience is enjoying the play just as much as the previous audience; they simply show their appreciation in a different manner.

Critics

Both director and actors want to have their production reviewed. It is better to have a bad review than to have no review at all. At the same time, the director may be faced with a problem when a reviewer praises some of the actors and criticizes others. Performers want to hear praise—even minor negative reactions may hurt their feelings—and critics often overstate their case in a cruel manner, describing a slightly weaker performance as if it was a total disaster. The director wants to protect the actors from anything that might interfere with the performance. Therefore, the director may have to meet with the actors to reassure them and rebuild confidence in their performance.

The director has to deal with negative reviews in a sensible fashion. Some criticism may seem justified whereas other reactions will seem to be totally absurd. Have confidence: If the comment does not make sense to the director, the reviewer is probably wrong. The director should evaluate the criticism, accepting that which makes sense and ignoring that which does not. A recent review of one of our musicals picked at some things, praised others, and was generally positive about the show. Overall, the review was accurate, clearly recognizing the weaker performances in the production. Nevertheless, the designer was incensed: "How can they send an incompetent like that to review a show!" Not an unexpected reaction; an artist who has spent months creating a work of art is not in the mood to hear criticism. The director, however, should be more level-headed, ready to control the damage, relieve the stress, and encourage the actors to give their best performance.

Curtain Calls

When the director is busy with rehearsals of the play, the last thing on his or her mind is the curtain call. The director will be reminded of this at the time of the technical rehearsal because there will be a lighting cue for a curtain call. Some theatre people do not believe in curtain calls—especially for serious shows— because they break the mood created by the ending of the play. However, the audience expects a curtain call. They want to applaud the actors; it is a tradition. A missing curtain call will defeat their expectations and leave them feeling uncomfortable. Often, the actors take the call in character, holding on to the final mood of the show. Even then, characters who have been killed must rise from the dead in order to take a bow. After all, the curtain call is not for the characters in the story; the audience applauds the actors for their performance. The audience expects the actors to step out of character, and the change of mood will not spoil their enjoyment of the play.

In staging the curtain call, the director usually tries to bring the actors in from a variety of entrances, in an order that allows those with leading roles to appear last. If the cast is large, the actors take bows in groups, with individual calls reserved for the leads. The one great sin of the curtain call is that it lasts so long that the audience becomes tired of clapping. Their arms and hands begin to ache, and the curtain call begins to spoil their evening of entertainment. Some professional groups milk the curtain call unmercifully—a painful experience—both literally and figuratively. The curtain call should be as brief as possible. It is much better to leave the audience wanting more, applauding vigorously through the blackout as the actors fade into the darkness.

Summary

In this chapter, we have discussed the practical problems of technical rehearsal, dress rehearsal, and performances. The director should realize that a large portion of his or her work goes beyond artistry, involving solid planning, organizational ability, and good sense. Choosing the play, discovering the practical problems presented by the script, and organizing the auditions require many hours of hard work from the director.

The director should take on the job of producing a play with confidence, trusting in the actors' creativity and in his or her own artistic ability. Whereas solid organization and planning will assure the director of a competent production, artistic creativity and instinct are the keys to a great production. Intuition is as important as intellect for the theatre director. Directors must approach this job in a manner that will provide them with the proper atmosphere for their own creativity.

PART

Further
Considerations

In the final section of this textbook, we shall attempt to expand our horizons beyond the typical theatrical play and the proscenium theatre situation. In the previous chapters, we have dealt with directors' problems which occur when staging a production for an audience that views the work from one particular and consistent direction. The different problems that arise when the audience surrounds the actors or watches them from three varied viewpoints will be discussed in Chapter 18.

Up to this point in the text, we have dealt with the nonmusical play, represented by such works as *Play It Again, Sam* and *Uncle Vanya*. In Chapter 19, we will look at the different problems faced by the director of a musical.

If the musical takes the director beyond theatre arts into the arts of music and dance, then motion pictures take the theatrical director into an entirely new art form, one with similarities to the theatre but with its own unique artistic tools and aesthetic. This author has had very little experience as a director of motion pictures; however, it is enough to be able to shed light on the basic tools of film directing and the ways in which movies present new and different problems for the director of theatrical productions. Thus, we shall venture into the art of the cinema in Chapter 20.

Each of these new areas of interest—arena staging, musical theatre, and motion pictures—present fresh challenges to the director. Nevertheless, many successful professional directors work easily and well in all three different directorial situations, transferring without difficulty from one to the other.

CHAPTER 18

CENTRAL STAGING AND THRUST STAGING

In this chapter, we will discuss **central staging** (also called staging-in-the-round or **arena staging**), a situation in which the audience views the production from all four sides rather than from a single side as in the traditional proscenium theatre. This new relationship between the actors and the audience will present practical problems in both the blocking of the action and the technical aspects of the production.

Blocking for Central Staging

Even though the audience views the action from all sides, the basic principle of blocking remains in force: Actors move toward or away from one another, creating movements which illustrate the emotional relationship between the characters. Now, however, all of the principles of movement that relate to the audience viewpoint and make it easier for the audience to see the actors' faces no longer have any meaning. Gesturing with the upstage hand, crossing downstage of another actor, standing with the body one-quarter turn toward the audience, and other rules of this type are meaningless when the audience surrounds the actors, and terms like upstage and downstage no longer exist. Obviously, there can be no rule about not turning one's back on the audience when almost every position on stage has the actor facing one section of the audience and turning his or her back on another section. In the proscenium theatre, the director tries to control the attention of the audience and make it easy for them to see all of the action. The director continues to control the focus of attention when staging in the round; however, making it easier for the audience to see the action is a whole new ball game.

No stage position taken by the actor looks good from all sides; every position creates an awkward situation from the point of view of some audience members. Therefore, directors must not allow their actors to stand in one particular position longer than is absolutely necessary. In central staging, the actors must change positions more often than in proscenium staging, moving and turning around as much as possible. The key to staging-in-the-round is that much more movement is required. Actors trained in the techniques of the proscenium theatre must now learn to sense the audience all around them, to give themselves as often as possible to all of the different sections of the audience.

Few places on the central stage are neutral locations where a character who has no lines can stand and observe the other characters who have both the lines and the movement. Actors who have no excuse for movement usually have two choices: They can stand in front of an aisle so they are not blocking audience view, or they can seat themselves on the furnishings of the set. The performer who is the focus of attention should be standing up so that he or she can move often, and the audience will be able to see that actor over the heads of the characters who are seated. Actors soon learn instinctively to find the aisles because they provide a good place to stand.

An alternative audience arrangement to staging-in-the-round is called **end staging,** in which the audience is located on three sides of the stage area, with the fourth side occupied by scenery. End staging has many advantages; one wall of scenery can provide doors or an archway for entrances and exits, even a stairway and balcony could be located there. When the actors are close to that end of the stage, they can be blocked as if they were on a proscenium stage. And, of course, that end of the stage provides a place where actors can stand without interfering with the view of some of the audience.

A recent experience with a production of *The Rainmaker* provided an example of end staging. The Curry farmhouse consisted of a sofa in front of the fourth wall, which contained an exit to the remainder of the house. In the center of the stage was a circular dining table and chairs. An aisle through the audience opposite the fourth wall served as the front entrance to the home. The small secondary sets were also against the fourth wall, on either side of the sofa. The Sheriff's office contained a desk and two chairs; the tack room, bales of hay and a sawhorse. When playing on or behind the sofa, the actors could operate as if they were on a proscenium stage; however, once they were out in the room, near the table or front door, they had to move in the manner of central staging. The only neutral areas where an actor could stand for any length of time were near the sofa or in the front doorway. As usual, the key to the blocking was to create a profusion of movement.

Scenery and Lighting

Because staging-in-the-round does not allow for scenic walls which would block the view of the audience, the director avoids much of the elaborate and expensive scenery required by a proscenium staging. A contemporary play—using borrowed furniture and the actors' own wardrobes for costumes—can be an amazingly low-budget production when done in the round. However, the requirements for lighting a central stage are more elaborate. The production must be well lit for members of the audience who are looking at it from every side; therefore, at least six or eight separate instrument positions will be required. And the angle of the lighting must be high enough to avoid having the light fall on the spectators in the front row, directly across from the instruments. Audience members may become uncomfortable being lighted well enough to feel as if they are onstage.

In earlier days, critics thought that the types of plays suitable for central staging were severely limited. For example, it was thought that because the playing space is small, large-cast shows and plays with multiple sets should be avoided. But the vast *Inherit the Wind* has been successfully staged on a tiny arena stage, as well as shows with multiple sets such as *Summer and Smoke*. This author has participated in end staging productions of *Oedipus Rex* and *As You Like It,* on stages no more than fifteen by twenty feet. Obviously, directors and designers of theatre-in-the-round are limited only by their own imaginations.

The Audience

In central staging, the relationship between actors and audience is very intimate. No audience member is more than five or six rows away from the actors and is usually closer. The production of *The Rainmaker* had only three rows of seats. The acting in such a performance must be extremely natural and believable, much like the style of acting required by motion pictures. Everything must be more subtle: makeup, costumes, projection, gestures, and the like.

Some people worry that shows in central staging might be too intense for the audience. The proximity of performers to audience might diminish aesthetic distance and frighten people. As stated earlier, aesthetic distance has little to do with the actual physical distance between the actors and audience, unless the actors are shouting in their faces or sitting in their laps—literally making physical contact with them. Aesthetic distance is a psychological attitude that the audience can maintain as long as they feel safe and anonymous—as long as the actors do not threaten them, or in the case of realistic plays, look them directly in the eyes.

Thrust Staging

Three types of staging with audience and actors arranged in different relationships are commonly used in the contemporary theatre. We have discussed proscenium theatres and theatres-in-the-round; the third type of theatre is a **thrust stage,** so called because the stage seems to thrust out into the audience. The audience is seated around the stage in a semicircle, usually rising up from the stage in a manner resembling the seating at a football stadium around one of the goalposts. A thrust stage is rather like an elaborate version of end staging in a very large auditorium.

Thrust stages were originally developed for companies that specialized in the plays of Shakespeare. The thrust stage supposedly resembled the staging arrangement of the original Elizabethan theatres of Shakespeare's own time. Actually, a contemporary thrust stage has a greater affinity with the theatres of the Greeks in ancient Athens. Nevertheless, the thrust is used for every kind of production, including modern realism. As with end staging, the blocking must be a combination of that which is appropriate to the proscenium theatre when the actors are upstage and that which is appropriate to central staging when the actors are downstage, nearly surrounded by the audience. Exciting theatre can be produced with any audience/actor relationship, as long as the

In the Director's Chair

Mike Nichols (b. 1931)

After an early career as a founding member of a successful comic improvisational group in Chicago and national success as a member of a stand-up comedy duo with his first wife, Elaine May, Nichols moved on to become a successful director. He staged most of the early plays of Neil Simon, beginning with *Barefoot in the Park* (1963), and he won his second Tony Award for his direction of Tom Stoppard's *The Real Thing* (1984). Nichols moves easily back and forth between Broadway and Hollywood. His first film was *Who's Afraid of Virginia Woolf?* (1966), and he received an Academy Award as best director for *The Graduate* (1967). Recent films include *Working Girl* and *Wolf.*

audience can see and follow the action of the play clearly. Director training usually emphasizes one particular arrangement simply because the vast majority of theatres are of the proscenium type.

Summary

Central staging and end staging present the director with new problems in both the blocking of the action and the technical aspects of the production. At the same time, arena staging provides the director with exciting new opportunities and the audience with a different, more intimate emotional experience.

CHAPTER 19

DIRECTING THE MUSICAL

In staging a musical, the director faces many new challenges. Not only are rehearsal schedules and casting issues different from those of the straight play, but totally new and different problems appear, such as the addition of orchestras and **choreography.** In this chapter, we shall discuss these new difficulties which must be overcome by the director of a musical.

Multiple Directors

The key difference between a musical and a nonmusical is that there will be multiple directors. Each of the major areas—drama, dance, and music—will have its own director. Not only must the director deal with the designer, costumer, and technical director, but he or she also works with a choreographer and a musical director. Often, the musical director has subdirectors as well: vocal coaches for the leads, a choral director, and an orchestra director. However, in small theatrical operations, a single musical director may well do all of these tasks. Although cooperation among the many directors is the key to success, the director should establish a clear line of authority. When a major clash arises, all must be in agreement that the director will make the final decision to which the other directors will defer.

Rehearsal Schedules

The director of a musical loses some control of the rehearsal schedule. He or she must schedule well in advance, having consulted with all of the different people who will be working with segments of the cast, such as the choreographer and musical director. Production meetings are particularly important with a musical. Because there are so many different elements that need rehearsal, inevitably the directors will start fighting against each other for time. For example, the choreographer will come to the director and say, "This number is taking far longer to rehearse than I thought it would; we have to have more rehearsal time." And the musical director will say, "These performers really need more rehearsal on these particular songs; when can we do it?" Therefore, the director should build extra time into the schedule to allow for these typical problems.

Directors must plan three different sets of rehearsals: dance rehearsals, musical rehearsals, and their own rehearsals. A director who is used to rehearsing every day must give up rehearsal time to the other directors. For example, a great deal of time is needed to teach people who are not trained dancers to dance well and feel comfortable. If a nonmusical play can be well-rehearsed in five weeks, then a musical will require six or seven weeks of rehearsal in order to allow time for these new aspects of the production.

In a traditional musical such as Rodgers and Hammerstein's *Carousel,* the chorus, dance corps, and leading actors can be rehearsed simultaneously in three different locations; however, because the solos, group musical numbers, and dancing are done by the same people in most contemporary musicals, rehearsals must be sequential rather than parallel. The director must talk to the choreographer, find out about that schedule, and plan to give up his or her own rehearsals for those needed for choreography. Occasionally, the scene designer might need the stage as well, in order to paint some elaborate backdrop that will take up the entire floor space of the stage. Rather than forego a rehearsal, the director should find an alternative location for rehearsal in advance to allow for such contingencies. The biggest difference between a musical and a nonmusical is the scheduling of all of these different elements of rehearsal—elements that invariably take more time than the choreographer, musical director, or scene designer think they are going to take.

Communication

At the early production meetings, the director must communicate his or her interpretation of the script to all of the other directors and designers. The concept of the show, the overall interpretation of the style of the production, must be shared by all of the creative personnel. Otherwise, when elements of the finished product do not fit with the rest of the show, the blame falls on the director alone.

The basic responsibility of the director is to serve as the unifying force of the production. Good communication among the directors at the beginning and throughout the rehearsal period is essential. In a typical situation, the choreographer comes up with elaborate dances that look fine and fit well with the show. The costumer designs and builds gorgeous costumes. Then, the director discovers that the dances that had been designed cannot be executed in these costumes. Obviously, such a problem derives from insufficient communication between the costumer and choreographer. The responsibility of the director is to make sure that this does not happen. Although the director cannot be everywhere, he or she should try to attend some choreography and musical rehearsals in order to be cognizant of the directions they are taking.

Casting

The director of a musical often has some difficult decisions to make when casting the roles. Actress X is a great singer but cannot act her way out of a paper bag. On the other hand, Actress Y is a superb actress, but she is not as far advanced in her singing ability as is Actress X. Which actress should the director choose for his leading role? The director is looking for individuals who, ideally, are talented in both singing and acting. In the amateur theatre, the director is often faced with some rather difficult compromises. Some roles absolutely require great vocal ability. Others, such as Rex Harrison's leading role in *My Fair Lady,* can be performed very successfully by an excellent actor who is not really a singer. When faced with the choice, the director might consider casting a balance of actors and singers, each of whom may be able to help the other achieve success in their area of weakness.

Another choice that the director of a musical must make is whether to use a full orchestra or a small group of two or three musicians. A full orchestra provides beautiful accompaniment, but a smaller group has its own advantages. Unless the performers are highly trained singers, the audience will often not be able to hear their voices over the sound produced by a full orchestra. Because an orchestra requires the director to rent full orchestration as part of the scores and scripts, the cost of the production will also be increased considerably.

Scripts and Royalties

In general, musicals are much more expensive to produce than nonmusicals. Royalties, based upon the size of the auditorium and the price of the tickets, tend to be excessive because the agents assume that the house will be full every night. Even more exasperating, both scripts and musical scores must be rented from the agents at prices that are greater than the cost would be if those items were available for outright purchase. For many years, the Tams Witmark agency had a virtual monopoly on the amateur rights for major musicals, and they developed a well-deserved reputation for treating theatre companies in a shabby manner. The musicals of Rodgers and Hammerstein are handled separately; Music Theatre International controls the rights to some of the better musicals with style and class; and the excellent Samuel French, Inc. has now broadened their scope to become agents for musicals as well as plays. Nevertheless, the cost of producing a musical is at least triple that of producing a straight play.

One problem created by the script rental system is that the actors are often supplied with "sides" rather than with full copies of the script. An actor's side contains the lines of dialogue of the character he or she is playing, as well as a few words of each preceding line by another character that will be the cue. A major character will have a rather substantial side, whereas minor characters might receive a side that contains only one or two pages—just enough to list their few lines of dialogue and their cues. Historically, this system of sides has not been in general use in the theatre since the nineteenth century. Before Bronson Howard and his fellow playwrights managed to achieve copyright protection for their dramatic works, producers tried to keep the plays out of print in order to avoid pirate productions which paid no fee to the original owners of the play. Giving actors sides rather than full copies of the script helped to achieve this purpose. The agents of today's musicals are trying to keep copies of the scripts out of

In the Director's Chair

Harold Prince (b. 1928)

Easily the best known and most successful producer and director of musicals, it would seen that Hal Prince has been associated with nearly all the famous musicals produced on Broadway from 1954 to the present day. He began as an apprentice and stage manager for George Abbott. His first stint as a producer was the hit *Pajama Game* in 1954. He began directing musicals in 1963 and has won Tony Awards for *Cabaret, Company, Follies, Candide, Sweeney Todd, Evita,* and *The Phantom of the Opera.* He is also known for his work as a producer and director of operas for the Metropolitan Opera and Lyric Opera of Chicago, among others.

circulation in order to protect their high rental fees. With just a side in hand, the only way the actor can know what the whole show is about is by listening to the read-through of the script by the cast at the first rehearsal. Even then, the actor is likely to forget the order of events or what the show is about, during the course of rehearsals. For this reason, the director may find it helpful to schedule an early run-through during the rehearsal period for musicals.

Special Challenges

For a theatre director, taking on a musical can be a major challenge. If directors do not read music, they become dependent upon someone else to handle that aspect of the production. If they cannot stage dance numbers, they become dependent upon an outside choreographer. Dance is so central to many contemporary musicals that their original productions on Broadway were staged by such people as Bob Fosse, Gower Champion, and Gene Kelly—famous dancers and choreographers—rather than by theatre directors.

Many musicals contain large dance scenes that must be choreographed and planned in ways that are not like normal directing. In our previous discussion of the staging of crowd scenes, we pointed out that the director does not want his crowd lined up onstage because it looks patterned and unnatural. However, in dance, the performers are often lined up on purpose; they are not supposed to look natural and unposed. Putting people in lines and having them dance is a kind of geometric game. For the most part, choreography operates on entirely different principles than does normal blocking. Even solo song numbers—which seem like monologues and are therefore amenable to normal blocking—often repeat the same lines over and over again. In a Mozart opera, the same line may be repeated twenty times in a row. The director will find it difficult to discover twenty different believable ways to block the same sentence.

Some years ago, this author staged a production of *Carousel* in which the major dance numbers were done by the dance troupe working with a choreographer. One big song number, "June Is Bustin' Out All Over," gave the director trouble. Everyone in the large chorus is having fun, singing about the wonderful weather; but the song does not move the story along, and there is no specific motivation for movement of any kind. The performers finally lined up, one behind the other, and did a snake dance all around the stage. The movement was lively and fun to watch, but it had little motivation in terms of characters or the story. It was something to do—just a game to play during the song. Unlike a straight play, musicals often present situations for which the director must invent movement that is not motivated specifically by the script. In other words, choreography often has the audience responding to movement for its pure kinetic beauty rather than for its function as symbolic expression of narrative or ideas.

Although most theatre directors are inexperienced in dance, simple choreography can be done without great expertise. Unless the director is working with skilled dancers, the choreography must be elementary; at the same time, a group of performers doing simple movements in unison looks amazingly complex. Dance is choreographed with much the same approach as preblocking—according to the dramatic situation, intent, and characters at that particular moment. The director should listen to the music and write a scenario. Then, he or she should divide the people into subgroups, plan their location onstage, and decide the number of counts or beats for which they will be moving. For example, let us take ten people and divide them into two groups of three and two groups of two. Working in floor patterns as if we were looking down on the stage or on a floorplan, we would place each of the four groups in a particular section of the stage. The music is divided by beats into patterns of eight counts. A series of different rhythms, or patterns of counting, are developed to those eight counts: one, two, three . . . , or one and two and three . . . , or one, (pause), three, four, ... Each of the four groups of people may work with one of these varied patterns of the eight-count. First, the dancers clap their rhythm in order to learn it. Then, still seated, they tap it out with their feet. Finally, they get up and march in place to their rhythm. All of dancing boils down to simple marching in terms of footwork—left-right-left-right—marching to the rhythm pattern of the eight-counts. Once this is learned, the marching pattern can be varied by doing it in place: moving forward or backward, moving to the left or right, or by simply turning around while marching to the rhythm. All four groups doing this in unison will be impressive. Two groups doing one pattern while the other two do something else will seem quite complex.

The director should not repeat the same step, even with simple movement variations, for more than thirty-two counts—four repetitions of the eight-count patterns. Therefore, most numbers would require three different step-pattern routines, each covering thirty-two counts. Careful preplanning is the key to success. The director should count out the music, writing down the number of eight-count sections. Then he or she should plan different variations of the eight-pattern for each small group, as well as the particular area of the stage each will occupy. A useful variation is to have the small groups exchange areas of the stage at some point during the number. Every director and choreographer does their homework first, sitting with a tape recorder and a score, and listing along the margin of the score: (1) a scenario, (2) particular step patterns, and (3) stage positions for each section of eight beats for each subgroup of dancers. All of this may seem difficult and complicated, but with a little practice and a lot of imagination, most directors will amaze even themselves with their choreographic skills.

Summary

In this chapter, we have discussed the new difficulties that the director must face when staging a musical. Multiple directors can cause problems in schedules and communication. Finding performers who can act, sing, and dance equally well may prove difficult. And, unlike blocking, choreography often requires the director to follow a new set of rules in order to invent some of the movement. Nevertheless, the musical is the most popular form of theatre with audiences everywhere. With competent and cooperative support from talented musicians and dancers, the theatre director should have little problem in staging a musical.

CHAPTER 20

DIRECTING THE MOTION PICTURE

In this last section of the textbook, we looked at various directing situations that differ, more or less, from the traditions of directing a dramatic production in a proscenium stage theatre. We have seen that directing for an arena stage is a variation of the basic techniques used for staging in a proscenium situation. Directing a musical is more complex than staging a drama or comedy, but, with the aid of skilled musical personnel and choreographers, the task seems to be reasonably parallel with that of directing the nonmusical show. Motion pictures, on the other hand, are an art form distinct from theatre and will require attention to new and different directing skills.

Motion Pictures and Theatre

In many basic ways, **cinema** and theatre are alike. A director's work with script and script analysis—understanding the story and foreseeing the manner in which the audience will perceive it—is a parallel process in both media. In both theatre and movies, directors work with actors, attempting to build personal relationships and provide a working atmosphere that will ensure the psychological safety of the performers and encourage their creativity. Our previous discussions of these aspects of directing are equally relevant to the directing of a motion picture.

Movie acting, however, differs from stage acting in significant ways. In many cases, the camera is much closer to the actors than a theatre audience would be. Because the camera acts as the eyes of the audience, its proximity requires actors to perform with greater subtlety, honesty, and deep reality. In other words, film acting must be more naturalistic in order to appear believable to the audience. The actors' relationship to the camera alters the entire process in significant ways. An actor may be directed to not move his head during a particular scene, because in that tight close-up, any movement will take his face out of the picture. Virtually nothing in the theatre resembles this typical situation in film-acting and directing. We will return to the subject of acting for movies at a later time in order to detail the essential differences with which the director must deal.

Artistic Distinctions of Film

Motion pictures differ from theatre in certain basic ways that are the foundation for the distinction of cinema as a separate art form. Unlike a theatrical production, which one views from a single, particular vantage point, a film story is seen from numerous points of view—close-ups, long shots, different angles, and the like. The dual ability of the camera to see the action from differing angles and distances and to move while viewing the action is truly unique. It is as if one were able to get out of the theatre seat and move around, circling the actors, walking right up to them to see their facial expressions; in this way, the camera magically transports the audience member in and about the action of the story.

The camera records the action from numerous points of view, and portions of these different perspectives will be joined together in the editing process to give the illusion of one continuous, uninterrupted action. However, the movie is never one continuous action in time and space as is the action of a play on the stage. And it is this very fact that allows the director of a film story to shape both time and space in an artistic, "artificial" manner. Moments in time can be made longer or shorter than they are in reality; a shocking event can be elongated, as if time were almost standing still, while other events—from a night out on the town to the construction of a skyscraper—can be condensed and shown in a few minutes. This ability to control time and space in an artistic fashion, to create an artificial reality, provides the film director with the basic tools of a unique dramatic art form.

Artistic Problems of Film

Theatre has certain advantageous qualities that cinema lacks. For example, the theatre is alive and three-dimensional, whereas movies are merely flat patterns of light projected on a wall or a screen. Because of this, film directors attempt to compensate for the lack of dimensions and depth—to create the illusion of three-dimensional life. Technically, the motion picture is a series of patterns of recorded light. Therefore, the film director and cinematographer attempt to develop the illusion of depth by controlling the lighting, which illuminates the action. Lighting control, in the making of motion pictures, accomplishes four basic goals. The first goal is photographic, making sure there is the proper amount of light to expose the film in the camera. The second goal is to create a three-dimensional look, a quality called **modeling,** which is achieved by the way an object is lighted. The brightest light, or **key light,** is usually aimed at the object (or person) from an angle of 45 degrees above and 45 degrees to the left or right of that object. The key light will create shadows on the opposite side of the object. A second pattern of light is aimed from the side opposite the key light to fill those shadows. This **fill light** is dimmer than the key light, depending upon the effect and look desired by the director. A third lighting pattern will be set to strike the object from overhead and behind. Often called **back light** or hair lights, the purpose of this lighting is to separate the plane in which the object stands from other objects behind it in the background, enhancing the sense of depth in the picture. Thus, the pattern of key-fill-back lighting gives the object a look of three-dimensionality.

The third goal of the lighting is to help set the mood, whether bright and cheery or dark and ominous. The fourth and final goal of the lighting is to aid in the composition of the picture, to help focus the audience attention on the particular object or person that is most important dramatically, to create the dominant contrast in the composition.

Blocking the Movie Action

All of the preceding information is intended as background for an understanding of the job of film directors. For motion picture directors, the blocking involves arranging the actors and choosing the angle of view of the camera. It involves choice of both actor movement and camera movement. The goal of all of this blocking is to record the action so that it may be reconstructed in the editing room into a story that seems sensible, continuous, and dramatically powerful. All the while, the dialogue is being recorded on sound tape. The dialogue will be edited along with the picture, with sound effects and music added in the process.

If this process appears to be different and complicated—it is. The amateur film director has great difficulty producing a professional-looking movie without the aid of professional **cinematographers, editors,** music composers, sound and film laboratories, and all of the other accoutrements that cause Hollywood films to cost millions of dollars. Nevertheless, in order to see the film director's job clearly, let us assume that the situation is a professional one, with cinematographers, editors, and the like all at the director's disposal.

The Film Director's Job

The director works with the actors, arranging their positions and movement. With the advice of the cinematographer, the director plans the camera positions and the camera movement. The cinematographer takes care of lighting the action, but the director must communicate clearly what the desired effect is to be. Professional sound-recording people will take care of recording the dialogue. The director's job is to see that the actors deliver that dialogue well; others will see to the technology.

Directing the Camera

By what means does the director decide what camera angles to use, when to use a close-up or a medium shot? One basic pattern can be described—a pattern of camera work that is used to maintain the continuity of the story from one discontinuous shot to the next. That simple pattern is: long shot, medium shot, close-up. One starts with a long shot—a shot that includes all of any particular action or group of people. This shot establishes the location and relationships of all parties to the action. The camera can then move into medium shots of one or

In the Director's Chair

Steven Spielberg (b. 1947)

A master of all the arts of filmmaking, Steven Spielberg has combined art and popular subject matter to become the most successful film director of our time. From the release of *Jaws* in 1975 through *Raiders of the Lost Ark* (1981), *E.T.* (1982), and the subsequent Indiana Jones films, Spielberg has had enormous popularity and financial success. Spielberg prepares a thorough storyboard for his films, and he is very active in coaching his actors in order to achieve the precise effect he has in mind. Spielberg's love for popular fantasy and concern with serious social issues led to a stunning coup in 1994 with the production of the amazingly successful *Jurassic Park,* followed immediately by the Academy Award-winning *Schindler's List.*

two people and on to close-ups of particular faces. The audience will understand these fragments of the picture—such as a facial close-up—because they can fit them into the whole picture—the long shot—in their minds. Thus, whenever confusion may arise or a new person enters the picture, the wise director returns to a long shot in order to reestablish the relationships and avoid confusion in the minds of the audience.

The pattern of long shot, medium shot, close-up, followed by reestablishing with another long shot, is simply a basic, minimal idea for the maintenance of **continuity** in the story line. However, if one takes the time to study some of the shooting and editing in recent films, one will discover that the number of shots, the quick volume of editing that has become the style of contemporary films, requires that the director shoot any scene from numerous vantage points so that they can be briskly edited from one to another during the scene. The number of shots to be edited goes well beyond those needed simply to tell the story in a continuous and interesting fashion.

An interesting parallel exists between the stage and cinema. In order to create a sense of dynamic pace, this author encouraged stage directors to increase the amount of actor movement in the blocking. This same principle is true of motion pictures. However, there are two distinct ways to increase the movement in a film. The first is to have the actors move more often, just as on the stage. The second is to have the camera move more often. This idea does include actual movement of the camera during a shot, but that is not the point. Each time the movie cuts from one shot to another, from one angle of viewing the scene to another viewpoint, the sense of movement is just as strong as that created by the camera or the actors moving during the shot. The more often and more rapidly we cut from one shot to the next, the greater the illusion of movement and pace and excitement that is created for the audience. Directors will discover that with the double ability to create movement—moving either the camera or the actors— less movement of actors will seem appropriate in the film situation. In effect, camera movement replaces some of the movement of the actors that seems so necessary on the stage. As a direct result, the director should plan to view any particular scene from a number of different angles and distances.

From which angles should any scene be shot? That clearly is the artistic choice of the director. There is a standard method of shooting that guarantees full coverage for the editing process. The director shoots a **master shot**; that is, the whole scene is shot in a fairly long shot that covers the whole story. Then, one shoots as many close-ups and medium shots as appear desirable. In the editing room, the editor can always cut back to the master shot if trouble appears and none of the detail shots seem suitable.

Directing the Actors

Working with actors is actually considered to be the central task of the film director. The production team contains experts in every other area who assist the director with camera angles and the like; but only the director is expected to have expertise with actors.

The key to film acting is the relationship of the actor to the camera. Experienced performers are always cognizant of the camera; without looking directly at it, but often playing as if the other actor were just to the right or left of the camera, they produce a performance that has exactly the correct level of subtlety and believability for that distance to the camera, that distance that is the distance from the performers to the eyes and ears of their audience.

In a number of ways, acting for movies is more difficult than theatrical acting. Because the director is moving both actors and the camera to a new viewpoint—a new **setup**—at the same time, actor movement must be more controlled so that it will fit with the choice of camera shot. Actors must hit their marks with precision and repeat the same movements and gestures over and over for each new camera setup. That same hand gesture of brushing the hair out of the eyes, for example, must appear in every take, every long shot, and every close-up. If it does not, the different shots will not match up in the editing process. Thus, film actors are often required to repeat the same scene numerous times. They never get to play through the whole story from beginning to end. Typically, they must film their scenes completely out of order so earlier scenes in their character's story may be filmed after scenes from the character's later life. Often, movie actors are lucky to get one rehearsal before the camera starts rolling. And that intimate bedroom scene, for example, is played with thirty or more crew members standing only a few feet away, just out of sight of the camera. Clearly, acting in the cinema requires wonderful concentration and equanimity. Helping the actors to achieve and maintain this level of concentration is an important task of the film director.

The Questions of Preblocking

The question of preblocking arises in the context of motion picture directing, just as it did for our work in the theatre. Great films have been produced by directors who encouraged much improvisation on the set and by directors who preplanned every shot in detail beforehand. The approach used will be influenced by a number of factors: Will there be time for the actors to rehearse with the director at some length prior to the beginning of principle photography? If there is, much creative work involving both actors and director can be included. Is the film well-budgeted with enough money to work on scenes and reshoot often, searching for the best moments? If it is, more creative activity on the part of both actors and director will be forthcoming. Unfortunately, however, large budgets and extra rehearsal time are not common in cinema. Cutting corners and shooting as rapidly as possible is more often the case. Therefore, under typical filming conditions in which time pressure is extraordinary, directors would be well advised to do as much preplanning as possible. Because directors control the movement of the camera, they must exert greater control over the actor's movement so that the two will be in concert. Many famous motion picture directors create a **storyboard,** a series of drawings that show each new camera viewpoint in sequence, from the first setup and shot in the film to the last. The storyboard is a preplanned vision of the entire film, showing every camera shot and the location of the actors at every moment.

Summary

A totally thorough discussion of the art of motion pictures and film directing is not possible in one chapter, or, perhaps, even in one whole book. Nevertheless, we have surveyed a number of basic concepts. After a comparison with theatre, we have looked at the ways in which the art of cinema is unique. We then discussed basic approaches to these artistic aspects of filmmaking for the director, some aspects of working with film actors, and the value of a storyboard as a strategy for the director of a movie. As we maintained at the opening of this chapter, motion pictures are a distinct art form from theatre. Whereas many of the director's techniques apply to both media, film clearly requires attention to some new and different directing skills.

GLOSSARY

Aesthetic distance   The psychological detachment between a work of art and those who respond to it.

Agent   One who acts as the business representative and negotiator for an artist.

Antagonist   The force that is opposed to the protagonist in the major conflict of a story. That force may be other characters, within the protagonist (for example, a personal decision that must be made), or some outside force such as nature.

Arena stage   A stage surrounded by audience. Synonymous with "central stage" and "theatre-in-the-round."

Arrangement   The composition or organization of visual objects in a particular space.

Back light   Cinema lighting from above and behind the subject, helping to separate the subject from the background and enhancing the depth of the picture.

Balance   The arrangement of objects so that their apparent weights seem equal on either side of the stage, either in perfect symmetry or in an asymmetrical arrangement in which lighter weights balance heavier by being farther from the center of the picture.

Beat   A section of the play script during which the characters have one consistent goal or desire and use one consistent tactic to achieve that goal.

Blocking   The organization of the stage movement for any scene or for the entire play.

Blocking rehearsal   A rehearsal in which the movement of the actors is developed for a particular section of the play.

Central stage   A stage surrounded by audience. Synonymous with "arena stage" and "theatre-in-the-round."

Choreography   The organization of the dance movement for any scene or for an entire play.

Cinema   A synonym for motion pictures or movies.

Cinematographer   The artist responsible for the lighting of a movie shot and the photography. Also known as the Director of Photography or "D.P."

Classic   Something that is of lasting value and importance, famous and long-established, such as the dramas of ancient Greece and of Shakespeare.

Classical paradigm   A term used to designate the style of mainstream fiction, drama, and films that have a narrative form with a clearly defined conflict and an action rising to one or more climaxes followed by formal closure in the ending.

Climax   The strongest point of emotional tension in a story, often involving the turning point in which the protagonist wins or loses the major conflict.

Closed form   A carefully and artfully arranged visual composition that has the sense of a completely finished, perfectly designed little world.

Commanding form   The underlying organization or form of the play that must be followed in order to accomplish the drama's purpose, as opposed to the many other elements of a production that are a matter of choice for the actors and director.

Conclusion   The final portion of a story, after the conflict has been resolved either in favor of or against the protagonist.

Conflict   The contest or struggle between the protagonist and the antagonist in a story.

Continuity   The coherence between edited shots in a motion picture that emphasizes smooth transitions so that the story seems continuous, unbroken, and sensibly and realistically believable.

Crisis   A major moment of high tension in a story, a point at which the conflict between the protagonist and antagonist seems to be coming to a head but concludes with that conflict still unresolved. A crisis is often a low point in the fortunes of the protagonist.

Dominant contrast   The area of any visual composition that draws the viewer's attention first, usually because of some visual contrast in lighting or composition.

Downstage   The area of the stage nearest the audience.

Dramatic pauses   A pause taken by an actor for dramatic effect.

Dramaturg   The official literary person or house playwright at a particular theatre. One who does research on the play and its author for the director and the actors.

Dress rehearsals   Final rehearsals before opening night that are done exactly as the play will be done for an audience, with full technical support and costumes.

Editor   The artist whose task it is to decide which film shot will be joined with the next in a motion picture. The editor recreates piece by piece the film story that the director and cinematographer have previously photographed.

Emotional key   The level of intensity of any emotional moment, higher key meaning of greater intensity.

Empathy   A quality of emotional relationship between spectator and dramatic event, usually defined by the spectator feeling the same emotions as the protagonist, putting himself or herself in the protagonist's shoes.

End stage   A theatrical arrangement in which the audience surrounds the stage on three sides while leaving a fourth side available for scenery and the like.

Evaluation   The process in which directors appraise their work in the aftermath of a production, hoping to improve their directing skills for the future.

Final rehearsal   The last dress rehearsal directly before opening night.

Fill light   Lighting that falls on an object in a motion picture and is utilized to fill, at a lower level, the shadows created by the brighter key light.

Focus   The area or object that draws the viewer's attention first; the focus of the viewer's attention; the dominant contrast.

Grace   Attractiveness in arrangement, manner, or movement; elegance in proportion; gentility in manner or movement.

Home position   The location of any particular actor in a carefully arranged group picture onstage, usually related to a crowd scene. After some general activity of the crowd, the actor can safely return to home position.

Identification   Relating to the emotional relationship between spectator and protagonist in a story, identification implies that the spectator sees himself or herself as the character, living the protagonist's life, having the same experiences.

Image   A metaphorical surrogate for the play; an overall symbol to help define the meaning of an artwork.

Improvisation   Impromptu creation of an acting scene or story without written dialogue or plot preplanned in any detail.

Initial incident   That event in a story that is the beginning of the major conflict for the protagonist.

Interpretation   The process of analysis of an artwork. Also, the conclusions drawn from the analysis of an artwork.

Key light   The brightest lighting that falls on any object in a motion picture, usually coming from a 45-degree angle above and to one side. Key light must be adequate to expose the film properly.

Line rehearsal   Rehearsals devoted to actors learning their lines. First rehearsals without scripts in hand and with a prompter to help when actors cannot recall a particular word or line.

Master shot   An uninterrupted long shot that contains the entire scene of a motion picture.

Memorized audition   A type of audition in which the actors are expected to deliver memorized speeches from one or more plays and to act out brief scenes or monologues.

Method acting   A style of acting developed by Stanislavski; common in America since the 1950s. The method involves emotional believability and "living" the part rather than mastery of technique.

Modeling   The quality of motion picture lighting that seems to give depth and three-dimensionality to objects being photographed.

Naturalism   The theory or practice in the arts of realistic representation. A theory of the world that emphasizes the scientific over the supernatural, envisioning human beings as creatures controlled by their heredity and environment.

Odyssey   A type of story structure named after the famous tale by Homer; it involves a series of episodes in which the protagonist faces one new adversary or problem after another.

Open audition   An audition at which any interested performer is welcome, as opposed to a closed audition that is by invitation only.

Open form   A visual composition that has a quality of spontaneity and a seeming lack of artificial organization. A fragment of ambiguous reality, as opposed to an artfully arranged closed form.

Open up   A command that tells actors to turn their bodies and faces toward the audience or the camera so that they can be seen more clearly.

Organic unity   A metaphor for the organizational relationship between the parts of a play or another work of art, organic unity implies a relationship in which each part is interdependent upon the others; each scene is necessary for the existence of the others.

Physicalize   A theatrical term that means to take the intentions and emotions of a character as given in the dialogue and turn them into actions, physical movement, and the like, which the audience can see and understand.

Pick up cues   An actor's cue is those lines spoken just before that actor must deliver a line of dialogue. Picking up cues means coming in with a line immediately after the cue has been given, leaving no empty space between the lines of dialogue.

Picturization   The arrangement of actors onstage so that the stage picture symbolizes the current relationships and emotions in the story. Thus, the stage picture tells the story in a visual analogue.

Play script   The published version of a story—words printed on pages—which the actors and director attempt to develop into a full-scale play production.

Polarization   A psychological characteristic of humans to become part of a group, joining in a group psychology and giving up their own individual differences.

Polishing   A theatrical term that refers to those rehearsals—after blocking and after lines have been memorized—where details of pace, emotion, timing, believability, and the like are of paramount concern in order to produce a superior or "polished" performance.

Postmodernism   A movement reacting against modernism, arguing that the meaning and significance of play scripts are open to much wider interpretation than has formerly been deemed acceptable. Postmodernism justifies a much wider range of possible production styles for any particular script.

Preblocking   The directing process of laying out all of the movement of the actors before meeting with the actors. The director preplans the actors' actions, and the actors simply imitate those movements given by the director.

Precasting   A process by which a director casts some or all of the roles in a play before the audition process begins.

Producer   In general, the producer of a film or theatrical production is the owner of the project. The producer puts the project together, purchasing the rights to the script, raising the money or finding stockholders or investors, hiring a director, and casting the major players. The essential aspects of the job involve control of the property and raising the funding for the project. In film, the person who works day to day on the artistic project along with the director is called the line-producer. Executive producers and others usually are associated with the funding and business dealings exclusively.

Properties   Commonly knows as "props," these are all the small items of decor on the set of a play. They include objects used by the actors, such as cups and saucers, and objects that are just decorative, such as pictures on the wall.

Proscenium stage   An arrangement of actors and audience that has all the audience watching the action from a single direction, with the actors on a stage, behind a frame or large arch. That frame is called the proscenium arch.

Protagonist   The main character in a story; the person who the story is about; the person who must face the major conflict and solve the problem in some manner.

Reading rehearsal   Early rehearsals in which the actors and director read the play script aloud and discuss its meanings, characters, and implications. Another name for these rehearsals is "table talk."

Realism   Realism is a style in literature and the arts that emphasizes fidelity to nature in representation. Typical characteristics of realism are: (1) characters who demonstrate three-dimensional psychology as opposed to simple stereotypes; (2) stories that minimize melodramatic events; (3) dialogue which sounds like everyday conversation, including, for example, off-color language, regional dialects, and slang; and (4) subject matter that emphasizes social problems, often those of the poor and disenfranchised.

Rhythm   A pattern of successive strong and weak movements or sounds. A regularly recurring sequence of events in time or objects in space creates a pattern which is said to possess a rhythm.

Royalty   A theatrical term that describes the amount of money to be paid to the playwright and his or her agents for each succeeding performance of his or her play by a particular company or theatrical group.

Sequence of events   In a play script, one things happens to the characters that leads to some other thing and on to another in a cause and effect pattern. These events follow one another in a pattern or sequence. Thus, the sequence of events is the very story being played out, one event after the other.

Setup   Any particular positioning of the camera and lights for a single shot in a motion picture.

Stage English   Stage English is a British dialect, specifically Southern British or "received pronunciation," which comes from an area south of London. It is the standard of high-class dialects, that which is taught in British schools and used by the BBC.

Stage left   The left direction as seen from the actor's point of view when facing the audience. Therefore, stage left is to the right of the audience.

Stage right   The right direction as seen from the actor's viewpoint when facing the audience. Therefore, stage right is to the left of the audience.

Story board   A filmmaker's technique for preplanning a movie. Shots are sketched in sequence prior to shooting, creating a visual outline or plan for both the director of photography and the editor.

Subclimax   Subclimax has the same meaning as *crisis* in story structure—a moment of high tension in the conflict that concludes with the major conflict still unresolved. Therefore, it is not yet the climax of the story.

Subplot   A subplot is an element of a story's structure. If the story has more than one conflict—each with its own protagonist, running along side by side—one of these conflicts is usually of major importance. The other is described as a subplot.

Subtext   A character's purposes and intentions; the dramatic implications beneath the surface dialogue that define the real meaning; the nonverbal communication behind the words.

Subtexting   A rehearsal process or game in which the actors verbalize the subject of their roles, moment to moment, during a run-through of a scene or the entire play.

Symbolic blocking   Actor movement that illustrates or symbolizes the emotional relationship between the characters at any particular moment, generally moving toward or away from one another to illustrate the relationship in an appropriate manner.

Synallaxis   A state in which all of the separate parts of a play script are seen as logically and consistently interrelated. An interpretation of a script achieves synallaxis when it integrates all of the separated elements in a logical explanation of the whole.

Synoptic response   The first response of any person to the play. The overall rational and emotional reaction (the holistic response) prior to analysis and critical thinking.

Tableau   Living performers in a still picture; a composition or arrangement of actors on a stage, frozen and unmoving.

Table talk   Early rehearsals in which the actors and director read the play script aloud and discuss its characters and meanings. Another name for table talk is "reading rehearsals."

Technical rehearsal   That rehearsal, late in the process, at which the actors finally have at their disposal all of the design elements of the production: settings, costumes, lighting, sound effects and music, properties, and the like.

Thrust stage   A theatrical arrangement in which the audience surrounds the stage on three sides. Thus, the stage thrusts out into the audience rather than remaining behind the proscenium arch. Thrust stages are often associated with the plays of Shakespeare. Staging on a thrust is the same as "end staging."

Touching rehearsal   A type of rehearsal or rehearsal game in which the actors touch one another in an appropriate manner while delivering their lines. As nonverbal communication, the touch helps to define clearly the relationship of the characters to one another.

Unity   Any pattern of organization which draws the separate parts together into a single entity or whole is said to unify, or give unity to, that grouping or artwork.

Upstage   The part of the stage which is farthest away from the audience in a proscenium stage arrangement.

Willing suspension of disbelief   An idea originated by Coleridge that describes the tacit agreement on the part of audience members to allow themselves to believe in the reality of the dramatic presentation, to suspend their disbelief and enjoy the show even while they know it is all an illusion with actors playing roles.

BIBLIOGRAPHY

Allen, W. (1969). *Play It Again, Sam.* New York: Samuel French, Inc.

Anderson, R. (1994, April). In Dan Sullivan, *Playwrights Panel: The Contemporary American Theatre.* Discussion conducted at the Wm. Inge Festival XIII, Independence, Kansas.

Bank, R. K. (1981). *Interpreters, dramaturgs, and process critics.* Paper presented at the meeting of the American Theatre Association, Chicago.

Bartow, A. (1988). *The Director's Voice.* New York: The Theatre Communications Group, Inc.

Benedetti, R. L. (1985). *The Director at Work.* Englewood Cliffs, N.J.: Prentice-Hall.

Best Plays or *The Applause/Best Plays* series; for example: Guernsey, O. L. and Sweet, J. (1992). *The Applause/Best Plays: Theatre Yearbook 1991–92.* New York: Applause Theatre Book Publishers.

Bevington, D. (1968). *Twentieth Century Interpretations of Hamlet.* Englewood Cliffs, N.J.: Prentice-Hall.

Brockett, O. G. (1991). *History of the Theatre.* Boston: Allyn and Bacon.

Brook, P. (1968). *The Empty Space.* London: MacGibbon & Kee.

Burns, J. M. (1978). *Leadership.* New York: Harper and Row.

Clurman, H. (1972). *On Directing.* New York: Macmillan.

Cohen, R., and Harrop, J. (1984). *Creative Play Direction.* Englewood Cliffs, N.J.: Prentice-Hall.

Cole, S. L. (1992). *Directors in Rehearsal.* New York: Routledge.

Cole, T., and Chinoy, H. K. (1954). *Actors on Acting.* New York: Crown Publishers.

———. (1953). *Directing the Play.* New York: Bobbs-Merrill.

Coleridge, S. T. (1817). *Biographia Literaria.* New York: Dutton, 1965.

Dean, A. (1980). *Fundamentals of Play Directing.* New York: Holt, Rinehart and Winston.

Dennis, J. (1982). In discussion conducted at The American College Theatre Festival at the University of Northern Iowa, Cedar Falls.

Dietrich, J. (1953). *Play Direction.* Englewood Cliffs, N.J.: Prentice-Hall.

Dmytryk, E., and J. P. (1984). *On Screen Acting.* Boston: Focal Press.

Doleman, J. (1946). *The Art of Play Production.* New York: Harper and Brothers.

Eisenstein, S. (1957). *Film Form* [and] *The Film Sense.* New York: Meridian Books.

Engel, L. (1983). *Getting the Show on: The Complete Guidebook for Producing a Musical in Your Theater.* New York: Schirmer.

Frerer, L. (1971). Bronson Howard: Dean of American Playwrights. Doctoral dissertation, The University of Iowa.

Giannetti, L. (1993). *Understanding Movies.* Englewood Cliffs, N.J.: Prentice-Hall.

Gross, R. (1974). *Understanding Playscripts: Theory and Method.* Bowling Green, Ohio: Bowling Green University Press.

————. (1981). *The Organic approach to the problem of style in acting.* Paper presented at the meeting of the American Theatre Association, Chicago.

Gunkle, G. (1963, March). Empathy: Implications for Theatre Research. *Educational Theatre Journal* 15: 15–23.

Guthrie, T. (1965). *In Various Directions.* New York: Macmillan.

Hackman, M. Z., and Johnson, C. E. (1991). *Leadership.* Prospect Heights, Ill.: Waveland Press.

Herlihy, J. L., and Noble, W. (1958). *Blue Denim.* New York: Random House.

Hodgson, J., and Richards, E. (1966). *Improvisation: Discovery and Creativity in Drama.* London: Eyre Methuen.

Houseman, J. (1979). *Front and Center.* New York: Simon & Shuster.

Humphrey, D. (1959). *The Art of Making Dances.* New York: Rinehart.

Kirk, J. W., and Bellas, R. A. (1985). *The Art of Directing.* Belmont, Calif.: Wadsworth.

Lange, J. (1990, August). Dialogue on Film. *American Film* 15 (no. 11): 16–17.

Lees, C. L. (1951). *Play Production and Direction.* New York: Prentice-Hall.

Logan, J. (1976). *Josh, My Up and Down In and Out Life.* New York: Delacorte Press.

Maholy-Nagy, L. (1947). *Vision in Motion.* Chicago: P. Theobald.

Nash, N. R. (1955). *The Rainmaker.* New York: Random House.

Pacino, A. (1979, December). "Playboy" Interview. *Playboy* 26 99–100.

Pearson, R. M. (1934). *How to See Motion Pictures.* New York: The Dial Press.

Prince, H. (1974). *Contradictions: Notes on 26 Years in the Theatre.* New York: Dodd, Mead.

Schechner, R. (1980). In discussion conducted at the meeting of the American Theatre Association, San Diego, Calif.

Sherman, E. (1988). *Directing the Film.* Los Angeles, Calif.: Acrobat Books.

Stanislavski, K. (n.d.). *My Life in Art.* New York: Theatre Arts Books.

Streisand, B. (1979). In discussion conducted at The Center for Advanced Film Study of the American Film Institute, Beverly Hills, Calif.

Sutherland, D. (1978). Interview concerning the film: *Invasion of the Body Snatchers.* Westwood Village, Calif.: Marco Baria and Associates, Inc.

Vaughan, S. (1993). *Directing Plays: A Working Professional's Method.* New York: Longman.

Williams, T (1963). *The Night of the Iguana.* New York: Dramatists Play Service, Inc.

INDEX